AID
SUTRA

AIDS
SUTRA

Untold Stories from India

FOREWORD BY AMARTYA SEN

INTRODUCTION BY BILL AND MELINDA GATES

PHOTOGRAPHS BY PRASHANT PANJIAR

EDITED BY NEGAR AKHAVI

Anchor Books
A Division of Random House, Inc.
New York

Library of Congress Cataloging-in-Publication Data:
AIDS Sutra : untold stories from India / introduction by Bill and Melinda Gates ; foreword by Amartya Sen; photographs by Prashant Panjiar ; edited by Negar Akhavi.
p. cm.
ISBN 978-0-307-45472-0
1. AIDS—India—Literary collections.   2. Indic prose literature (English)—
21st century.   I. Akhavi, Negar.
PR9497.28.A33A33 2008
823.'01083561—dc22
2008028184

www.anchorbooks.com

Printed in the United States of America
10   9   8   7   6   5   4   3   2   1

To the community members who stood up and gave voice

CONTENTS

CONTENTS

INTRODUCTION
Bill and Melinda Gates

A few years ago, we went to downtown Chennai, India, to talk with a group of women about AIDS. We all sat together on a white mat in a small hotel room. There were about a dozen women there, wearing their best saris, gold necklaces, flowers in their hair, and bindis on their foreheads. As they talked about their lives and dreams—the things they wanted for themselves and their children—they sounded like they could have come from any walk of life.

In fact, they were all sex workers. They had come together as a community to learn how to protect themselves from HIV and slow the spread of the disease. We were there to learn, in turn, from them. We knew a lot of statistics from our work with Avahan, our foundation's AIDS prevention programme in India, but we wanted to hear firsthand what made women like them so vulnerable to the disease, and what could be done about it.

They all had turned to sex work because they desperately needed money. But often the income they earned still wasn't enough, and they ended up living hand to mouth. One woman, a mother, told us about the terrible choices she had to make, such as whether to buy milk for her family or get medicine for her sick child.

Some of the women had been forced to give up on more promising pursuits. One young woman had been a star student in school, but when her father came down with a debilitating illness, she dropped out so she could earn money to support the family. When they fell further into debt, she turned to sex work.

This group of women had all been ostracised by their families and neighbours. One woman had hoped to keep her work a secret from her husband and children. But when word got out, her daughter was disowned by her friends. The girl was so distraught that she committed suicide.

This kind of stigma is cruel and senseless. There are nearly 3 million Indians living with HIV today. If we're going to stop AIDS, we have to embrace every one of them—regardless of social class, line of work, or circumstance. That includes those who are especially vulnerable to the disease, such as sex workers and their clients, the transgender community, and injecting drug users.

It starts with telling their stories. That's why we are so grateful to the distinguished writers who have contributed to this anthology. Their work shows the human side of this disease, and it lives by the words we saw written on a poster in that room in Chennai: 'Open your eyes to HIV/AIDS.'

AIDS
SUTRA

FOREWORD
Understanding the Challenge of AIDS[1]
Amartya Sen

Human ordeals thrive on ignorance. To understand a problem with clarity is already half way towards solving it. Confusion distorts individual behaviour as well as social action, and ignorance of the effectiveness of societal intervention contributes greatly to resignation, fatalism and, ultimately, callousness. This is as true of the global epidemic of AIDS today as it has been of other major human disasters, in the past.[2]

It is a great privilege for me to be asked to present some introductory remarks for this anthology of wonderfully engaging essays on the terrible epidemic of AIDS, which afflicts India as well as the world. This global calamity has hit India just when the country is fervently seeking a place in the sun, away from the age-old gloom of poverty, illiteracy, ill health, and nasty, brutish and short lives.

Given the magnitude of the new problem, the challenge that India faces is, of course, gigantic. It not only requires informed and determined action, but demands, first of all, a broader and more foundational cognisance of the nature of the affliction that attacks us from its safe haven of dense fog.

---

[1] I am grateful to Pedro Ramos Pinto for discussion and research assistance.
[2] *Oxford Textbook of Medicine* (5th Ed, Oxford University Press, 2008).

We have to understand better the nature of the disease, what it does or does not do, how it spreads and how that process can be arrested, how the victims of the disease can lead good lives, and how the epidemic can be stalled as it awaits eradication through medical advance and social action. No less importantly, we have to appreciate that the understanding of a complex reality not only demands facts, figures and empirical details, but also the use of our responsive imagination to interpret what is going on, so that crude facts can be transformed into informed comprehension.

Literature has played this mediating role over the millennia everywhere in the world. It has been, in this way, even a great ally of science in making us discern the world better—a hugely important contribution that still does not get adequate recognition. If Kalidasa succeeded in making us grasp the richness of the diversity of 5th century India through the poetry of *Meghadutam* [The Cloud Messenger], it is not merely because there is a wealth of graphic description of various communities, lives and cultures that the poet outlines to the cloud messenger: what the elevated courier will find on its way across the country to the exiled communicator's lover. What Kalidasa makes us perceive about the country comes from his characteristically luscious description of the sights and sounds that stimulate the imagination—and involvement— of the readers themselves. A millennium and a half later, the poetry is still animated by proximity and illumination.

We, the readers of this book, are fortunate that the organisers of this ambitious work, impeccably planned by Avahan of the Gates Foundation, asked some of the finest and most innovative authors of the subcontinent to write essays on different aspects of the challenge, seen from distinct perspectives, and from disparate regions of the country. Even as the contributions excel in their literary quality, they also lead us to a fuller understanding of the epistemology of the AIDS epidemic, thereby opening the door—since epistemology is so central to a well-founded ethics—to informed reflections on the social and political commitments that the calamity inescapably demands. If we move from depiction to perception, and from reflection to compassion and resolution, all this happens, as in good literature, without self-conscious effort. This is a huge achievement.

The Size of the Epidemic

Much about the nature and reach of this disaster is unclear. It is even hard to be sure of the size of the population affected by AIDS in India, or by its biological precursor in the form of HIV positivity which leads to AIDS over time. The essays are, rightly, concerned with more complex problems of knowledge and understanding than the mere telling of numbers in 'the AIDS category', but the magnitudes are also important in appreciating the relevance and reach of this insightful collection of essays.

As it happens, the number game of sizing the affected population has been something of an elephants' burial ground, not least in India. While the Government of India remained committed for many years to insisting, typically rather loudly, that there was no serious threat of AIDS in India, the CIA's National Intelligence Council in the USA saw India as the largest conquest of AIDS in the world. In 2002, the CIA convinced itself that there were going to be 20 to 25 million—no less—AIDS cases in India by 2010. If the complacent Government of India failed to take any notice of the early signs of the growing epidemic, the magnified and frightening estimates of the CIA, which numbed all who believed them, showed how easily an organisation dedicated to intelligence can fail to give much evidence of it.

Since it was clear enough that official India's underestimations were as wrong as were the terrifying numbers coming from some foreign agencies, a compromise was struck, with

3

something around 5 million being taken as a kind of a mediated estimate of the HIV affected population in India. The United Nations did its best to popularise their calculation of 5.7 million affected population in India. Much of these estimates were, of course, pure guess work, which is not to be scoffed at: what else can you do other than guess when there are no hard numbers?

However, recent statistical studies, most notably the National Family Health Survey (NFHS), have given us a much stronger basis for actual estimation. Surveys conducted in 2005–06 by the NFHS form the basis of the standard recent estimates that the HIV affected population in India lies between 2 million and 3.1 million. In mid 2007, the United Nations came in line with this statistical picture and did a kind of a mea culpa on their previous numbers, and cut down their figure of 5.7 million to take on these new and substantially lower estimates. The range of 2 to 3.1 million affected population is the basis of the most repeated assessment, situated in 2007, that there are 'perhaps 2.5 million people' affected by HIV in India.

While this may look like a small proportion of the huge Indian population of more than a billion people, it is, in fact, a gigantic number of people whose lives are threatened, battered or ruined. Further, the prevalence of AIDS varies from region to region, and in some states (such as Manipur, Andhra Pradesh, Karnataka, or Maharashtra), the incidence is very much larger than for the country as a whole. For example, Andhra Pradesh has nearly one fifth of the total cases of HIV incidence in India, despite having only 5% of the country's aggregate population. And when the data are broken down by districts, the variations are truly enormous: we find 118 districts with more than 1% of the population affected by the disease (1% prevalence is usually taken as the cut-off point for a 'generalised epidemic') and 14 districts with more than three times that cut-off rate. It is good that the organisers of this anthology have encouraged the authors to visit differ-ent regions of India and write their essays informed by local problems and perspectives. This helps the reader to get an appreciation of the territorially diverse challenge that India faces and the great variety of forms that the tribulations can take.

Ignorance and Half-understanding

While exact numbers are hard to pin down, unfamiliarity with the total numbers involved may not be quite as punish-ing as the ignorance of the nature, impact and implications of the epidemic. We can typically get by well enough without being sure of how many people are suffering from this afflic-tion at this time. But innocence about the infection both promotes the spread of the disease and hampers the use of well established measures for prevention, including regular and appropriate use of condoms. Other problems of ignorance are less appreciated. For example, the fact that exaggerated fears of catching the disease can—and do—lead to discrimination against the patients, which is not only barbarous in itself, but which also directly contributes to the reluctance of the possible victims to undergo testing, and furthermore, severely discourages HIV positive persons from disclosing their status to others.

In a recent survey in Maharashtra, 'People Living with HIV/AIDS' (PLHA), it is found that 56% of the afflicted people have not disclosed their status to the community, and 79% have not disclosed their status to their employers. These, in turn, facilitate the spread of the infection and hamper the care that is needed. If *underestimation* of the infectious nature of the disease can kill, so can *overestimation*. There is no safety on either side of the truth.

At the policy level too, the contribution of ignorance and lack of precise knowledge can be disastrous for the making of programmes and procedures. One reason why the question of knowledge is so important for social policies to combat HIV/ AIDS is that, unlike in the case of other ailments, many of the biological ravages of the disease may not be overtly visible. In this respect, AIDS is not like malaria, which is another major killer across the world, and, of course, it is very unlike leprosy. This not only leads to a vast ambiguity about the seriousness of the AIDS epidemic and reduces the appreciation of the urgency of dealing with it right now, but it also makes it harder to generate an understanding of the routes and reach of transmission and the ways and means of countering them and of organising medical and social care. The essays in this book have much to offer in providing insights into these critically important issues.

There are other problems where the need for further scrutiny seems to me to remain strong. These include difficulties that arise from half-knowledge and half-understanding, which can play havoc with our reasoning. As Martin Luther King, Jr put it in his 'Letter from Birmingham Jail': 'Shallow understanding from people of good will is more frustrating than absolute misunderstanding from people of ill will.'[3] This may be a bit tough, but there certainly is some disturbing shallowness in the thinking on AIDS in the public media, which needs scrutiny and significant emendation.

Putting Economics in Its Place

Concern is expressed, rightly, about the economic consequences of the AIDS epidemic. There are losses of economic production because of morbidity and disability. There are costs of care and prevention. There are high expenses of treatment with effective drugs. AIDS orphans need resources in order to have reasonable chances of a good life. And the

---

[3] 'Letter from Birmingham Jail', Open Letter to Clergymen, April 16 1963, *Atlantic Monthly*, August 1963.

economic ruin that families face when earning men come down with the disease vastly magnifies the econo penalties of the illness. There are many other ways as wel which AIDS imposes economic costs. And yet the persistent attempt to see the epidemic as an economic crisis cannot but be misleading, and sometimes even dense and vulgar.

It is critically important to recognise that the AIDS epidemic is primarily a crisis of human lives: people suffer and are disabled, lose their freedom to do things, become dependent on others, and a large number of the victims die prematurely. It is not principally an economic crisis, even though there are important economic components in the human disaster, which add to the adversities involved. It is, of course, sensible enough to ask how the AIDS epidemic will reduce the growth rate of Gross National Product (GNP) in India (a study by the United Nations Development Programme presents calculations to suggest that the annual growth rate of the Indian economy will go down by 0.86%). But this cannot be the main story in this human crisis. Indeed, for a country that is growing around 8% a year, with ups and downs each year much larger than 0.86%, this is not a catastrophe in the same way in which the massive suffering and helplessness and unnecessary deaths are. Eliminating that 0.86% growth loss through some clever economic policy would, of course, be a very good thing, but it would not radically alter the nature and magnitude of the human disaster.

Economics is a great subject, and as a member of the profession, I am proud of what the discipline can, and often enough does, achieve. And yet we must avoid crassness, and also need a sense of proportions. A limited focus of vision can transform careful economic analysis into crude articulation. John Hatcher's historical study, *Plague, Population and the English Economy, 1348–1530*, brings out how 'the Black Death' raised the wages of labourers through reducing the supply of labour by killing off people. There is certainly an interesting relation to be seen here, and yet there is something hugely problematic, as Hatcher notes, in going from there to the often-repeated conclusion that 'in these terms', the 15th century 'was truly the golden age of the English labourer'.[4] A golden age? Despite the fact that a great many of those labourers suffered and died even as wages rose? As Hatcher argues: 'Clearly an age which relies for its prosperity upon large numbers of its members dying at an early age, and suffering the frequent losses of spouses, children, relatives, friends and colleagues, is somewhat less than golden.'

Economists must eschew their diagnosis of any kind of age—'golden' or whatever—if they cannot look beyond wages, prices and incomes. The temptation to put economics at the centre of the stage even when it does not belong there is far too strong at a time when economic consequences have a tendency to swamp thoughts on other subjects. Indeed, it is not absurd to question the sense of proportions when another leading economic historian sums up the Black Death thus: 'For the survivors, the 14th century famines and pestilence were, no doubt, on personal grounds, inexpressibly grievous. But they unlocked a cornucopia. England was given a sort of Marshall Aid on a stupendous scale.'[5] Marshall Aid coming to England through the massive death of Englishmen? This is a grimly upbeat forward march from Anna Akhmatova's bitter irony about the Russian purges of the 1930s: 'It was a time when only the dead smiled, happy in their peace.'

The central point is this. Economic effects of the AIDS epidemic are important not so much on their own but primarily because of their consequences on human lives and happiness and freedoms. This does not make the economic issues unimportant, but we have to see why and how they are significant.

---

[4] John Hatcher, *Plague, Population and the English Economy, 1348–1530* (London: Macmillan, 1977), p 73.

[5] AR Bridbury, *Economic Growth: England in the Later Middle Ages* (Harvest Press, 2nd ed, 1975), p 91.

Economic Aspects of the AIDS Epidemic

There are indeed crucial economic issues to be addressed in dealing with the AIDS epidemic. One of the central ones is the need to devote much more resource to tackling the epidemic—on prevention, on treatment, on care, on rehabilitation, and no less importantly, on education about the disease.

There is a peculiar—and rather bitter—irony in the fact that no country has done more than India in cheapening the production cost of known antiretroviral drugs (CIPLA is something of a world leader in this), and yet most HIV affected people in India cannot afford to get and use these drugs. India's role in supplying cheap lifesaving drugs to the world is, of course, to be much applauded (if anything demands cooperation across the national boundaries today, the global AIDS epidemic surely does), but this country itself should also have a more effective system of delivery and use within its own borders. There are, to be sure, the barriers of organisation and medical assistance, but the costs of the drugs, even when lowered by domestic production, tend to be well beyond the means of the less affluent patients.

There is a very strong case for a much larger deployment of public resources in changing this terrible situation through making the treatment more affordable, and also for spending more on hospital facilities, medical advice, social care, and community organisation. There are, of course, other demands on the government's money, but it is important to recognise that the rapid economic growth of the Indian economy is not only expanding many people's income (though it is still giving the lion's share of the gains to the relatively affluent themselves), but it has also been raising public revenue in the hands of the government at an unprecedented rate. Governmental revenue must, of course, grow very fast if it keeps pace with the rapid economic growth of the economy. In fact, however, government revenue has persistently grown substantially *faster* than the growth of gross domestic product (GDP): the annual growth rates of the GDP of 7, 8 or

9% have been exceeded by the expansion rates of price adjusted public revenue of 10, 11 or 12% per year. Just as it is important to keep these growth rates high, it is also totally crucial to make intelligent and humane use of the funds that are flowing rapidly into the government's hands.

The economic aspects of the challenge of the AIDS epidemic include a great many other issues that take us well beyond the expenses of medicine, health care and social services. Let me give an example. Since the spread of AIDS has been greatly hastened by long distance road transport and the role of truck drivers in picking up the infection and passing it on to their families, it is easy to see that one of the important aspects of the classic 'road versus rail' choice was missed when the new road lobby in India managed to swamp the geriatric pro-rail school. There is, in fact, considerable evidence that even without taking into account the connection of road transport with the spread of infection, the railways were given far less of a role than they deserved in the fast expansion of transport in rapidly modernising India. Calculations of relative costs and achievements done by a team led by Dr S Sundar of The Energy and Resources Institute (TERI) in Delhi brings out how much of an economic opportunity was lost through an over-reliance on roads and the relative neglect of rail transport. And if the AIDS implications are added to that picture, as they must be, the conclusions are even more clear and momentous. This is not to say that we do not need more roads. Of course we do. But we should try to put a much higher proportion of our goods traffic and also passenger movements on the rails, not merely because it is cheaper to do this, and more friendly to the environment, but also because this would be a contribution towards slowing down the spread of the new epidemic.

Economic issues raised by the new epidemic include a great many considerations of this kind, which may initially look rather far away from the policy implications of fighting an epidemic. This is not the occasion to launch into the many aspects of Indian economic thinking that should take on board the vast ramifications of the HIV prevalence in the country. But, in general, policy making has to come to terms with the reality of a substantive presence of this new calamity in India and its far-reaching implications for so many different aspects of economic and social life in the country.

The Role of Responsibility

If the economic implications of the AIDS epidemic raise complex considerations, so do the ethical and political consequences of the challenge. The ethics of responsibility has been a big subject in analysing the social aspects of AIDS. The point has been made, with considerable influence, that since HIV infection is primarily contracted through voluntary acts, such as unsafe sex, it is the individual rather than the society that should take responsibility for avoiding the disease and accepting the consequences of irresponsible actions. This way of seeing the social ethics of AIDS would have vast implications for what an afflicted person can or cannot expect the state to do for the ill. In their combative book, *Private Choice and Public Health: The AIDS Epidemic in an Economic Perspective*, Thomas Philipson and Richard Posner have argued forcefully that the demands on the state and on the society by the affected persons would have to be critically limited in this light.[6]

This line of reasoning is rarely presented as systematically—and as well—as Judge Posner and Professor Philipson do, but the basic argument has a very wide resonance and appeal. The idea that somehow the afflicted person bears the responsibility for his or her own unfortunate condition, since the infection could have been avoided through changing

---

[6] Thomas J Philipson and Richard A Posner, *Private Choice and Public Health: The AIDS Epidemic in an Economic Perspective* (Cambridge, MA: Harvard University Press, 1993).

personal behaviour, is indeed quite prevalent—not just in advanced countries like the USA, but also in India. There is certainly an element of narrow plausibility in this general outlook. Many of the actions that may lead to the infection are certainly within the person's own control, and the role of personal responsibility is indeed an important connection to bear in mind in planning strategies for prevention, through greater availability and use of information and more social education and advocacy. And yet to see this as an 'open and shut' case of just personal responsibility also misses the nine tenth of the iceberg that lies below the water, hidden from view.

First, infection can come to a person in a way over which he or she has little control. This applies not only to those who get the contagion from blood transfusion, but also to children who get the disease before they are able to run their own lives. Less obviously, the same lack of control applies to members of the family who get the ailment from their spouses or partners when they are not in a position to ascertain the infection status of their consorts. Women are particularly affected by this lack of control, and among the millions of arguments for women's empowerment, the fight against this epidemic has a clearly defined place.

Second, while ignorance of the law cannot be taken to be a legitimate excuse for a legal lapse, lack of knowledge of the process of transmission and of the ways and means of prevention can certainly rob a person of the ability to relate actions to consequences. The presumption of 'rational choice', which plays a large, direct and indirect, role in the arguments presented by Philipson and Posner, is compromised by many limitations, one of which—an important one—is clearly linked with informational ambiguity.

Third, even when there is a general understanding of the risks involved in certain types of actions, individual conduct is often swayed by the prevailing modes of behaviour. For example, in the success of the sex workers' unions in Calcutta

(or Kolkata) in moving the vulnerable population tow[...]
100% use of condoms (one of the essays in this coll[...]
explains how this initiative has worked), a critical diffe[...]
is made not just by the dissemination of information, but
also by developing group-based behavioural norms that individuals can follow without having to muster unusual resolve
and willpower in each behavioural choice. Personal responsibility is indeed a big part of the fight against AIDS, but the
routes to its exercise go through many related territories,
including knowledge, understanding, individual resolve, and
group norms.

Fourth, people are influenced in their behaviour not only
by well-reasoned advocacy (the role of clear reasoning was
clearly very strong in the Calcutta initiative just mentioned),
but also by what may look like 'thrilling' behaviour. This not
only applies to smoking, which is another area of huge health
adversity, but also to drug taking, which has played a very
important part in the spread of HIV infection in parts of the
country (for example in Manipur, on which there is also an
illuminating essay in this collection). Easy availability of
drugs can play a big role in enhancing the exposure to that
type of temptation (as it indeed did in Manipur). The exercise
of personal responsibility varies radically from one community to another depending on the social circumstances,
and it would be rather simple-minded to see these variations
as endogenous diversities in personal decision making, divorced from the way society influences the choices and actions
of individuals.[7]

Fifth, while it is easy enough to advocate 'just say no' in
any field with any kind of danger, living a life does not consist
only of invariably choosing the safest courses of action. While
the purist ascetic might find the entire field of sexual activity
to be suspect territory, the fact is that the spread of HIV

[7] Some of the connections between individual reasoning and social circumstances are discussed in my book *Rationality and Freedom* (Cambridge, MA: Harvard University Press, 2002).

infection is closely linked with one of the most powerful propensities of human beings. Love and physical relations are not activities that are themselves base and sordid—indeed the world would have been immensely poorer in poetry and culture if the inclinations that go with them were absent in human psychology. So this is not an area of life that can be simply 'censored out' through reasoning, but something where behavioural modification is needed in line with the dangers and threats that arise, as and when they do arise. Throwing the baby out with the bath water can hardly be the object of the exercise.

Finally, the criminalisation of some types of human relations can contribute to driving them underground, which makes it very difficult to bring them into standard public discussion—much needed both for the dissemination of information and for open discussion of safer behavioural norms. In particular, Section 377 of the Indian Penal Code offers the possibility of 10 years of imprisonment as a fitting penalty for gay sex. This provision of the penal system was imposed on India in the 1860s, during Victorian British rule, and while the British have liberated themselves from their Victorian past, the Indian officialdom seem to have found their own reasons in favour of retaining this bit of imperial legacy. When that law came into force, America was just trying to liberate itself from the institution of slavery. Section 377 is presently being debated in the Indian courts, and one can only hope that the liberation of gays from prospective police threat (and blackmail) will come before long, even if 150 years late. Openness has a huge role in the use of knowledge and shared reasoning, and among the many implications of the AIDS epidemic is the need to normalise a kind of sex that many people find perfectly normal, no matter how distressed some others are even at the thought of such relations.

I conclude by reaffirming the need to take personal responsibility seriously (it certainly must have a big role in tackling the HIV epidemic), but along with that, by emphasising how dependent the exercise of personal responsibility is on a variety of social circumstances—informational, behavioural, organisational, economic, and legal. Those who want to 'rely' on personal responsibility, divorced from social contingencies, may be, in one respect, better informed than those who fail to see the role of personal responsibility altogether. But partial understanding can also be the source of very serious misdiagnoses.

Nearly 2000 years ago, philosophers of the Nyaya school in India pointed to the fact that the familiar case of mistaking a rope for a snake, much discussed by classical Indian epistemologists, occurs only because of half-knowledge—not full ignorance. One needs an understanding of the 'snake concept' to take a rope to be a snake. Someone who had no clue about what a snake looks like would never mistake a rope for a snake. We have to avoid the errors of half-understanding as well as those of ignorance. It is important for us to see a rope as a rope, and a snake as a snake, for they are both parts of the world, including the world of AIDS. But first we have to stop blaming the victims and stop looking for reasons for leaving them to look after themselves. We are in it together.

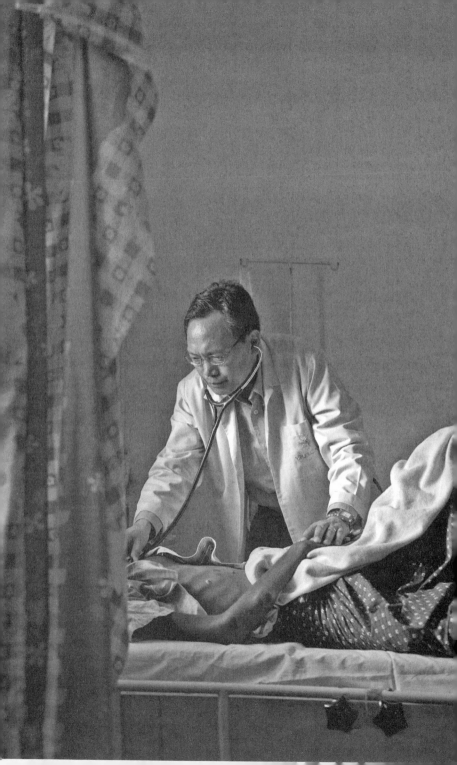

MISTER X VERSUS HOSPITAL Y
Nikita Lalwani

I am with him in his workspace, a narrow box of a room, as
he talks. The room is clean, fresh and comforting; controlled,
yet welcoming. As there are very few objects in the room, I
wonder if these defining characteristics are coming from
Toku himself. He is seated at his desk in the corner, a doctor
in his early forties, of northeast Indian origin, with very clear
skin the colour of light pine, high cheek-boned, hair arranged
with a tidy side parting, silver-framed spectacles. His face,
which has a certain 'do not disturb' quality at rest, creases
confusingly with the very opposite quality when he smiles.
'People call me Toku,' he says, when I refer to him as
Dr Tokugha.

There is a knock behind me. I get up quickly to allow the
door to open—my chair, by his desk, takes up most of the
free space in the room. Toku engages warmly with the patient
who enters—a slight, quiet man in his thirties with patchy
white bristle on his cheeks, dressed in a dark work shirt and
slacks that roll up to reveal bare feet. They speak in Tamil,
but I can sense that they are talking about medicine and treatment. The phrases 'three times a day' and 'after food only'
form part of the conversation. As the patient leaves, Toku
gets up to follow him out.

'Be comfortable,' he says, noting my nervous, slightly tense
posture. 'Be my guest.'

He flashes a modest smile of impressive teeth before exiting. I look around the room for more clues. To my right, a makeshift bed has been formed from a sheet and pillow laid on top of a chest of drawers. On the wall is a poster for a twenty second general conference of some kind, entitled 'Enduring Beyond'. The image is of a warrior ready for battle. Above that, a few trophies in a glass cage. To their left, a picture of a park in eighties film colours—heightened greens and flushed fuchsia blooms. 'God Bless You' is inscribed on a wooden plaque on the top shelf, below a rusty air cooler, set into the wall, which touches the ceiling. A Bugs Bunny peg near the door, for a coat. A sink, with Dettol handwash at the back. His name written in faded gold on a thin length of wood by the computer.

What am I looking for? I am confused by my desire to document these objects. Why do I imagine that I can find something intimate in them? Maybe it is because Toku seems so contained that it is difficult to imagine that our meeting is going to reveal anything that has not already been written down somewhere, by someone else. I think of the newspaper cuttings that I have seen, in which his story was appropriated and printed without his consent. I think of the case study I have received from the Lawyers Collective in Delhi, in which the ramifications of his battle for justice are meticulously detailed.

'How can I help you?' he asks when he returns.

I decide to be as straightforward as possible. It is the only way to avoid the fudge of possible meanings.

'How did you discover that you were HIV positive? What was it like, the... discovery?'

The words come out of my mouth, and I feel their inadequacy. They are too vulgar, hanging in the air without context, like underwear on a washing line. We look at each other. We both know that Toku's story is out of the ordinary. That he has suffered key abuses of the kinds of human rights that

20

many of us take for granted, most notably the loss of privacy. I am, of course, part of the fallout from those abuses. I know his public story. That is why I am here, trying to understand his private space.

'First of all, I need to tell you something,' says Toku.

I nod.

'I have a very painful tooth. I have had three root canal operations. I am disheartened. So I may not be in the mood to talk. I may feel, how to put it... withdrawn.'

I nod again. Of course. 'It is understandable,' I mumble. 'The root canal is a very tender and exposing operation, isn't it?'

'But this is how it was...'

And then, just like that, Toku begins at the beginning, and tells me exactly what it was like.

'In 1995 I used to work in a Nagaland hospital as an eye consultant. It was the biggest hospital in the state. My father was the village headman, I had finished my studies and was an eligible bachelor. Everyone has to settle down, and it was time. I'm forty two now, then I was thirty. A few suggestions were made to me, and I had a couple of ideas myself. Then I proposed to a girl.'

'So, would you say it was arranged?' I ask. 'Not really,' he replies. He met her three or four times, and decided to propose. He liked her. His family was also keen for the match. His brother-in-law, his cousin's husband, especially encouraged it—he was a government minister, just like the girl's uncle. They set a date for the wedding to take place just weeks after the engagement.

'I made a trip with my fiancée and her mother to get the wedding dress stitched. They wanted to go to Hong Kong or Bangkok. The marriage was the big talk of the town, you see. In the end, we decided on Kolkata. We commissioned the dress—both being Christian, it was a long white dress with a veil—and two weeks later I went back to pick it up along with the invitation cards. I got it in a closed box—the tailor said it was very important that I did not see the dress before the wedding, I remember that.'

'Did you look at the dress?' I ask. 'No,' he replies, smiling. He knew not to do that.

'I flew back to Nagaland, and descended from the plane. Normally, if I returned from a trip, quite a few family members would come to pick me up from the airport—come along for the ride, help with the luggage. This time it was just my sister. As I approached her, I could see she was very sad.'

Toku lists the fears that entered his head. They are the same worries that haunt us all when away from loved ones: mostly touching upon the vacuum of unexpected deaths. His mother? His fiancée? A car accident? But his sister would not reveal anything on the journey home.

'I arrived at the house to see all of my family assembled there, maybe twenty people. My brother stood up in the centre of the room and said, "Your wedding has been called off because you have AIDS."'

He smiles again, and pauses for me to laugh out loud, should I feel like it. The drama of the scene is both chilling and faintly absurd.

'That is how I found out.'

Six months prior to this, Toku had travelled with his brother-in-law, the minister, to Chennai to help him organise an operation. His brother-in-law's uncle was ill and needed to get to a large hospital, for the treatment of his abdomen. Toku discovered that the patient needed major surgery, and a blood transfusion. They needed a donor urgently, and so he volunteered to give his own blood.

'I didn't know whether it would be the right blood type, but I said "Look, I will give my own blood." I don't know whether they used it, but I stayed for the whole thing and went into the operation theatre with him. I was very pleased that the surgery was successful. The minister left and I stayed back to help with the aftercare—remove the sutures of the patient, keep an eye on him.'

Toku has become more agitated. He speaks quickly now, leaning forward in his chair.

'The doctors there ran tests on my blood and found that I was HIV positive. But they disclosed my HIV status to the minister, my brother-in-law, instead of to me. And then, he chose not to disclose it to me until six months later. After encouraging me to get engaged and helping me decide on marriage, he waited till the day I returned with the wedding dress and gathered everyone I knew, to make the announcement.'

When he went back to the hospital to confirm the rumours, Toku says he was treated with disdain by the doctor who tested him. He was told that he would die soon, that there was no cure, and was asked to leave the room after a few brief questions about his sexual behaviour. He tried to find someone in the hospital who could tell him how the information had been leaked, but no one would give him an appointment, or listen. Finding himself on the other side of the doctor–patient divide, and with a disease that aroused disgust and moral judgement in his wider circle, Toku lost his voice overnight.

'I had many thoughts on my mind. I will die soon. How will I face my father? What about the shame? Of course, I withdrew from the wedding myself. After checking the results with another test, I told my fiancée that we had to call it off. She cried. I was in shock. Everyone knew. But it should have been my decision. I would not have searched for a girl and proposed if I had known. Why did the hospital tell the minister, and not me? This was a breach of confidence. And that it was my brother-in-law. I donated my own blood for his uncle—I gave my own blood for him.'

I ask if he knows the reason behind the betrayal. He shakes his head. Even now, 12 years later, Toku says he is not going to dig it up. He has his suspicions. It could have had to do with his brother-in-law's career, rivalry with his fiancée's family, who knows? But his brother-in-law's betrayal is irrelevant compared to the actions of the hospital which disclosed his secret.

'With AIDS, there was such a stigma then. People didn't understand the issues. He was a big minister, but I had just become someone with AIDS. Who was going to listen to me? They all knew my status in Nagaland.'

I nod. Sitting in his office, and listening to him, it is difficult to imagine Toku commanding anything other than respectful attention. But it is a reminder of what we are doing here together, a small paper cut of sharp feeling when it comes to thinking about how we name and identify each other with regard to this particular illness. He is talking about something that happened a decade ago, but of course I have asked him to tell me his story because he is HIV positive.

Whenever he uses the word 'status' to refer to the result of the blood test, it feels so collapsible as a word. In effect, because of how he has told the story, I have an idea of his 'status' in society before he found out that his blood was marked in this way. He has used the same short cut signs and signifiers most of us use—his vocation, age, location, familial background, the impending union with another person and their family. After the revelation of the blood test, in this narrative of his life, just as in the hospital where he supervised an operation, those indicators become irrelevant—he becomes a man whose whole status is HIV positive, and nothing else. Even now, as he talks, he seems aware of this fact. He is a little louder, more insistent than before, as though the danger of being dismissed is never gone once the labels come out of the bag.

'Then it begins. I can't sleep, nothing. They all know my status in Nagaland. And there is such a stigma, so much shame; I know I have to leave there. I don't have my job any more. People are criticising me. Then I start thinking I want to disappear. I think it is very difficult to disappear. I start to question myself—how to disappear.'

He closes his eyes and frowns almost indiscernibly.

24

'I think, is it a dream? I pinch myself.'

Silence.

He opens his eyes and presents the impossible nature of the question to me, throwing his hands into the air with sudden vehemence.

'How to disappear? How is it possible to disappear? I think maybe I'll go to the jungle, live there, or go to another state and live quietly. But if people know I am a doctor, they will wonder why I am so quiet, with no ties. They will find out, and I will have to leave again. I thought maybe I would go to Nepal; help people who have no hospitals. But then I would need a visa, medical tests—it becomes difficult. Where to hide?'

There is an impasse between us. It is as though he genuinely wants an answer to the question, and I am with him, trying to imagine how I would act if thrust so suddenly into such a fugitive skin. Having been silenced internally, I would of course, like him, want to erase my outer, visible self—it would be a matter of survival.

He registers my stasis and laughs, urging me to join him.

'It is not so easy to disappear, you know?' he says.

I concur. My chest feels tight. No, it is not so easy to disappear.

Anand Grover, the lawyer who sent me to meet Toku, has likened human rights to the green leaves on a tree:

> If a fire is lit in the forest, which of the trees will catch fire and perish? Obviously, the one without the green leaves. The one with the green leaves, with the rights, will survive. Those without rights are therefore most vulnerable.[1]

Grover, who met Toku in 1996, has been at the centre of the battle for human rights for people affected by HIV, for the past two decades. A charismatic and provocative man,

---

[1] 'A Tryst with Dominic', Lawyers Collective, March 1 2001, www.lawyerscollective.org/content/tryst-dominic-0.

known for being fearlessly outspoken on issues of personal freedom, Grover is one of the directors of the Lawyers Collective, a group of legal professionals and activists, who donate their time together in the form of legal aid and lobbying for legal reform. Much of the work of their HIV/AIDS unit centres on marginalised groups—women who are evicted from their family home, or separated from their children when discovered to be HIV positive, drug users, sex workers, and the large number of positive people who are impoverished—having very little money and, therefore, very little access to treatment, information, or the courts.

After confirming his HIV status, Toku stayed in Chennai without knowing how or what he would do to survive. He met with an old college friend, who expected him to be on his honeymoon.

'He wanted to know where my wife was,' says Toku, with a laugh. 'I said, "Oh I am in big trouble. My marriage is cancelled because I am HIV positive." He was shocked when I told him, and very supportive. He said he knew of just one place that gave help to positive people, and we searched for that place for two days. No one seemed to know where it was.'

The place turned out to be the YR Gaitonde Centre for AIDS Research and Education, the hospital in Chennai where we are now sitting, host to over 11,000 patients a year with HIV and AIDS related issues. The director of the place, Dr Suniti Solomon, would become his future boss.

'She changed my life,' he says. 'She said she would respect me as a doctor, not just see me as an AIDS patient. And incredibly, she said she would hire me.'

Dr Solomon, who documented the first AIDS case in India, in 1986, has since pioneered major breakthroughs in AIDS research and education. In 1996, when she heard that Anand Grover was in town, conducting a workshop on HIV and human rights, she sent Toku to attend. Grover remembers meeting Toku at the end of the workshop.

'He was very sincere and well mannered,' he says. 'His story evoked empathy on my part. He wanted to take legal action, which surprised me—I was apprehensive as the issue raised was an untested area of law in India.'

Inspired by Toku's story, Grover took his case to the National Consumer Redressal Forum (NCRF), which deals with cases of consumer protection, in an attempt to sue the hospital that had leaked Toku's HIV results. But the NCRF was not interested in the confidentiality issues around testing for HIV.

'Their attitude was that if you are positive, the whole world should know about it,' says Grover. 'After a lot of hostility towards HIV positive people, the Forum decided that it was not the appropriate forum to decide the issue.'

Unwilling to settle for this, Grover took the case to the Supreme Court.

Meanwhile, Toku began to write, and campaign on the newly emerging issues around AIDS. After a trip to the XI International AIDS Conference in Vancouver, he got involved in the creation of a network for people living with HIV in India. INP+ was founded in 1997 by Toku and 11 other HIV positive people, and now has over 100,000 members, with a network in almost every state in India. Back in those early days of dialogue and awareness, he went to a workshop near Pune to take part in discussions.

'It was in the jungle,' he says. 'It felt like it was far from anywhere, an isolated place. The place was full of HIV positive people and representatives from NGOs. So imagine this… Early in the morning, first thing, on the first day, I meet a woman.'

He laughs.

'I meet her, and immediately tell my whole life story to her. Just standing there. It was 7:30 am.'

I look up at him from my notepad. Is he saying what I think he is saying? He laughs again. The sound is relaxed. But careful. It feels like it contains something valuable.

'The whole thing. I don't know who she is. Whether she is positive or negative. But I just meet her, and straightaway I tell her my life story.'

He shrugs his shoulders. He seems pleased that this is inexplicable, and I am moved by the simple warmth and thrill that her introduction into the story seems to bring. It is so unexpected. 'Did anything happen?' I ask. 'Why do you think you told her everything?' He acknowledges my questions with a grin, and brushes them away.

'Wait! After three or four days we have become close friends. She is back in Goa then, where she is from. We like each other, but marriage is not in my mind, for many reasons. Then we begin to write to each other. We start to meet often, but we do not know if we are making the right decision. We understand the feeling, but we can't tell each other that this is in our minds. Then gradually, we talk. First, there is this: I am living with HIV. I can give her no children. She herself is negative. People will think that she is mad, marrying an HIV positive person. I was worried. How could I expect her to cope with these things?

'She was very supportive. She said we could have an adopted child. "Life is in the hands of God," she said. "What is short or long? It is the sweet memories that matter. You can have a hundred years of bad times. Or some good ones."'

'Why was she at the workshop?' I ask.

'She was a psychologist with an organisation for positive people. But still, I was worried. We thought that we would seek different opinions from different NGOs. We may be biased, we thought, and they can help. They were all supportive. They said, "As long as your own mind is clear, you should proceed." Still, it is very difficult to know what is right. So we decided to break off, and give ourselves time to think.

'This was at the end of 1996. The plan was to have six months with no phone contact. If we could forget each other, then fine. If not, then... well, let's see, we thought.'

He smiles, eyes mischievous.

'After almost four months, I phoned her. I couldn't help it. I was supposed to go to Bangkok for a work trip. My supervisor told me to take a team. I thought to myself, maybe she can come.

'I call her and tell her that. But she says "We are not supposed to talk about this for six months," and then she puts the phone down. Tak! Like that, she bangs it down!'

He shakes his head.

'Oh no, I thought. Oh dear. Then I waited. And after six months, I called her on the appointed day, and she said she still felt the same. We met, and well... on October 10, 1998, we got married.'

I am visibly relieved. But he moves on quickly.

'We began living here in Chennai, and a few months later another bombshell comes—from the Supreme Court case. You know about that, yes?'

Yes. This is the part that I do know about. When the case was finally heard at the Supreme Court, it was entitled 'Mr X versus Hospital Y'. Grover's argument was that the hospital had not honoured basic confidentiality rights, and that leaking Toku's status to the wider community, instead of giving him the information, had resulted in the destruction of the fabric of his life—social exclusion, humiliation by friends and family, the loss of his post at the Nagaland eye hospital, the dissolution of his reputation, and life as he knew it.

In spite of the fact that the hospital had not informed Toku of his condition, and even though he called the proposed wedding off himself, the court ruled against him, decreeing that the hospital's release of the information to the minister without his consent had 'saved the life' of Toku's proposed fiancée.

The case had an unfortunate and far-reaching side effect. The judge decided to include, as part of his verdict, comments that suspended the right for HIV positive people to marry. The court sought to protect the rights of potential marriage partners who could contract 'the communicable venereal disease', unawares. But instead of pinning this to informed consent between parties, the idea that a positive person should declare their status to a prospective marriage partner, thereby allowing them to make the decision and take necessary precautions should they still want to go ahead, the Supreme Court deemed that marriage itself was not appropriate for someone with HIV.

For the first time in judicial history, anywhere in the world, a court had taken away the right of an individual to marry. Newspapers raged with debate under headlines such as 'Right to marry not absolute!' Grover was furious. He called for a national campaign against the judgement, expressing the need for public protest. At a meeting organised to rouse support, he argued that a blanket ban on marriage took no account of the fact that many positive people commonly got married with full, free and informed consent of their partner, who might or might not be HIV positive. His speech was reported in *The Indian Express*:

> The restriction on the marriages of HIV infected persons can have serious repercussions. The isolation of such persons will drive the epidemic underground, as doctors and hospitals will not maintain confidentiality with regard to their HIV status.[2]

The right to marry and found a family is a fundamental human right, and recognised internationally—under Article 23 of the Universal Declaration of Human Rights, and Article 16 of the International Covenant on Civil and Political Rights. It is part of the right to life, which is recognised under the Indian Constitution, Article 21.

I sit in Toku's office, and hear about the throttling legal details of his battle so soon after the simplicity of his love story, and think about how heartening, almost fantastical, it is that the right to marry has ended up as part of the Universal Declaration of Human Rights. Aside from the obvious links between marriage and stability, or procreation, there is

---

[2] 'Lawyer Calls for Protest on SC ruling in HIV Marriage Case', *The Indian Express*, September 4 1999, www.indianexpress.com/res/web/pIe/ie/daily/19990905/ige05033.html.

something hungry and romantic about the assumption that this aspect of human companionship is recognised as a basic need, along with the right to liberty and freedom of person.

Toku's case, however, had inadvertently curtailed these rights for positive people in India. The news of the ruling spread quickly through the HIV community worldwide. This decision must have horrified him, I say. Especially as his case was, of course, about privacy, and not marriage. And he had just got married himself, after so much soul searching. Although the status of his marriage was not officially affected by the ruling, as it had already taken place, the judgement must have shaken Toku and his wife.

He frowns, looking down as though he is thinking of a way to encapsulate the magnitude of the feeling it brings up.

'But of course! I was very upset. For so long we were afraid to get married, and a month after we had done it, this happens. People were reluctant to accept us. "How can you marry a negative woman?" they asked.'

Then, in a perverse and peculiar twist, the case produced exactly the same breach of confidentiality that had led to its existence, and Toku's personal details were leaked to national and local media. When the story hit the press it was no longer Mr X versus Hospital Y.

'They published my name and address in every single paper!' says Toku.

'They told me that my identity and name would be suppressed. I did not file a case for marriage—it was for confidentiality, and then they themselves abused those rights. All the newspapers published my name. From Nagaland to Chennai, to Delhi. All of them. It was there even in the local papers. Even on the radio.'

He clenches his fist, and strains against the words, which come quickly.

'My new mother-in-law went to Delhi to take a flight to visit her grandchildren in Australia. She was staying with her relatives. It was a Sunday, and she saw the papers. Every supplement carried my name. She was so shocked. She called

31

her daughter and asked, 'Did you know he was HIV positive?' My wife said yes, she knew. Her mother said to her, "You people do what you want." Her relatives said my wife should take me to court. Then her mother stopped talking to us.'

There is a sombre quality to his voice.

'For those two weeks we cried in the night, and in the day. Then, the relief. My wife's mother called back. She said they would support us, and asked us to come and see them. I went back to Goa for Christmas, to their family home. I felt very uneasy going there. But they didn't treat me differently. They said they would be there with us. In fact, my mother-in-law became the ambassador between us and the rest of the family.'

Over the next few years, the Lawyers Collective worked consistently to battle the new ruling, filing several petitions for the judgement to be reconsidered. After four long years, they succeeded in getting it dismissed, restoring the right for HIV positive people to marry in 2002.

'And what about Toku?' I ask. 'What happened to him at the end of all this? How has it left him?' He says Grover took him back to Nagaland recently, after more than ten years away. Grover said, 'It is time for Nagaland to welcome its son, which she had abandoned, back home with open arms.' Toku went back to the hospital where he used to work, and gave a talk on coping with HIV. The hall was packed. Everyone had turned up to see, in effect, how he himself was coping.

'All of the doctors from nearby came,' he says. 'They came to see how I looked. You could see them standing, watching and thinking, "How is it possible that he is HIV positive? How can he talk like that?" They didn't listen to me, just stared! Then gradually, they came to their senses and started to listen. They thought I would be incapacitated, living in a dingy place. They didn't imagine that I would seem so normal. Or empowered.'

And indeed, I think, this is the first thing that strikes you about Toku: his spotless skin and demeanour, the infallible quality of seeming to be in very good health. Like his root canal operations, any sense of physical weakness is hidden— something you have to be told about, rather than glean for yourself. I wonder if it was always this way, or if it has gradually become part of his armour for living.

'One or two of my old friends came up to talk to me afterwards,' he says. 'They said if I had not become HIV positive I could not have achieved what I have managed. They admired what I was doing.'

And what about his family? I ask.

'Oh, we have two sons—we adopted one when he was three years old, now he is eight, and then also adopted his brother last year, who is now nine. In fact, I have to go and pick them up from school soon!'

He looks at his watch, and smiles.

It is an abrupt end, but one that feels fitting for a conversation that began in a similar fashion. I make some comments of gratitude as I get up, an attempt to try and provide some kind of wrapping after such an emotional ride. I try to convey my thanks for his patience and lucidity, in spite of the pain from his teeth.

He gestures to me to wait.

'I want to show you one thing before you go.'

We walk up to the top floor of the hospital, and I see 50 faces photographed in hero and maiden poses, on park benches, and in studios. They are typical portraits for potential suitors, adhering to the grammar of this particular genre—the gaze of the subject unsmiling and intent on the lens, each expression inviting an array of possible interpretations by the viewer. The photos are attached, by a staple or paper clip, to a personal handwritten statement including their 'Biodata' and 'Needs'.

Toku has begun matchmaking for his patients. All of the people in the folder are HIV positive. He tells me that when first diagnosed, patients are often reluctant to give him their details for these marriage files. They may be young widows who are worried about what people will say, or fear that they will not be alive for much longer. He tells them to return after three or four years, that it is now possible to live a long life, and that companionship is important. And indeed, many of them come back.

I speak to Annie, who makes the matches and organises the meetings. She tells me that the most recent marriage boasts the safe conception of a baby, free from the virus, as a result of the recent developments in treatment.

The people in these pictures are often poor, and many come from exactly the kind of vulnerable groups that Grover talks about as being most susceptible to rights abuses, those without a canopy of protection:

> The trees without the leaves are like the vulnerable groups in our society: women, children, sex workers, injecting drug users, men having sex with men, prisoners, etc. They are already stigmatised and marginalised by society. They are often poor and illiterate. Either they do not have rights, or, even if they have them they are not able to exercise them.[3]

But even more of the people in the folders, like Toku, do not technically fit into this list. If forced to articulate their 'status', I would probably have to just put them into the generic category of 'middle class men'.

I wonder what the story has been for each person, as I leaf through this bundle of social strata, united by blood: teachers and plantation workers, engineers and market traders. I even start to wonder if the small business owner on page 7 would go well with the young mother on page 15, in spite of the fact that he is looking for a Pentecostal Christian, and she is nothing of the sort. She is photographed in a kitchen

---

[3] 'A Tryst with Dominic', Lawyers Collective, March 1 2001, www.lawyerscollective.org/content/tryst-dominic-0.

next to a stove, and has a half smile that suggests a curt sense of mischief, a lack of pretension. She has written that caste is not important to her, in the section entitled 'Needs'. I catch myself before getting fully immersed. It is time to go. Toku has to pick up his sons, after all.

I take the lift, alone. It has a large folding door, a heavy accordion of metal that is quite difficult to open. Inside, it is dark and noisy on the journey down; pipes rattle and wheeze as the machinery gets going. Lights are going off around me as I find my way to the front of the building, and people leave for the day. I think about how Toku is trying to actively restore this right to marriage as part of his own patients' right to life—by attempting to reignite that part of the human psyche that maybe we all share. The part that believes that we own the right to love in that particular way, and be loved in return.

NIGHT CLAIMS THE GODAVARI
Kiran Desai

'Hindu vegetarian breakfast,' proffered the stewardess, but a cold wind had blown the fog from about the Delhi airport, and before we'd finished, the plane landed, unexpectedly on time. The city was dug up for the new metro, looking subversive, broken. We drove past the sadness of poverty at night, slums of plastic bags barely off the ground, gunny sack doors battened against the freeze. I climbed up the stairs between houses all turned into apartments since my childhood. Where one family lived, there were mostly eight, with offices in the basement, servants on the roof, underground, atop the water tanks.

I climbed to our flat, sure that it remained as always: the inauthentic, but beautiful painting of a blue-robed scholar painted over an old Persian manuscript; my narrow bed with its mattress worn into my childhood shape; the photograph of all of us before we left: two silent brothers, two talkative sisters, and a dog who is smiling, his teeth a shining, grinning star. Our love for him was the love that first taught us about death.

My father was waiting in his brown dressing gown, familiar to me over years, but oddly, he was also wearing gloves and a hat. His smile arrived slowly, as if from far away. Tonics didn't help, nor the homeopathic, the ayurvedic, the herbal. He was sinking; the body gives way so fast, so fast. We lived in hospitals that were in a constantly unsettled state between decay and renovation, thronging with people from all over the third or renegade world—Afghanistan, Iran, Nigeria.

Together in a broken parking lot—men and women doing namaaz; sleeping by the defunct fountain; a train station's worth of bedraggled bundles lying about—we waited hour upon hour for the loudspeaker to announce the name of a relative in emergency.

Our family coordinates first displaced by migration, were being displaced again. This illness—it felt like leaving home in the first place.

When I came back from the hospital, I was quite alone with the family bookshelves. The library now relied on memory and love—to find a book you'd have to have known the titles from before the orange and pale green-blue spines faded. It was still an antidote to open those pages now smelling of tobacco, dust, a mustardy pungency distilled by age.

I remembered how an educated madman, living in the ruined seam of a mosque behind our house, used to pee an arc under the moon and scream 'India–Pakistan—Arrrghaaa!' probably in reference to an anguished journey that never resulted in a home. In the distance, there was still the familiar grinding of trucks driving turnips and cement, chickens and bathroom tiles, across the nation; unsettling the night with the sound of endless, rushing travel.

I read a Márquez story my mother had admired: 'The Incredible and Sad Tale of Innocent Eréndira and her Heartless Grandmother'. Exhausted Eréndira, who has laboured hard to bathe her fat and terrifying granny, falls asleep with her candle burning, and a wind of misfortune catches flame to curtain. To repay the debt of the cindered hacienda, she is prostituted across the landscape; she services client after client, but never makes enough; across the desert they go, following men, being followed; the granny-pimp holding a giant cross, and Eréndira in a grand bed carried by porters.

A bit wobbly in the soul, I travelled to coastal Andhra Pradesh, to the delta region of the Godavari river. On the streets of a village we drove through, I noticed an overabundance of beds. Beds being delivered, new old beds, makeshift stage set

40

beds, cheap beds being varnished in the sun, mattresses in the dust. Around this strangeness of beds proliferating, village life seemed as benign as Narayan's Malgudi stories that had created my idea of what it meant to be Indian in this world, in the sweetest incarnation possible. Little shops for cigarettes and sweets; cows wandering; men riding cycles on their way to the banana market by the river's edge, bananas tied to the handlebars, their colour macaw shocking—green and yellow, green and yellow, the greenest green and the yellowiest yellow. Sound of water pouring into pails, out of pails. A jeep going by with some policemen poking their heads out. This world was normal.

Except it was really entirely something else.

The women getting children ready in tiny shorts and mini-ties on elastic bands were all sex workers. The children with their homework were the children of men who stayed five minutes for a 'shot'. The cycle rickshaw men were pimps who'd found extra business when auto rickshaws drove down their income, the gas station men were also pimps, and so were the dhaba men. A 20% or 30% cut. The lorry drivers, the coolies—were clients. Others in the street were 'brokers', some 300 of them. Men coming back with groceries were 'temporary husbands'. The old lady at her gate was a brothel madam, haggling over the price of girls she was buying from desperately poor parents. Coloured Christmas stars over bungalows revealed a missionary drive to save the fallen. The policemen were slowing down, hoping to catch someone soliciting. They'd let her go again in exchange for free sex.

Say 'Peddapuram', and every man grins. This is a village of 'high class' sex workers from the Kalavanthalu subcaste, hereditary courtesans and temple dancers famous for their elegant beauty. Almost every family is involved in the trade. They trace their lineage from the days when they were protected by royalty, priests and landowners, all the way downhill to a franker prostitution as patronage crumbled in a modernising India of another shade of morality. 'There is still a lot of money in this dhanda (business).'

41

The price of a high class sex worker in Peddapuram: all the way from Rs 200 ($5) a shot, and Rs 1500 ($37) for a night, to Rs 1000 ($25) a shot, Rs 10,000 ($250) for a night; depending on beauty, fairness of skin. 'Shot' always said in English, with movie swagger. All ages were sought after, from teenagers to 'auntys', for younger men feel safer with 'auntys', explained a sex worker. And, guffawing hard: 'Those policemen are smiling at you because they think maybe you're a new girl with lipstick on especially for them.'

Andhra is red earth; chillies; virile moustaches—lush, verdant, moist and black—on every man's face. A state famous for pickles and chutneys.

'And other hot stuff.' Frank humour of women with other women.

'It's the chillies.'

'No it is the music. The beat of the music.'

'And who likes the sex?' asks one of the aid workers. 'Any of you girls?'

'She! She! She! *She does!*' they point at one woman with frustrated, accusing faces.

The woman begins shouting, 'Why do you all say that? I *don't.*'

'*Yes, you do! Admit it.*'

At the moment it seems it will break out into a bitter row, the accused begins to laugh and cover her mouth, and they all convulse into giggles while still attempting to maintain anguished and stern expressions.

The statistics indicate Andhra Pradesh is at the top of the list in people having multiple sexual partners. In rural Andhra Pradesh, 24% of men and 9% of women claim to indulge themselves beyond the restrictive parameters of marriage, up from the meagre national average of 10% of men and 2% of women.[1]

---

[1] Andhra Pradesh State AIDS Control Society (APSACS) TRU Behavior Surveillance Survey 2003.

But, I wondered if, more than titillation, Peddapuram proffered home comforts. I had imagined stripy tiger sheets, spooky and suggestive lighting, mirrors in strange places, women posturing with bottoms and breasts first—my naiveté? But there wasn't the slightest attempt at titillation or mystery. The women were in conservative sari blouses, almost no makeup, gold and diamond nose rings and earrings in traditional flower shapes. Peddapuram strove to provide simple middle class contentment on the road.

'We are famous because we are the descendants of courtesans and royalty, so we have that poise, those fine looks,' the Kalavanthalu women say.

'No special tricks?'

'No tricks. We are known for our good manners. We treat a man like a king. We'll cook non veg, we'll give oil massages and baths. We turn on the fan. The men bring the whiskey, the McDougal's—but everything else we provide, and when they leave we beg, 'Don't go, please don't, oh, don't go, oh…'—we do all of that play acting. We spoil them.'

Inside a brothel so high class, they say film stars and even Americans go there, was the stuffiness of a middle class home: melamine; fridge; food smells; cabinets full of plastic flowers and china dolls; bed done up in pink with a poster of the Sydney Harbour over it. The only odd thing was that, for privacy, sheets printed with flowers and zebras had been tied across the grill gates, blocking anyone attempting to peep into the compound. The brothel owner, like a prosperous and overly mannered housewife, large tummy spilling over her sari. 'Don't even call them sex workers, don't mention prostitution here,' I was warned. Her parents were oriented towards each other in the manner of people who'd been married most of their lives, and were finishing lunch thalis of rice.

'There is a temple where the Godavari meets the sea. Here, each year, a Kalavanthalu girl is married to Shiva. That night she spends alone with the deity.' This I'm told at a gathering of sex workers training to distribute information about HIV prevention. 'Every year they select one girl. Her family is given 2–3 acres of land by the village council. They look for a girl who is beautiful and poor, so she will fetch a good price, and so her family will benefit. The ceremony was just held— on December 11th, celebrated lavishly as any wedding by the elders of the Kalavanthalu community. We heard she was bid on for 5 lakhs ($12,500). She spends that night sleeping in the temple, the next day she goes to the man who won the auction for the "first night".' 'First night' is always said in English. 'The girls dance in traditional festival melas to advertise themselves. In the old days, they would put a betel leaf in the girl's hand to indicate a future assignment, now they exchange cell phone numbers.'

A sex worker named Ragini, charging her phone from a socket behind her chair, tucked it back between her breasts and departed to cook goat curry. 'Meat from the legs,' she specified, for her 'temporary husband' to take with him on a trip to Hyderabad. 'Temporary husband' is another English phrase, always uttered with pride at having attracted loyalty within a system conjured for betrayal.

Most Kalavanthalus are not married in temples any longer—the symbolic ceremony attempts to bring a whiff of distinguished past, of religious approval, to the present. Mostly they are married off to their father's sister. Marrying deities and banana trees, I'd heard of before, but not one's aunty!

'Yes, the father's sister is the one who gives the mangalsutra.'

A tremendous amount of discussion about mangalsutras. It seems so sad—all the sex workers have this necklace, this sign of a married woman, about their necks. Everywhere you sense a desire for structure and ritual, for normality in lives singularly without it.

'The whole family—grandmother, mother, even the father if he is around—decides who will have "first night". The nails are filed; the married uncle gives the toe rings. We do most things just like any other wedding. Three things we do not do. We don't step on each other's feet, which is part of a usual ceremony; we don't shower rice and turmeric over each other's heads; or cumin, jaggery, flowers; we don't bow to the Arundhati star.'

One family of sex workers, grandmother–mother–several daughters, proudly displayed each picture in huge albums, of the 'regular marriage' they had worked to give one daughter, no sign of resentment at the vast cost of this sister's beaming happiness, paid for by the rest of them.

They told me they trace their lineage all the way to the three celestial dancers who tried to distract the sage Vishwamitra from his meditation.

Today, the women dance at fairs to advertise themselves, but in the old days, the first performance was the gajjela puja; the anklet puja, when a girl, ready for market, danced before the Shiva lingam.

One grey-haired lady took us to the temple where she performed at eleven. Her house is hung with portraits of Jesus, John David—a local missionary, Sai Baba, and a temporary husband. Four good men, all of whom, obviously, could not save her.

But even now, the priest's wife greets her as 'sister-in-law' and applies the tika, indicating how much these women are accepted.

'For us, the first man would give the mangalsutra. Unless the first man was the raju [king],' she said optimistically. She herself was sold to a chowdhary (a landowner), for Rs 500 ($12.50), 55 years ago. He had sex with her for a few days, then left her to solicit.

If they are not married to the deity, or to their aunty, they are married to a sword. At least seven in a group of 50 sex workers here claimed this initiation.

'At puberty, I was asked if I preferred marriage or the dhanda,' said a girl in pink chiffon embroidered with mirrors.

'My mother eventually married, but her husband drank, and they were very poor. She learned it was better for a woman to make her own money, no man would support you, you'd just be in the dhanda anyway, and supporting him as he drank and visited prostitutes. So at fourteen, they put the mangal-sutra first around the sword, then around my neck.'

What choice could she have at fourteen? Of course her mother took the 'first night' money. She is a 6th generation sex worker. 'My great-great-great-great-great grandmother was the dasi [courtesan] of the king.' Her home, that she built herself, is airy, all white, steps rising steeply above the dirt. Even the light appears to be at peace here. Peddapuram is full of proud women, women who build their own homes.

But there are homes and homes. On the other side of Peddapuram, in a dusty patch full of rubbish, lives Laxmi, all alone. She says she is eighteen, she looks far younger. Laxmi grew up in nearby Kakinada, mother a maid, father a rick-shaw puller. A woman from their town took her to Bombay promising to find her work, took her to a club, told her to wait; vanished. A while later, the brothel seth entered and informed Laxmi, entirely innocent of sex, that the woman had been paid for Laxmi to work into the future without pay. A police raid uncovered her after a year and sent her home, whereupon she was thrown out by her ashamed parents. She came to Peddapuram.

The 'class' girls don't talk to her, she says; they resent others muddying the famous Kalavanthalu name; they have glam-our and 'colour', name themselves Kareena Kapoor and Sonali Bendre after film stars, without it seeming absurd; they leave the brothel only if a client sends for them in an air-conditioned Maruti car—otherwise you never see them.

Her friend, Sridevi, comes over to share a bit of winter sun. Sridevi's mother is a brothel madam, and while she takes a 50% cut on the girls who work for her, or takes them on con-tract, paying their parents, say, Rs 10,000 ($250) for two to three months of their daughters' sex work—with her own daughter she can recoup 100% of the girl's earnings. Sridevi seems too overcome by this simple sense to be resentful. About her neck, a Virgin Mary in gold. They are both Christian converts.

'Do you go to church?'

'How can we go to church?' they laugh. 'We are prostitutes!'

Opposite, they say, lives a girl with a temporary husband who stays with her because her earnings allow him to play cards: 'He blows Rs 1000 ($25) a time.'

For love, or at least company, they will support married men, drunks, gamblers.

No simple emotions result. One woman said she had sex once with a man who, ever since, has sat outside her door crying. But she has a temporary husband as well as clients. 'One of them I love, and one I cannot bear to see sad.' How to work one's heart out of that predicament? So the man who cries continues to cry.

Another woman, you can see how beautiful she must have been once—before she desperately slashed her arms and wrists upon seeing her temporary husband flirt with another girl.

When we visit Ragini (preparer of the goat curry), in her village of Dowleswaram, 30 kilometres from Peddapuram, it turns out her temporary husband is also her blood uncle. A child, who must be twelve or thirteen, is sitting in Ragini's lap—like sisters they have their arms about each other. The girl ran away from home with a man who seduced her with stories of love, then sold her to Ragini's mother, the haggard, unsmiling owner of one of five brothels near a cinema house. They tell me of another child forced into sex work by her parents, so as to earn her own dowry. She'd marry and hope her husband would never uncover the truth.

Generations of struggle, and this is what they have: one trunk; a few battered pots; an ancient, dusty, cloth umbrella; a black and white TV, picture wavering, from the first days of television; a few cosmetics, safety pins, a toothbrush lying on the earth; all in a hovel of ruined thatch and mud, more sieve than shelter, two dark holes into which they carry a mat, should a client appear.

In homes all over the district, secret housewife sex workers wait for their cell phones to ring. One woman and her daughter-in-law transform into a brothel as soon as the son and husband leave for work. 'There is so much demand, and not everyone can afford a Kalavanthalu.'

'Do the men know?'

'They don't know, or maybe they know and don't ask. You see, they can't earn enough to pay the bills.'

Their clients are students, daily wage labourers, stone cutters, fishermen, factory workers, hawkers, farmers, port workers, coolies, sari purchasing businessmen, plant nursery men, Oil and Natural Gas Commission men, water engineers who work at the barrage, the military and navy, sailors from China, South Africa, Croatia, Sri Lanka, Madras—ships docking for weeks sometimes, transporting urea from Nagarajuna Fertilizers, sugar from Deccan Sugars, rice, smuggled DVD players, imported beer, and 'drugs!'—the women assure me.

Brokers arrive in towns like Peddapuram; take the girls out to the ships in little boats. The captains get the Kalavanthalu girls. The drudge sailors get Laxmi or Sridevi. 'We depend on sign language, don't understand what they say, but we like to go—they pay us with lipsticks, perfumes and dollars.'

My hotel, by the side of the Godavari river, offers a 'torpedo deck' for business conferences and 'mind-boggling water slides' in a water park, 'a scintillating place to while away your time with the near and dear ones'. It is full of businessmen on their own and they are mostly at the bar above the Captain's Table. It is painted brightly in an attempt to be jaunty, but nothing can rid it of a flavour of something else. Tinted glass in the windows; mosquitoes coming at you through slowly swirling cigarette smoke. The night has claimed the Godavari.

A nice waiter says: 'No, no no, oh no, we don't make tandoori as nobody asks for it and if you want continental, it will take twice as long, as, you see, continental takes so much longer to cook,' and so we are all eating the same fish curry, with not enough liquor to drown out this diseased gloom, and any attempt to lighten things, sinks one deeper, because of course, the truth is that there is something else going on in this bright, rich India. This taking off India, this rising giant, this Incredible India!—seems heavy. Eastern Europeans, men from Japan and Hong Kong, Russians, American desis—they are travelling, the news is spreading, they have arrived for it—and the new India is often nowhere.

In the rooms, hotel TVs play music videos that show half-clad bodies, tongues and fingers doing gasping, grasping things.

On the highway, truckers go barrelling through the void, their minds becoming convinced of rumours: *If you sleep with a virgin and a donkey you won't get AIDS.*

And in the dark, by the side of the road, invisible women are signalling with torches. 'We'll go into the jungle.'

Enough of several languages to say this much. 30–34% of about six million truckers and helpers have commercial sex.[2] Two million truckers may be on the road, away from their homes, for as long as one to two months at a time.

Andhra Pradesh is the Indian state with the third largest number of migrants. Sex workers cater to them, but they are also part of this migration, travelling to towns like Peddapuram to work off its fame, travelling so they might be anonymous, travelling to urban centres where women from coastal Andhra are considered desirable, madams dropping off girls in Bombay, Hyderabad, Chennai, Goa, for lucrative contract work—Rs 20,000 to 30,000 ($500–750) a month.

---

[2] Family Health International (FHI), Department for International Development (DFID), *Healthy Highways Behavioural Surveillance Survey*, August 2000.

95.4% of sex workers from East Godavari moved once; 90.4% moved at least twice.[3]

We travel more; the world grows lonelier and bigger; a disease like AIDS waits for the spaces between us, for people displaced, for so many not travelling in the way of shiny advertising, whose journeys are not about freedom and pleasure in the wide world—but about being squeezed into a small place. In the past, there were repressive regimes; there was slavery, the Holocaust—terrible methods of dehumanisation. In today's world, we have bitter patterns of migration, of illegality. Refugees and exiles of war and poverty, moving from rural landscapes to urban centres, from poor countries to rich countries—the kind of journey that undoes one's spiritual, one's personal place in the world, making anyone uprooted from home exchangeable with anyone else, leading to betrayal in myriad forms, economic to sexual.

Off the highway, a group of women carry a folded examining table, a sterilised speculum, a flashlight and a broom, into a derelict weed-filled compound belonging to the forest department. They are followed by a young doctor, an ophthalmologist. 'But this is my interest,' she smiles. How many would volunteer for this? Two times a month, they gather up the women scattered on the highway, searching for 'hot spots' near petrol pumps, eating stalls. Sometimes they find 40 to 60 women, or 20 to 25. The percentage of HIV prevalence among female sex workers in East Godavari is reported as 26.3%,[4] compared to 1.25% in the general population of Andhra Pradesh.[5] They do not automatically do HIV testing

---

[3] Population Council, 'The Patterns and Drivers of Migration and Mobility of Sex Workers and Male Migrant Workers on the Move and Examining the Links with HIV Risk', 2008.

[4] National Interim Summary Report (October 2007), Integrated Behavioural and Biological Assessment (IBBA), Round 1 (2005–07), Indian Council of Medical Research & Family Health International.

[5] 'HIV Fact Sheets Based on HIV Sentinel Surveillance Data, 2003–2006', National AIDS Control Organisation (NACO), Ministry of Health and Family Welfare, November 2007.

in these clinics, as they do not offer treatment, and the logic is simple: how would anyone survive a loss of livelihood, a life of pus and ruin, if you offer no medicines and no alternate income?

Yet, on the other hand, the cost of discretion: AIDS is flaming down these highways. Four to 10 clients a night, sometime 20, sometimes 40. More traffic on festival days. Pongal, for example, when women traditionally visit their mothers' homes.

'Don't you get tired?'

'When I see the money, I don't get tired.'

Many of the women are balding, with weeping sores, blisters ringing their mouths. Some with a dullness about their beings, an inside out look to their eyes, as if they are gazing beyond the highway, the table with the speculum in the ruined hut, and the broom by the side of the rubbish it has just swept up. Who would pay to have sex with them? They are checked for STIs, given condoms, released back to the highway.

If you have sex with a Dommarisani, a sex worker from the Dommari street acrobat community, your crops will be good and you will be healthy all year.

'Wives invite us in for their husbands.'

Some of the women in this highway clinic are skilled in somersaults and back flips. They can slither up a perpendicular stick and revolve in the air, balanced on a single point. Through summer they travel from village to village in a caravan, performing. In winter, they make palm mats to sell—we are sitting on them now. They come from nomadic communities now settled into villages like Chilakaluripet in Guntur district. The women are forced to have sex for free, and the community is paid collectively from the village fund.

'The men?'

'Men don't work in their community,' the outreach workers say matter of factly. Yamini tells me she was performing gymnastics when a mechanic gave her parents Rs 300 ($7.50) for first sex.

But they insist other sex workers exist in much more desolate vulnerability. Such as the women by the sea.

Eight women, holding used rice sacks, work from a sliver of jungle between the highway and a flat, dead-looking ocean; middle aged women with heavy bodies. Jayati began at twenty, when her husband abandoned her and their children. She's been here every day for 15 years, working for Rs 50 ($1.20) a shot. There are no brokers for there is no money to be made off these women. But a merry toddy seller has set up his stall near them, a frothy, batty expression on his face. The women come out of the forest like refugees, tentative, shy— then in a rush of affection and eagerness—ready for photographs, jokes, to tell absolutely everything. They pull me by the hand down the network of paths, to shallow pits in the sand. 'This is how.' One woman lies down on her rice sack— an old, fat, sad woman lying in a pit among plastic packets, cigarettes scattered about, with legs spread, sari pushed aside to reveal breasts poking up. A lifetime of this, and each year she will be more worn, the rash will spread like a fungus, the sari will have more holes and stains, she will have more grey in her hair, more wrinkles—and her price will drop.

As the stories mount in an overwhelming tidal wave of disaster, I think of the sadness and defeat inherent in feminism, the humiliation of waving a banner: 'Well, I believe women should earn as much as men, and men should help with housework etc etc…' when men from Oslo to Rajahmundry, are walking out of the back door, in fact, out of the front door, to seek out girls sold for less than the cost of a bottle of beer.

Yet these women have not succumbed. Their friendship gives them dignity. They used to suffer terrible violence, they say, drunken men in gangs coming to the forest, demanding certain angles, postures, roughing them up. A sex worker can't go to the police.

The lady who runs the centre that opened to help them presents herself as an ordinary middle class woman, in sari and glasses—but extraordinary enough to travel away from her cricketer husband and her son to protect the women from thugs in this desolate place. The sex workers at least have each other, their children, and their toddy friend coasting upon his personal wave. She lives in one dim-lit room at the unbuilt edge of town; no company for a woman like her here. She invites us in; the emptiness gapes; nobody about in the silent night; and not even a television. One cannot overestimate her chosen loneliness.

'Do you use condoms?' she asks, seriously, but with a sort of introverted humour.

'Yes, yes, yes!' The jungle sex workers pull out the packets from between their breasts and wave them madly like flowers in a festival.

There is buoyancy about this answer that suggests the truth may be otherwise. This is so we can all be happy together. 76% of sex workers from East Godavari report consistent condom usage,[6] but what happens when women like these are on their own, negotiating out of hunger and debt, dropping their price, as even the climate conspires against them. In the monsoon, they say, they go from Rs 50 ($1.25) to 25 (63 cents) to 15 (38 cents), anything so as to pay their rent. Go out with their sacks over their heads in vicious rain.

Then, their voices suddenly hush. They are not the most desolate of sex workers, they tell me. There are mythic creatures of misfortune that actually exist. Doomed creatures even the sex workers hesitate to speak of, as if doing so, would make it impossible to continue their own lives with any life spirit. These are the yoginis; branded witches, chased to the outskirts of the village, often widows whose property is then stolen by greedy relatives. They are considered communal

---

[6] National Interim Summary Report (October 2007), Integrated Behavioural and Biological Assessment (IBBA), Round 1 (2005–07), Indian Council of Medical Research & Family Health International.

property, free for any man to enjoy. 'But not common here. Inland. In Karnataka…'

The morning I left, I woke up early. At first light, the Godavari river is the colour of widowhood, a final departure.

Spilling over sand banks, it is wide enough, pale enough to soothe difficult human emotions, to suggest a journey more peaceful than this earthly one. Many people are gathered here, staring out.

Some buffaloes interrupt the scene, though, swimming out to a grassy island. A priest sat on the bank, in the sun, in front of the over pink Krishna Consciousness centre, amidst washermen washing, washing; so much washing going on, it seemed a metaphor for cleaning deeper things. He said there was a Telugu saying that translated: 'Well, you go all the way to work so as to eat, and by the time you've come all the way home, you've undone the food in your tummy.'

Turning away from the water, the landscape is overrun by red again.

'The beloved may absent herself from existence, but love does not,' John Berger quotes Naguib Mafouz, while meditating on the emotion of the colour red.

'Could it be that red is the one colour,' he wonders, 'that is continually asking for a body?' That refers always to the human form? The emotional music of love and the end of love blares from every lorry. River, sea, road travel beyond the eye's horizon. Coconut palms reach extravagantly all to the right or all to the left.

And a delicate sex worker sings in Kakinada, 'Why aren't you singing? Why aren't you singing to my eyes? To fill the vacuum my heart cannot express.'

My father opened one wise eye when I saw him again in his hospital bed, now sadly diagnosed with cancer. The nurses, he told me, were really skilled actresses, temple dancers being trained by the government towards a new vocation. Every evening they had put on a play, he said, philosophical discourses, songs—and he watched for hours, he got no sleep; their unusual talent, he felt, might take them all the way to England. His poor mind was seeking the refuge of imagination.

What I had seen, really seen, were lives lived with the intensity of art; rife with metaphor, raw, distilled. The emotions of love and friendship, you'd assume would be missing or rotten, in these communities—existing even more so for their being sought amidst illegality, fragmentation and betrayal. These were lives lived beyond ordinariness, insisting on a personal story, not exchangeable with any other. 'Tell each one properly,' said the women in the jungle by the ocean.

'Receding into a private existence, Murad plotted his next move. Emerging from his hiatus he announced his incipient departure from India. No one was interested in making his kind of cinema. The Indian arts scene was conventional, unadventurous, docile. Moreover, the boys in Bombay were dull as dahi, unable to make good on either a night of delicious raunch or a rogue ballad of something more permanent. New York, with its titanic, neurotic energy, with its tease of a dirty, luscious salvation, was the perfect island. His bags were packed. A special visa had been approved. He was ready to pitch camp in a new land. But the few select buddies who knew of his health were afraid to let him go. Would he finally take the life extending drugs he needed in New York? Or would he continue to hang on to the mumbo-jumbo that AIDS did not really exist?'

Siddharth Dhanvant Shanghvi

HELLO, DARLING
Siddharth Dhanvant Shanghvi

Every time my friend Reba Khan spoke of Murad, her voice, darkly nostalgic, was like a jazz tune on the run, at once spirited and melancholic. Murad had large, wandering brown eyes, she said as her face lit up with memories; a limber, athletic body and the sort of manner that made all the straight women in the room suspect—with a sigh of regret—that here was another man, invulnerable to their advances. 'I don't remember the first time I met Murad,' Reba told me, 'but I remember the first time he invited me over to his house, on Worli Sea Face, where he lived with his parents in a penthouse. He had a gorgeous room and one wall was glass, so you could see the sea, and only the sea.'

Reba paused to look out at the cars on the street. We were driving down from her graphic design studio in Colaba to a restaurant in Bandra.

'Murad was the original flamboyante. He was more than life. He was a filmmaker, raconteur, vintage poster collector, an outrageous flirt. He never just went to a party—he always arrived, and then quickly became the party. He was generous and funny and clever, and he always said, *hello darling*, in a way that made me come completely alive. I guess,' she said, her eyes squinting, 'you think it's a cliché or that it sounds queeny, but coming from him it was like a bolt of light, and you felt, well, priceless.'

Over our meal, Reba asked me why I was so intrigued by Murad.

I replied saying that although I did not know anyone personally who had died of AIDS, I had researched the subject for my master's thesis, parts of which had been rewritten and published in newspapers in India and America. My interest, initially scholarly, deepened significantly after a character in my new novel was diagnosed with AIDS, and, eventually, succumbed to the condition. The aspect of AIDS that fascinated me most was its reinvention, for those who could afford medication, into a long-term health condition—as opposed to the death warrant it was thought to be in the eighties and early nineties. Edmund White, perhaps the finest chronicler of the impact of AIDS on art and artists, wrote in his essay, 'Esthetics and Loss', that by inflicting doom upon desire, AIDS had put the fire out of corporal pleasure. Sex, which had once provided 'a daily brush with the ecstatic', was now no more than a 'death trap'. Artists were falling like flies, and within the rapids of their suffering and eventual passing was lost their art and all its fury, consolation, splendour, argument, tenderness, provocation. But White wrote his essay in 1987, almost a decade before the 'cocktail' of life-saving drugs became available and altered forever the vocabulary of AIDS mortality. By the mid nineties, new drugs came to dock, signalling hope for millions, slowing down the obituaries that routinely littered the newspapers during the tail end of the eighties. In the nineties, activist Urvashi Vaid used AIDS as a lens to gaze on the direction of the sexuality movement in America. Vaid's book, *Virtual Equality,* observed how the passing of an entire generation of men from AIDS helped give rise to the modern idea of homosexuality: thousands of men had to die, in fact, to have been seen as alive in the first place. Fascinated by White's idea of the art lost along with the artist as well as Vaid's lament for an era of men who had to die to come alive, I knew I could explore these two filaments of thought in a novel. The character I wanted to create

60

would bear witness to both ideas—the death of an artist from AIDS, as well as the price that sex eventually extracts from us. This task took me about four years to pull off. During this time, whenever Reba spoke of Murad, which was often and always with robust affection, I felt as if I was revisiting in conversation what I had previously met only in my musings: now the character in my head was suddenly and dramatically writ large in reality.

Reba, who had met Murad in the heady days of Bombay in the early nineties—media had just arrived; the economy had opened up; the internet had rearranged the furniture in the living room of our head—did not know him in his childhood. But Lata Shroff did. They had both gone to school together, in south Bombay, and both hailed from affluent backgrounds—from a gilded milieu where men like Murad were accepted, but teased. 'Murad was frequently the target of mean jokes, and he hated it most when someone called him "faggy",' Lata told me during our meeting at her apartment. 'One evening at the club, someone called out "faggy" at him and he started to yell hysterically and kick the air. What a spectacle he made! And no one knew how to calm him down. It wasn't even funny how grossly in denial he was of his sexual orientation as a teenager.' Murad was not effeminate—certainly not a 'flamer', to resort to slang, as much as an unusual combination of striking good looks, a posh accent and bitchy repartee, all of which were noticeable from a tender age. The other boys at school naturally assumed he was not 'on their team'. Of course, Murad himself thought he was straight, and even had a girlfriend for one summer. His denial was not simply because homosexuality was—and is—viewed as aberration in India, but also because Murad knew that his father had reservations on the matter. 'Perhaps that's why,' Lata hesitated to add, 'Murad left for Australia to study film after a few years of college in Bombay—around 1987 or 1988. He needed some time away to figure himself out.' In Australia, Murad tried hard to convince Lata that he had a girlfriend, Alexandra, who later turned out to be Alex, the boyfriend. 'I didn't mind his little fabrication,' Lata said with a grin. 'I took it as part and parcel of the aesthetic of our friendship. We'd both been over the top. I mean, when we were sixteen we would reminisce over our "youth", and then cry our hearts out as we listened to "Those Were the Days"…' Lata, now almost forty, rolled her eyes at the absurdity of their crying jag: two teenagers mourning the innocence of their lives as twelve year olds. Although such a memory seems incredible, it's also exactly the sort of detail that fills Lata with anguish each time she listens to the song again; after all, her accompanying singer is no longer at her side.

If it has never been easy to be openly homosexual anywhere in the world, it has been particularly harrowing in India. Not only is homosexuality frowned upon culturally, but Indian law—Section 377, a colonial curse imposed in 1860—punishes anal and oral sex, even when it occurs between consenting adults. It states:

> Whoever voluntarily has carnal intercourse against the order of nature with any man, woman, animal shall be punished with imprisonment for life, or with imprisonment of either description for a term which may extend to 10 years, and shall be liable to fine.

It might be easy to assume that men from Murad's echelon might be exempt from Section 377 and its draconian tenets. After all, men who have sex with men in the open—in parks or on the beach—are far more vulnerable to cops, who invoke Section 377 and then promptly demand bribes to let them off. But the law has a strange way of catching up with the rich. Several years ago, at a party hosted by a diamond merchant on Madh Island, sexy clusters of muscular men were dancing the night away when police sirens rang over and above the electronic throb of music. Panic enveloped the air.

Cops disembarked from vans. A retinue of constables arrived on the scene. And one guest overheard the inspector ordering his constables to 'Go, get the rich one, quick!' If extortion is the advantage of threatening arrest under Section 377, then nailing the man with the moolah is crucial. When affluent married homosexuals have sex on the sly, their toy boys often turn around and threaten public exposure. 'Some of the blackmail rackets are clearly looking for well-off, closeted targets with who, perhaps, they could get into long-term blackmail situations,' says the Bombay based writer and activist Ravi Mehta, who has known of several cases when a male escort called on Section 377 to wrest money from his partner. 'I know a lawyer—a lawyer, for god's sake, one practising in the High Court—who paid a lakh of rupees [\$2500] over a couple of years before finally discovering his backbone, and telling the guy to get lost.' To be outed, particularly under racy circumstances, terrifies so many wealthy men that they readily pay up to safeguard social status, marital life, and their stake in the family business. The real power of Section 377, however, is not limited to the threat of its enforcement; its existence fosters a climate of hatred toward homosexuals in India. After all, as Foucault noted, law is not external to an individual and its real power lies in how it is internalized: prohibitions are not always enforced by the law, as much as self-imposed.

The nineties dawned, Murad wound up film school in Australia and returned to Bombay, fully reconciled with his sexuality. Oddly enough, his parents had also come to accept him, and his mother, in particular, doted on him, convinced that her son would make a name for himself. In 1993, Murad made his first documentary, noted for the boldness of its themes, as well as for its camp and feminist undertones. The film, widely reviewed and keenly discussed, resulted in extraordinary, premature praise for Murad, whom the press dubbed a 'Young Turk' of independent cinema. In those days, as Reba pointed out, it was difficult to miss the dapper

63

gent, with his loud, welcoming *hello darling*, his careful coiffure, cigarette in hand, wrist bent ever so dandily, and eyes that focused on their subject like a spotlight. Photographed at society soirees with film stars and socialites, Murad togged up with splash and shimmer, dishing out catty quotes to journalists, who were so bedazzled by his persona that they happily overlooked what some critics had written off as a mediocre talent. Although his early success gave him the guts to take the tentative steps from being privately homosexual to being publicly so, he remained cautious, extending the news of his sexuality only to friends. In San Francisco, in 1994, on a panel discussion on South Asian films, the moderator asked him about his sexuality. Murad had already confided to the moderator that he was homosexual, but when questioned before an audience he balked and said that his private life was his business.

But only two years on, Murad was no longer as protective of his privacy.

His next film, six polemic vignettes on homosexuality, adapted from verse, announced his coming out with aplomb. If he had kept his homosexuality out of view so far, then now, all of a sudden, it *was* the view. A slick ensemble of short, interlinked films gave him a patina of notoriety, and his newly minted celebrity swiftly piloted him into the pages of the Bombay press. Some activists believed Murad's following was not a result of his output but of his public homosexuality as he was, in one sense, the polar opposite of the closet, from which countless Indians sought liberation—which only a few achieved with as much panache as Murad.

While his peers in the film industry envied his social status, as well as the press adulation, in an infinitely more competitive sexual cosmology, the beautiful boys of Bombay wondered with awe how Murad managed to seduce just about any man he set his eyes on. His eclectic coterie of arm dandies, ranging from the highly stylized to the slightly thuggish, came from the realm of theatre, media, advertising, and, of course, film. One famous Bollywood star discovered, much to his chagrin, that Murad was sexually voracious—but discerning to boot. When the star failed to make the grade in the sack, he was promptly packed off home in a battered old taxi. Murad's sexual innings were chalked up to his significant charm, his ability to give attention, as well as to hold it, to his good looks, and to his fame—which he hunted out hungrily. 'He sought out publicity like no one else I knew,' observed one of his friends. 'Although there's nothing wrong with soliciting public attention, it also resulted, ultimately, in his undoing. Murad seemed to believe what the press said about him, and his ego gradually inflated. Far worse, his expectations of himself seemed to crescendo, and, quite frankly, it was never clear if he could deliver on what he expected of himself.'

Fame, it would seem, had become yet another narcotic in Murad's life.

Animated by the glitter of celebrity, Murad was a klezmer band of a companion at any party. 'Once, Murad was doing a retrospective of his movie posters at a gallery, I think, somewhere in Marine Drive,' remembered Reba. 'I sat up nights designing the posters, the invites. He said he didn't know how to thank me. I said he didn't have to. I, you know, *loved* him. I arrived at the retrospective late—as usual! Murad spotted me, and, almost instantly, he started to applaud. Hearing him, every single guest at the gallery followed suit. I felt like a thousand watt bulb lighting up. I'd never expected to arrive at *his* show and feel a superstar. He just knew how to do that.'

A year after his second documentary, which had come out in 1996, Murad and one of his pals underwent HIV tests. Murad's friend was fearful that he would test positive ('I was quite popular with the Irani boys,' the friend said to me over lunch). Murad was confident he would be fine. Fate reversed the odds. That afternoon they went home, altered forever. News of the infection paralysed Murad. He was in his early thirties, and he felt as if a death sentence had been handed out far too early, far too cruelly. But his dread would have had greater poignancy a decade earlier, when HIV really did translate into a death sentence.

By 1997, when he had tested positive, HIV was seen as a long-term health condition for those who could access the new drugs.

Murad started to sleep during the day and rise at night, scouring the internet for news of a cure. The more time he spent on the net, the more he grew vulnerable to rumours that AIDS was only a conspiracy unleashed by pharmaceutical giants to make money off homosexual men. His belief in them was based on little more than the persuasive hogwash that eventually vanishes into the footnotes of urban mythology. Although adequate medical information was available at the time, the doctors Murad met with were not competent at calming his myriad, manic anxieties. Ever the nonconformist, he resolved to deal with HIV in his own way: he would not take any treatment. Murad's sepulchral and inexplicable decision confounded—and terrified—his friends. Did Murad really believe AIDS was only a rumour started by pharmaceutical companies to rake in the pink rupee? What could they say or do to make him change his mind?

Receding into a private existence, Murad plotted his next move. Emerging from his hiatus he announced his incipient departure from India. No one was interested in making his kind of cinema. The Indian arts scene was conventional, unadventurous, docile. Moreover, the boys in Bombay were dull as dahi, unable to make good on either a night of delicious raunch or a rogue ballad of something more permanent. New York, with its titanic, neurotic energy, with its tease of a dirty, luscious salvation, was the perfect island. His bags were packed. A special visa had been approved. He was ready to pitch camp in a new land. But the few select buddies who knew of his health were afraid to let him go. Would he finally take the life extending drugs he needed in New York? Or would he continue to hang on to the mumbo-jumbo that AIDS did not really exist? Reluctantly, with their hearts in their throats, they watched him take off for America, unsure how he would fare, or if he would return. 'I was terrified for his health,' said the friend who had been with him when they had gone to get tested. 'And amazed that he would push himself like that… under the circumstances.'

Before Murad left Bombay in 1997, he went to see Reba. 'He said he wanted business cards, and would I design them? Of course, I would!' Reba exulted. 'He wanted 2000. But I was on a roll, and said I was going to offset them, and so I had to do 5000 minimum. When he came over and saw the sheer volume of the cards, he was overwhelmed. As he was leaving he said, "5000, you made 5000…" And I said, "Sure babes, knowing you, you'll have handed them out in a week!" And he said, "I won't need 5000. I won't need so many in this lifetime." At the time, I thought he was being modest. I had no idea that he was trying to tell me something that would, much later, break my heart.'

But New York proved to be a letdown, especially for a man who had been a pretty cool canapé, if not the toast, of Bombay society. Going from being featured in weekend papers, and making appearances on talk shows, Murad now worked part-time at a copy shop, in addition to a slightly more stable job. One year, Lata Shroff and her companion called on Murad in New York. 'We dressed up for dinner, under the assumption that a night out with Murad had to be an occasion. The restaurant was nondescript, but pleasant. We arrived on time, and I asked the maitre d' to lead me to the table booked under Murad Shah's name. The maitre d's eyes widened. Then, I saw Murad in the white and black uniform of a waiter. He was serving someone, and he looked over his shoulder and winked at me. He was trying not to blush.'

So, why did Murad really go to New York?

Practical reasons could have driven Murad off. As Ravi Mehta explains to me, 'It's certainly true that some poz guys have chosen to go abroad because of the superior medical care—or more precisely, perhaps the awareness of dealing with HIV positive patients that exists abroad. Here (in India) there's a big NGO/medical structure built around prevention and testing, and, to some extent, giving first line treatment. But I think the awareness of dealing with long-term positive patients, and all that that implies—for example, how to treat them for other opportunistic infections, or surgery that is not necessarily related to their HIV, but is affected by their being poz—is much less here. I certainly know people who have, quite recently, decided to move abroad, and their being poz was very much a factor in their decision.'

'Ironically,' Ravi adds, 'going to the US doesn't mean being able to be more open about being HIV positive. Thanks to the US visa regulations, still in force, which would allow being openly HIV positive as grounds for rejecting someone's visa, many people who go to the US are driven into secrecy about their status for fear of being deported, or denied a visa extension. They'll tell their doctors, who will respect their confidentiality, but they can't be more open. I know a guy who would really like to be more open about his status, to help his friends back here, but he can't, simply because of his fear of being denied the visa which he feels he needs in order to get the level of treatment he wants.' The US continues to classify HIV as a communicable disease, similar to TB, even though it is neither airborne, nor is it transmitted through casual contact.

Homosexual men with HIV have to combat not only the stigma that attends to their sexual origins, but also their health condition, yet another bridge to have to cross. The disgrace shrouding HIV in India provokes menacing acts of hatred, reserved, in another era, for lepers; and the self-loathing it encourages in the individual is often only a reflection and elaboration of the loathing that society fosters for HIV.

During the course of my research for my thesis on AIDS, in 2002, I met any number of middle class men and women at government hospitals who told me that they preferred to be dead than alive with HIV in India. 'We have been treated worse than stray dogs,' one man said to me, his eyes sparkling with rage. 'When the doctor touched my hand, it was as if he was spitting on me.'

Hospitals in India are infamous for their despicable treatment of the infected. One 2006 study noted institutionalised discrimination towards positive patients. Denial of healthcare, mandatory HIV testing, lack of counselling, and the public disclosure of HIV positive status were some of its troubling conclusions. Nurses often wore double gloves, and doctors donned masks unnecessarily when treating positive patients. The linen of positive patients was burned. Such prejudice is probably due to ignorance surrounding HIV transmission. Over half of the healthcare workers believed HIV was transmitted by touching someone positive. Nearly half were under the impression that the breath of a person with HIV could spread the disease.

Often enough, the worst sort of segregation is self-inflicted.

Andrew Sullivan, writing about AIDS in his memoir, *Love Undetectable*, found that after he tested positive, not only did he hide his status, but he also retreated socially. At the same time, his friend Patrick had also been detected positive, and Patrick too vanished from the radar.

> In this, we both participated in one of the unsung rites of AIDS. Not so much the fear, or the shame, but the fusion of the two, the uniquely isolating and self-punishing crucible in which the disease often announces itself.

One man, whom I interviewed for a piece I wrote in 2003, said that he had long accepted his homosexuality, but, after testing positive, he believed it was punishment for his sexuality; later that same week, a heterosexual bus driver told me that HIV was his punishment for sex. The subtle difference between the two confessions was almost lost on me at the time.

Guilt about HIV can also cross over into the most gothic forms of self-destruction.

Activist Ravi Mehta recalls the tragic story of a young man who walked into the sea in Goa after learning that he was HIV positive. A widely criticised article, published in *Rolling Stone* in 2003, exposed a small subculture of men who actively sought HIV. At 'bug parties' in America, positive men called 'gift givers' would bareback—have unprotected anal sex—with 'bug chasers', men who desired to be HIV positive only so they could finally overcome the constant threat, and terrible doom, of possible infection. Perhaps neither stigma nor fear—nor the profound, complex intermingling of the two—forced Murad to New York. His future as filmmaker seemed increasingly bleak as it was hard to source funding for a 'gay film', and nearly impossible to line up an acting crew unfazed by the subject matter. More worryingly, Murad's own directorial prowess was under question. His initial spark now seemed to have run into an ignition problem. Murad's debut documentary, charged with flashes of brilliance, may have been admirably outré, but its substance was always suspect. Similar complaints had been lodged against his subsequent two endeavours.

Lata Shroff conjectures: 'On the strength of his first documentary Murad travelled from one film festival to the next, gaining admirers across the world. But not even the fawning notices in the press could help him make a film that could establish his name as a serious filmmaker. The idea that his career would not take off in the way he had expected now consumed him with a grief that even HIV could not inflict on him.' There is an implication that Murad had grown conscious of one key problem with his spectacular public persona—the lack of any substantial talent. He was smart enough to gauge that he was good at what he did, but the greatness he aspired to was one elusive eel. Unable to deal with fate's tumult, Murad fled to New York to search for suitable work projects and also to live his life on high tilt—artistically, independently, hedonistically. When even New York failed to honour his genius, AIDS presented itself as the perfect exit clause—operatically tragic, a dramatic farewell symphony.

Passing on the drugs that could have extended his life, one friend remarked, was like suicide in slow motion.

Although New York was tough on Murad—he was often broke and he had to work long hours—it gave him the nerve to come to terms with his HIV. On a brief visit to Bombay, he told Reba about his condition. 'I was at my friend Firdaus' house in Colaba,' she recalls. 'I was the only girl at a party of boys, sitting on a seat by the door. Murad was also there, sitting across from me. He said, "I want to share something with you." And I said, "Sure babes." And he came out with it: "Reba, I've got HIV." There was a lot of music. I thought I didn't hear him properly. He repeated himself. I left the party because I had to go back to work. As I was driving back home, from Colaba to Juhu, it started to sink in. For the life of me, I couldn't imagine that it would happen to Murad; actually, I couldn't imagine that it could happen to any of my friends. It's not the kind of disease you ever *want* to happen to your friends. At the time, I just kind of blotted it out. There was no other way.'

After four years in New York, life was cumbersome for Murad. The jobs, insulting to start with, were drying up. Artists all across the city were glamorous and troubled variations on the same theme. Everyone was defiantly unique, touchingly liberal, hustling for immortality—and therefore, ironically, a part of the mainstream.

By September 2001, after the towers had come down, the romance with New York was wearing off swiftly.

India, meanwhile, had donned new colours in his absence. The arts scene was newly dynamic and lucrative, auctions hiking up the value of paintings. Writers were winning awards and acquiring readers across the world. Funding was pouring in for independent films, which were often made by young Indian directors who had also tried their luck in foreign pastures, but returned after failing abroad. It seemed a relief, more than anything else, to quit the Big Apple. He set sail for home, and arrived to the loud cheer of his friends. Delighted to have Murad back, they were also unsettled to see that his health was faltering visibly. He had resolutely hung on to his belief that HIV did not exist, resisting medication even as his body was caving in. and the ones who were never told were curious why he looked as if he had rickets. 'It was as if,' Reba reflected wistfully, 'Murad was packing it all in. He was going out, meeting artists, attending shows, inviting people over to discuss films over dahi puri. He was living like there was no tomorrow—maybe because there was some truth in that.' Back on the home turf, long nights of partying until dawn recommenced. The possibility of work on an international project enthused Murad. If he had considered chucking his life because his career was going nowhere, here was a reason to carry on now, to go fighting into the night, with strobe lights on the swirl.

But in spite of the gung-ho, the disease had chewed into his indefatigable spirit. Reba recollects: 'After he came back from New York, he was sick now and again. But that never stopped him from partying. He went to one party in a bright saffron sarong. Eyes turned. Jaws dropped. Murad looked stunning—but skeletal.

'That September, it was his birthday, and I called him a few days before and asked if he had any plans. Very sheepishly, he admitted he was alone. So I called up Anupama, a pal we had in common, and we agreed to meet up for drinks at Olive. That was the first, and only, time I saw that Murad was out of it. He was kind of blue, but a real dark, awful blue. He was not Murad. Not any longer.'

Shortly before Murad died, in November 2003, Lata Shroff called on him. They talked avidly about cinema, the changing face of the arts in India, the possibility of working together on a world class film. 'I remember walking away from his house thinking that Murad had got it back, his wild stamina for life. His optimism, and his love for cinema, seemed to be larger than he was.

'I had no idea that he had HIV. I hadn't been told—and I was one of his closest friends. Murad, who had always been so open about his sexuality, his sex life, was secretive about his HIV. Did he not trust me?' Lata asked, her eyes welling up. 'His concealment made me very bitter about our friendship, and I've never really come to terms with the fact that I'd been kept in the dark.'

Two days after Lata Shroff's last visit, Murad died.

'Shortly before Murad succumbed, I'd rung him,' said Reba, her voice flaring up with ache. 'I said I wanted to meet him. He said he was in hospital. I told him I would come and see him. But he was quite chirpy, and asked me to come see him at home on Monday, when he was to be discharged. I relented. I put the phone down. I kept thinking back to the night of his birthday, two years prior. How exhausted he'd looked. That weird sadness in his brow. I glanced out the window of my office, and something in my heart kind of burst up. I knew then that I would never see Murad again.'

There is no way of knowing what Murad's films, if he had been given a chance to make them, would have been like. For illness, when survived, furnishes profound questions and inspiring conclusions, as it did for Susan Sontag, who wrote *Illness as Metaphor,* following her fight with cancer. Would Murad's films have been love stories? Stark, stylish provocations, much like him? Or disdainful, existential kahaanian of mad, mad Bombay? More poignantly, there's no way to know if he would have used his HIV status—when reconciled to the magnitude of its experience—in a public sphere. During one of his hospital stays in Bombay, he mentioned to a friend that he had 'to do something about this HIV thing in India'. He wanted, he said hesitantly, to speak up, talk about what was chewing him up as if he was supari. Murad could have articulated not only the perils of HIV but also its incandescent hope, thereby compelling millions living with HIV in India to feel safe in their own skin. Just as he had once talked about homosexuality with a bravura honesty, he could have also gone on to become not so much a spokesperson of the condition but the rock star of survival, and, along the way, inspired in others an acceptance of self, so they too might find faith, relearn humour, and trust in love again—which is also a kind of a gift to pass on, a gospel, galvanic legacy.

As I struggled to imagine the pain Murad's friends had nursed, the memories collected, and that specific, permanent empti-ness in their hearts, it occurred to me that Murad need not have died. He had resources to avail of the healthcare he deserved as well as his family's unflinching support. To disbe-lieve AIDS ever existed may have been one way to confront its behemoth scale, but what he was really unable to come to terms with was thwarted ambition, dreams denied, art that could not redeem its artist. Having given filmmaking his best shot, and failing nonetheless, the dark music of HIV played in the background as the echo of salvation. As this final concerto faded into silence, the truth emerged in stark, ambiguous particulars—neither sexuality nor ailment claimed Murad, but the minor deities, who permit art to breathe through mortal figures, had asked for him back.

In some ways, Murad had become my novel's real life alter ego.

As expected, both subjects impelled me to consider what, then, is the sum of one life? A patch on a quilt. A photograph on the mantelpiece. A letter from another summer. All these join together to become beads on the turned-occasionally rosary of personal memory—of how we remember our dead (although it might be equally conceivable that, perhaps, this is how the dead remember us). But, and I hesitate to ask, do these passages and symbols of life add up to a life? Murad, who had been adored so uniquely and ardently, was sieved down to a constellation of anecdotes, absurd and bitter, sexual and poignant, outrageous and heart halting. Writing a novel teaches you one key lesson: that death might not be the opposite of life, but to be excised from narrative certainly serves as one form of abolishment. So, if the story is eternal, a contract with time and timelessness, then it is equally conceivable that Murad lives on in the stories his friends shared of him. Life curates the past and its inhabitants in the coral of anecdote and incident, and if this is the sum of one life, it is also a kind of life, a continuity unto itself.

(All identities have been changed in this essay.)

MAARNE KA, BHAGANE KA
(Beat Them, Kick Them Out)
Sonia Faleiro

The sari smells of dried blood. I bring it up close; imagine what it must have been like for Savita that night. She was waiting for a train home, when three railway policemen dragged her off the platform, kicking and slapping her for distributing condoms to other sex workers. Her red glass bangles speared her wrists. Blue cotton soaked up her blood.

Savita is physically assaulted by a policeman about twice a week. She pays hafta, bribes, as often. What most women would consider rape is, for her, 'free sex'—the price she pays to avoid arrest or further harassment.

When a policeman's demands become excessive, Savita will change her site of work. Hiding in the shadows, making herself inaccessible to the police, she also makes herself inaccessible to the HIV prevention efforts of outreach workers who provide her with free condoms. Savita receives as little as Rs 30 (75 cents) for sex. She will go without condoms if she must pay for them, placing herself at risk of acquiring HIV, the virus which causes AIDS. Unable to identify its symptoms, and with no access to a health clinic, she will stay untested and continue to work without protection.

The Bombay police are not alone in their mistreatment of street communities. Nor is their role in the spread of HIV new—the link has been documented since Bombay's first known AIDS cases in the late 1980s. It is only now, however, that the police have begun to question their behaviour. This is not about ethics. For if sex workers are victims of the virus, so are their partners. These include policemen.

At 5'10, with a heart-shaped face and wide cheekbones, thirty one year old Savita is a head turner. She is aware of this, accentuating her beauty with gold earrings and liquid eyeliner that give her the appearance of an old time movie star.

Like me, Savita is a migrant, but from Karnataka. We arrived in Bombay around the same time, four years ago. Although she admits it with less reservation, we are here to make money. And she is doing her best. She speaks Marathi, the language of her customers. She is fluent in Hindi. She has also learnt new words to label herself with. If she talks to me when she has not encountered the police for at least 48 hours, she may call herself a 'sex worker' and 'social worker', terms she has been taught by the NGO where she works part time. Otherwise she refers to herself as 'randi'—a Hindi word so disparaging it has no English equivalent. Neither whore nor hooker, prostitute nor tart.

One day, I went to meet Savita at Good Luck, a shabby café in Oshiwara, where we drink tea and share bhelpuri. A policewoman walked up to our table and said to her, 'I know what you are.' Savita looked her in the face. 'I'm not that anymore. I'm a social worker.' The policewoman smirked. She bent towards Savita. 'Rand,' she whispered, and calmly walked away.

The Immoral Traffic (Prevention) Act of 1956 (ITPA) is the primary statute that deals with sex work in India. It was meant to curb the recruitment, transport, or sale (defined as trafficking) of women and children for sex, and to punish the trafficker and financial beneficiaries. It criminalises neither sex work nor sex workers, but makes solicitation in a 'public place' illegal.

While ITPA is meant to rein in trafficking, not voluntary sex work by adults, police have greater success arresting women like Savita. Traffickers are part of complex cross-national webs that are nearly impossible to break, and given the evidence needed, rarely convicted. Arresting floating sex workers, however, satisfies demands from senior officers to fulfil a set quota. They address complaints from the public, upset by their presence in the neighbourhood.

Now, Savita knows the inside of a cell the way she does the order of spices on her kitchen shelf. She recounts the humiliations—constant and innovative. If she asks to use the toilet, she is told, 'Drink your urine.' So she carries an empty bottle with her wherever she goes, and fills it up before she enters her cell. If she starts her menstrual cycle, she tears off a piece of her dupatta, a garment meant to shield a woman's modesty, and places it in her underwear. The next day, she replaces it with another piece of her dupatta.

Long after she has been released, these memories keep Savita awake at night. Her head pounds as fast as her heart. Given a choice between silently accepting a policewoman's abuse—'Cocksucker, why is it that dogs find work, but you cannot?'—and courting arrest by standing up for herself, she will choose silence.

Savita is also vulnerable to the Bombay Police Act (1951), which governs the state force, and describes its powers. The act is broad and vague, and outlaws everything from frightening cattle to letting loose a horse. Section 110, or 'Behaving Indecently in Public', has been used by the police to great convenience, and as a supplement to ITPA. It makes 'behaving indecently' an offence, punishable with arrest and a fine of Rs 1200 ($30). The definition of 'indecent' has been left to the discretion of the arresting officer.

When a member of the legislative assembly, for example, is expected to visit, the station's senior inspector will want the adjoining roads clean. In a ravenous swoop, sex workers who had for months been standing on that road as the police

81

passed by will be arrested for 'behaving indecently'. The women do not protest or argue. Fine, jail, judge are their equivalent of my newspaper, laptop, library.

On occasion, Savita cannot pay the fine of Rs 1200. It is as much as she earns in a week. A policeman tells her, 'Then suck it.' She gives him oral sex.

As brutal as Savita's experiences are, male sex workers (MSW) and men who have sex with men (MSM) argue that theirs are more so. That policemen derive greater pleasure from exploiting their vulnerability to the law.

Like their female counterparts, MSWs work for money. They may not be homosexual. MSMs, on the other hand, cruise for masti, pleasure. Societal bias against homosexuality forces them out of their homes, plunging them into the darkness of unfamiliar streets. They are of all ages; some are educated and trapped in marriage. Their sexual trysts take place in cruising areas that are poignant metaphors for their marginalisation—abandoned parks, public toilets.

Social prejudice against homosexuality is endorsed by Section 377 of the Indian Penal Code, entitled 'Of Unnatural Offences'. It criminalises even consensual sex between adults, making sodomy punishable with a fine, and imprisonment up to life.

Banning sex between consenting adults is as likely to succeed as banning alcohol, another reality, and some would argue, natural impulse of adult life. Prohibition did not convert 1940s Bombay into a city of teetotallers. People drank in secret, in remote areas. They endangered their lives with spurious alcohol. They also laid themselves open to the abuse that is now emblematic of the relationship between police and sex workers.

Section 377 was enacted by the British in the 1800s, a reflection of an existing law in England. While it has not been amended in India since, by 1967, the British decriminalised homosexuality.

Like Savita, Ashok is an outreach worker. Educated about HIV/AIDS, outreach workers are a link between street communities and NGOs. They distribute free condoms, and offer access to health services such as HIV testing.

To Ashok, being an outreach worker is an achievement as precious as his own life. It dulls some of the horror of living off the streets. When he is explaining to other sex workers, his peers, how HIV is contracted, the twenty eight year old appears taller than his 5 feet 5 inches. He wears an air of temple gravitas.

His friends call Ashok 'bevda', alcoholic, and that is telling for they drink too, and with an uncontrolled relish. It is not a problem, he assures me. He has no other vices. He does not smoke, chew tobacco, or have unprotected sex. He must have something to calm him, if he cannot have someone to hold him.

An MSW like Ashok, awaiting customers in a park, is approached by a well-dressed young man who asks, 'Chalta hai?' (Coming along?) Ashok replies in the affirmative, and the two walk out holding hands. Waiting for them at the park entrance are three or four policemen in plainclothes, one of whom immediately grabs Ashok by the groin, and squeezes. 'Arre handsome,' he smiles as Ashok screams in pain. 'I hear you're sweet as jaggery. Can I have a taste?' Ashok is not expected to answer. His wallet is snatched, the money immediately distributed amongst the police and the young man, who in Bombay street parlance is known as a 'smart boy'—a person blackmailed by the police into doing this specific job. If Ashok is carrying his bank card, he is driven to the nearest ATM and forced to empty his account.

Ashok will not register a complaint. If he did, his elderly parents would receive an anonymous phone call revealing to them the truth of their son's sexuality and employment—secrets he holds close as fear, as carefully as a knife.

MSM and MSW are not only targets of blackmail and extortion, but also sexual assault. Those I have spoken with cannot say if their tormentors are homosexual. One AIDS activist believed sexual violence was meted out as punishment. 'Female sex workers may be pursuing the world's oldest profession,' he told me, 'but male sex work is a cultural glitch policemen cannot accept. It outrages their concept of masculinity.' At a police HIV/AIDS sensitisation workshop this February, a group of inspectors in their thirties were asked their opinion of homosexuality. One young man scorned, 'Humko nahin mangta. We don't want it. As long as there are women why should men have sex with men?'

Ashok maintains: 'Those who rape us are gay. They pretend to punish us while pleasing themselves.'

Sankar Sen, former director of the National Police Academy, believes the only solution to abuse is a written complaint. 'NGOs only talk about the problem,' he argued. When asked to whom the complaint should be addressed, Sen's answer was revealing. 'No one at the station,' he said. 'We must appoint people who liaison between the police and NGOs. That's the only way violence-prone officers can be tackled.'

Savita and Ashok are treated like criminals even when they are innocent of wrongdoing—sitting in a café with friends, for example—not just when they perpetrate the crime of solicitation in public. It is no wonder their frustrations flow fluent as sweat. Or that they blame the police for all their problems—a bout of gonorrhoea, missing a six monthly HIV test.

For them both, sex work is frail armour against destitution. Unable to work on Monday because of police harassment, on Tuesday Savita will feed on tea. On Wednesday, she will accept more than her desired average of four customers, even after she is tired, or does not like the look of the man she is following into the shadows.

Savita's enviable beauty, I realised too soon, was poor camouflage for the basic characteristics she shares with most sex workers—illiteracy (or in her case, semi-literacy), poverty, and little chance of ever finding for herself a place, on the streets and in society, that she cannot be beaten away from.

Neither the law nor law enforcers recognise the vital connection between sex work and survival. The law enables police harassment of sex workers. The public, viewing them as vectors of disease and immorality, supports it. The majority of sex workers, like stray dogs, either accept their maltreatment without objection, or fail to realise it at all.

Now Savita refuses to speak with the police, an interaction that is, in fact, part of her job as an outreach worker.

It would surprise her to know that some policemen feel similarly disempowered.

'If we arrest sex workers they complain,' Constable Anant Shirodkar,[1] told me. 'If we don't arrest them the public complains. Either way, politicians complain.'

Politicians can suggest transfers for policemen—from high level commissioners down to constables on the street. This is done through the offices of the chief minister and home minister. Between July 1, 2005 and February 28, 2006, 170 recommendations for police transfers were made by politicians in Bombay.[2] Up to 40% were passed.[3]

If a politician were to decide that safeguarding the morality of the youth was an election winning mantra, then he could, with the assistance of the police, ensure the harassment of young men in dance bars, and of couples exchanging cards on Valentine's Day. The Bombay Police Act is a useful tool for this purpose, for when 'indecent behaviour' is a matter of interpretation, a policeman could choose to be shocked by anything.

---

[1] A constable is the lowest ranking officer in the police force.
[2] 'Political Interference in Police Transfers Case—A Guide in the Process of an Application Leading to First and Second Appeal'. www.satyamevajayate.info.
[3] 'Why Politicos are Cops' Best Friend'. www.rtiindia.org/forum/387-why-politicos-cops-best-friend.html#post1265.

But it is not merely the enforcement of the law that has made the relationship between sex workers and the police contentious. It is also the criminal behaviour of some law enforcers. The demands for sex and hafta which directly impact the health of an estimated 100,000 sex workers in Bombay.

I wondered what this khaki-clad, imitation Ray-Ban-wearing lathi wielder thought of women like Savita.

'She has to eat, I know,' conceded Shirodkar, with a shrug. 'I feel sorry for her. I just don't want her to stand near me because I'll have to take her in.'

Actually, constables like Shirodkar will not arrest sex workers on sight. Police stations would fill up too quickly; paperwork would pile up. This decision is taken by the station's senior police inspector, who is influenced by his boss, the deputy commissioner of police. He is answerable to the assistant commissioner; and he to the commissioner; and all of them, in some measure, to politicians.

When senior officers are sympathetic towards sex workers, or see no reason to add to their workload by arresting those who will, almost immediately, return to work, they will, unless there are complaints, ignore solicitation. If their quota of arrests looks as though it will remain unfulfilled towards the end of the month, however, Constable Shirodkar is sent out.

Either way, the threat of arrest gives the police enough leverage to extract what they will.

I asked Madhav Rao, a senior inspector at a platform on one of Bombay's busiest railway stations, the same question—his opinion of sex workers.

'Maarne ka, bhagane ka,' he replied. They're to be beaten, to be chased away. Then he scrunched up his face, in what I suppose was in imitation of a woman crying, and said, 'I tell my men to beat them on their bottoms, and send them packing.'

One policeman understood the sex workers' dilemma, but knew his duty. For another, duty meant assault. But in beating sex workers he not only acted on his personal opinion of them, he became, like sex workers caught soliciting, criminally liable himself.

Policemen's attitudes mirror that of the society from which they are drawn. If the average policeman comes from a small town or village where people generally equate sex work with promiscuity, disease, and lawlessness, then he will, unless his training teaches him otherwise, carry those sentiments to work.

What makes this mirror image dangerous is that the police have the power to act on their bias.

A man like Rao, who equates illegal with immoral, will uphold the law with his fist. He will pass judgement on crime as well as character. He will, as happens often in India, administer justice outside the court. So a sex worker is arrested for selling her body, but slapped for being a bad woman. She is fined for solicitation, but raped because she is a whore and wants some. There is a dangerous zeal to this righteousness, and in pursuing it, Rao has become the criminal he should loathe.

But unlike Savita, who thought twice before revealing to me that she was a sex worker, or Ashok, who makes excuses for his work, Rao described his approach with pride. As though what he was doing was something we should all do.

Why was this? Why was Rao not afraid that I, in turn, would complain about his behaviour?

The answer, of course, is that Rao is a policeman. And as experience has taught those who have tested the force's clannish code of loyalty, one policeman will not readily file a complaint against another.

Police maltreatment has instilled in sex workers a terror of authority. Ashok's friend Munir, a masseur who offers oral sex for a small extra fee, told me that the first time he tried to enter a police station, he was stopped at the door and asked to return 'tomorrow'. The answer did not change for a week. On another occasion, a policeman who guessed that Munir was illiterate asked him to write down his own complaint of abuse by a policeman—'Give me every detail,' he winked. Such a response would naturally discourage sex workers from approaching even potentially honest and honourable policemen.

Rao and those who extract hafta and free sex, know with the certainty of sunrise, that they will not face trial for their crimes. The possibilities this realisation present are staggering.

Solutions are necessary as much to protect sex workers as to safeguard the police. Sexual assault and liaisons with sex workers, combined with in the line of duty injuries, make the police more vulnerable to HIV than the general population.

The police I had spoken with insisted they no longer demanded 'free sex' without a condom, because they fear HIV. Sex workers interviewed for this piece refute this.

Rao had this insight for me: 'What if you gave a vaishya [prostitute] a condom? What if her bag got stolen on the train? What if the thief was a young boy who got hold of the condom? Wouldn't he then go straight to the randi bazaar [market of whores] and have sex? Wouldn't he catch HIV? So how do condoms help regular people?'

If more men and women in the force share Rao's confusion about the role of condoms—that they cause people to have sex, and do not prevent HIV—then it is not just policemen, but society which is in jeopardy.

About 18% of female sex workers and 8% of MSMs in Bombay are HIV positive.[4] If they pay the police with sex, or are raped, then HIV could enter the force, spread to partners, wives, and unborn children—the larger population.

Although no specific data supports this thesis, there have been two revealing reports. In 2004, a Joint Commissioner of Police told the media that 450 members of the almost 50,000 strong Bombay force were HIV positive.[5] The figures appear

---

[4] According to HIV fact sheets (2006), based on HIV Sentinel Surveillance Data in India (2003–06), National AIDS Control Organisation, Ministry of Health and Family Welfare.

[5] 'Over 450 Mumbai Cops HIV Infected: Police', *The Times of India*, January 9, 2004.

low until one realises that the entire force was not tested, and the numbers collected haphazardly, over ten years. It is likely that only a small subset was tested, and that this estimate of 450 represents a very high infection rate. It places an undeniable question mark over the health of the rest of the force. That same year, 15 of 150 policemen tested randomly for HIV emerged positive.[6]

There have been no reports since, and not one uniform examination. This is the approach of almost all government institutions in India. They believe that mandating HIV testing would lead to further stigma and discrimination.

Their concerns are not unfounded. In 1999, a young man was dismissed from the Karnataka police force after testing positive for HIV. He had passed the entrance examinations, but was yet to start work. Having sought legal assistance, he was reinstated seven years later. In 2007, an HIV positive constable from Andhra Pradesh was denied a promotion to the post of sub-inspector after testing positive. His case is under appeal.

Even policemen who receive a measure of support from the force face problems. This March it was revealed that the police hospital in Bombay's downtown Nagpada area had, for over a month, been running short of Anti Retroviral Therapy (ART), the drugs which inhibit the replication of HIV.[7] The 300 policemen who allegedly receive ART would have either had to interrupt their treatment—which is generally considered unsafe—or change hospital, compelling them to disclose their HIV status again. This is not a choice they should have to make.

Late last year, the Karnataka State Police became the first in India to implement a workplace HIV/AIDS policy accepting that employees with HIV share the rights and responsibilities of other staff members.

[6] 'Bombay Police Launch HIV Scheme', BBC News Online, July 1, 2004.
[7] 'Police Hospital Faces Shortage of Free Drugs For HIV+ Cops', *The Times of India*, March 20, 2008.

ST Ramesh, Additional DG of Police, Karnataka, has been an officer for 32 years, and was a seminal force in formulating the policy. 'You don't have to be a genius to know that AIDS is an important issue for contemporary society,' he told me. 'So although there hasn't been an empirical evaluation of the relationship between AIDS and the police, considering certain factors—the aggressive nature of the police, their high sexual drive, contact with sex workers, and above all their contact with blood—the policy was a logical step.'

In Maharashtra, NGOs, with government help, have started various programmes to deal with this issue. Two have been significant. In 2006, the state's six training schools conducted a pilot HIV/AIDS programme—sensitising the police to the disease. Its success encouraged Rakesh Maria, then Inspector General of Police Training, to conclude that it should be permanent. Maria acknowledged, 'The nature of our work makes us reach those groups that are vulnerable to HIV. Thus there is an opportunity for vulnerability among the force.'

That same year, sex workers across the state agreed that the solution to their harassment should not be left to its perpetrators, but devised by the sex workers themselves.

Radhika, twenty seven years old and small as a pixie, solicits three stations down from Savita, on the Central Railway line, and is one of those women. She is part of the Rapid Response System (RRS) created by an NGO to intervene in potentially explosive interactions between the police and sex workers. The project has 264 task forces in Bombay, and in each, five sex workers are responsible for the others in their neighbourhood.

Radhika gave me an example: 'There was a policeman who'd routinely take money from a woman I knew. One day, I caught him just as he was pocketing Rs 100 [$2.50], and asked, "Sir, why are you snatching food from her children's mouths?" The sex worker got scared and said, "Radhika, leave it." She didn't want to deal with him after I left. I replied,

"Why leave it? And don't you dare run away. We'll both stand here until this problem is solved." Then the policeman felt small. He said, "I just took money today because I caught her with a customer." The sex worker now became bold. She yelped, "Only today! Don't lie! Every time you see me you demand 100 rupees." People started gathering. You know what the policeman did? He quietly took out her money, and gave it back. We never saw him again.'

This system shames the police from breaking laws they are trusted to uphold. But it also attempts to heal a historically fractured relationship.

Radhika visits at least four police stations a month. She requests, in writing, permission to park the NGO's mobile health clinic nearby—to hold a meeting, of about ten sex workers, on the railway platform. They discuss everything: herpes, babies, the price of vegetables. Seeing her so often, realising that she causes neither extra work nor trouble, the police have come to accept her presence. A few trust her; they ask for condoms. Radhika also attends legal literacy sessions, arranged for by the NGO she works with. She has been taught that even 'a woman like me' cannot be taken into custody after 7 pm; she knows to ask an impudent constable for his badge number.

'Now here's a funny story about how these things help,' Radhika told me. 'Having enjoyed himself, a policeman refused to pay up. When the sex worker objected he said, "Get lost randi, or I'll arrest you." So you know what the woman did? Because she'd learnt that a policeman can be identified by his belt, she snatched it and ran away. The next day she went into his station and in front of him asked his senior officer: "Please ask your constable why he isn't wearing his belt today!"'

Radhika's confidence did not wilt in front of the men who had, for years, placed her life in jeopardy. Eager to introduce me to someone she liaisoned with, she strode ahead in four inch stilettos. At the entrance of the police station, she beamed 'Good evening!' in English, to a constable. He smiled and politely replied, 'Good evening madam.'

The previous night that same constable had seen Radhika with a customer. When their eyes met, she turned and walked away, leaving her amazed customer behind. 'If a policeman catches me soliciting it's his job to arrest me,' she explained. 'I can't tell him how to do his job, just like he'd better not tell me how to do mine.'

Radhika seeks peers and customers in the same neighbourhood. As an outreach worker, she wears a badge and a chic blue coat that suggest the quiet efficiency of a nurse. At nightfall, she will discard these accoutrements and stand beside buckets of red roses and blood orange gladioli by the flower shop outside the railway station. A man will sidle up to her and under his breath ask, 'Chalegi?' She will reply, 'That's why I'm here.' They will quickly negotiate a price, decide on a lodge, and move down the street.

The same policeman she greeted when we were together, who regards her as an activist, someone to fear, but also admire, must now see her as one of the neighbourhood's hundreds of sex workers asking for trouble.

It is a fragile, curious relationship. And yet, so far, it has worked, because the policeman and Radhika both agree that he has to do his job.

Sex work affords Radhika her livelihood. Outreach work, on the other hand, has given her a self respect whose value, for her, is above price. This confidence translates into a greater willingness to take care of her health, which includes taking precautions against exposure to HIV.

'Do you know how I feel to be called madam?' she asked. She lifted her scrawny arms high above her head. 'Ten feet tall.'

The HIV sensitisation programme in the state's police training schools is significant for different reasons. It will educate new recruits, some as young at eighteen, at a time in their life when they are evolving, and more likely to embrace new ideas.

Although the park we met in was crowded with picnickers, and Constable Ram Naik was in civilian clothes, his straight, unstrained gait, determined eyes and a sharpness that belied his snub nose, made it easy for me to pick him out. He had perfect teeth, straight and white; but one, right in the middle, was yellow as butter. Every time he smiled, it flashed, drawing my attention away from his words.

Naik and his siblings are the first generation in the family to be educated. His mother's signature is a thumbprint. A housewife, she spends her evenings sewing her youngest daughter's trousseau. Naik's father, a clerk in a phone company, relaxes beside her when he returns from work, switching between news channels for his pleasure, and soap operas for hers.

Perhaps because they did not have the opportunity to study, Naik's parents value education above everything else. The one bedroom in their ground floor apartment in New Bombay is not for the child who needs sleep, but the one who has to study. Everyone else lies outside, on the floor.

Growing up in the village, Naik did not watch Hindi films. He did not cheer the good cop of *Zanjeer*, boo the bad cop in *Khaki*. In the town nearby, the appearance of the police encouraged people to cross the road, respectfully doffing their khadi caps. The boy understood that the police had power. It was spoken in the bang of their lathis.

When Naik graduated college, his parents urged him to consider a government job. It offered stability, a pension. If he died, his son or daughter would be given work. Naik remembered the swagger of the police, his childhood wonderment at their uniforms, crisp as newspaper. He was young and athletic. He thought, why not? Had he failed recruitment, as did several of his friends, Naik would have returned to the village to grow wheat and vegetables on his family's five acres of field. A life as fragile as dust. Every eight hours the burden of debt forces a farmer in the district to commit suicide. When he visits now, his relatives preen in the glow of his success. They tease, 'Sahib, can I make you some tea?' Farmers his father's age converge for advice. School boys beg a look at the uniform he has brought along. He sees his friends, backs bent like curling leaves. He knows he should be proud of his achievement.

But this is not so. For from his first day in training, Naik has seen around him corruption deep as a well.

'Not smart enough to pass the recruitment?' he asks, staring down at his sandalled feet. 'Use your contacts to put pressure on the examiners. Want a holiday but don't want to lose pay? Slip a ten rupee note to the constable in charge of the attendance register. Running short this month? Demand hafta from your juniors.'

It has been two years. Naik suffers swings of mood—sometimes miserable, at other times resigned. His parents watch from the background. He is their only son, but they are afraid to confront him, worried of what the answer may be. On his days off he cannot stand to be around their anxious faces, and rides a bus downtown to attend free events advertised in the morning's newspapers. Seed exhibitions, flower shows—he is not discerning. In his civilian clothes he is anonymous, one of thousands pushing and shoving, and so he can stare at his peers as they smoulder in the heat of packed streets, idle along shop fronts, waiting for he knows what.

He recalls the policemen of his childhood. His wonderment appears a joke. 'What is this life I have chosen?' he asks himself.

Naik's parents urge him to get married. 'A wife will be company,' his mother says; she will take his mind off work. He isn't spoilt for choice. For young men from Naik's conservative social class, interaction, never mind familiarity with the opposite sex, is discouraged. He did not play with girls as a child, has scant occasion to speak with his female colleagues. At home, as mother cooks or watches television, sister studies—conversation is limited.

So here is the irony. The women Naik knows best are the sex workers of Mahim whose streets he patrols. Some he calls by name—Asha, Lata, Priya—with a polite 'ji' appended, and they chat for a moment; nothing special, just a comment perhaps, on the heat. He knows where they hide when they have been tipped off about a cleanup, and that the loiterers will scatter like pollen when the sirens start their song. He can recognise them even when they get off work; faces clean of makeup as they stroll for toys and trinkets, children skipping happily by their side.

He tells me, 'The police think women have a higher sex drive than men. That's why they're in sex work.'

'And what do you think?' I ask.

'That they're not randis,' he replies. When he says it, he makes the word sound polite. 'Sure, some of them like having sex. Others make more money in a day than my sister would earn teaching for a month. But mostly, they're just very poor, pathetic people. And this talk of free sex? I would never. Not with HIV killing people like they were diseased cattle.'

'So what do you do?' I ask, my meaning clear.

He bites his lip. 'I read the Friendship Wanted pages in the newspapers. Every day. I have free outgoing calls on my cell phone, so one morning I called one of the numbers. The woman gave me a rate list. All kinds of sex. One person. Two. Massages!'

Disappointment sat on his face.

'Not friendship at all.'

Will you call again?

'Maybe,' he replies. 'That's better than taking what's waiting out there.'

'So this is how it will be,' Naik tells me. He will not torment sex workers on his beat, he never has, and when he sees policemen who do, his clear disgust sours their enjoyment. 'I can't stop them, but at least I can make them feel bad,' he says. It is the same with hafta, another whip that drives sex workers underground, even though he insists, 'there are reasons why we do these things'.

While many policemen take hafta because they can, some will say they have no option. A constable earns Rs 3500 (about $86) a month, excluding benefits. That is about half of what I earned at my first job out of college, at the age of twenty one. It is as much as a full time maid is paid. Economics aside, demanding bribes is as endemic to India's streets, as it is to the glass-fronted superstructures that look down on those streets. It is a culture upheld in the station itself, where some seniors demand hafta from their subordinates. Of every 100 rupees a policeman extracts from Savita or Radhika, 70 goes to his officers.

Statistics offer more insights. In Bombay, a policeman dies every 48 hours.[8] He succumbs to heart attack, stress related illness, accidents. Or he kills himself. It was only this year that the city police started granting its lower cadres a weekly holiday. Although there have been improvements, even since the time he joined, Naik still works shifts of 48 hours. After 10 pm, it is said, the police start drinking; they claim the streets as their own.

One man. What can he do?

I ask Naik if he will quit. He thinks about it. Looks down. Then he asks me, 'Can you imagine how bad I feel coming home from work, when I replay all the things I have heard and seen that day?'

I nod.

'And yet somehow when I wake up in the morning, I feel new. The way I did when I applied to the police. When I got in. I believed then that I could do some good. And I still feel that way. I still feel I can be different.'

On the surface, Naik is evidence of the fact that training and working within the law can help the police deal better with sex workers. It could reclaim Savita and Ashok's dignity, and Madhav Rao's integrity.

---

[8] 'Cop-ing with Trouble: A Policeman Dies Every 48 Hours', www.rtiindia. org/forum/1849–cop-ing-trouble-policeman-dies-every-48-hrs.html.

But change will not come easily. I know this as an outsider. Does Naik?

So I tell the young man a story about Ashok the MSW. It illustrates that no matter what position sex workers may carve for themselves as outreach workers, they are still at the mercy of the police, until the police decide it is time to change.

When I finish, Naik is silent. Around us the clamour continues, but, it seems, with greater clarity. Overfull buses honk, children scream with laughter, a woman giggles lovingly into her cell phone.

By the time we say goodbye, several hours later, after discussing other matters, Naik still has not responded to the story.

This is what I told him.

One evening, as I sat with Ashok and a dozen other sex workers, he recounted an incident involving a friend.

The friend was picked up in a park by a 'smart boy'. The policemen awaiting him were drunk. They took him to their station, to their colleagues who were also drunk, on anticipation and rum. He was stripped and shoved into an empty cell. The policemen formed a line. One after the other they forced him to give them oral sex. The friend begged them to stop. They demanded anal sex. He was bleeding, delirious. The policemen continued through the night. Not one of them used a condom. When the shift changed at dawn, there was a new line. Then one of the policemen had a 'good idea'. He stuck one prong of a wire into a socket, and with the other administered electric shocks to the 'friend's' genitals. The cell, still warm with the smell of blood, now reeked of scalded fat and burnt hair.

Ashok's eyes filled with tears. I realised who the 'friend' was. I looked away. What I saw made me want to lower my head into my hands. The other sex workers were mirror images of one another.

'Yes,' said their faces. The nod of their heads. 'Yes, this has happened to me too.'

(Names of all sex workers and police officers, with the exception of Sankar Sen, ST Ramesh and Rakesh Maria, have been changed on request.)

AT STAKE, THE BODY
CS Lakshmi

The body is not talked about. Hidden in its crevices are untold dangers for a woman. The body has to be trampled upon, and conquered as if it is a demon to be slain. The idea is to live with the body as if the body does not really exist; it is never discussed, nor openly mentioned. It is with such conflicts that a girl bears her body and grows with it, in most middle class homes in India. It takes a long time to accept the body with a lightness that is natural and logical; to look at the body for what it is. Sometimes it takes an entire lifetime. When that happens it is like reading a story with a happy ending. Everyone loves a happy ending, but not all stories finish well. When they don't, endings have to be turned into beginnings, our idea of happiness has to be redefined. I met some women who have been courageous enough to make endings into beginnings, and find a different meaning for happiness. They are street sex workers in Chennai who have hidden in their bodies the secrets of their lives.

> She does not remember her mother talking to her in gentle tones, or putting her to sleep with a lullaby. She does not remember the family sitting down to a meal, or when they laughed together. She stopped going to school very early, and joined a garment factory for work, like most girls did then. Garment factories, making clothes for export, had readily available jobs. That is when she

realised that she had a body; not just a body with which she breathed and lived, but also a body that could fulfill the desires of others—the supervisors, and other minor bosses who asked for sexual favours in exchange for promises and safety from their threats. She called it love the first time, ran away with the boy who desired her body, and 'married' him in a ceremony of sorts. There came a time when she was with two children in a small hut that did not have a door. There was only a soiled gunny bag in its place. She was only seventeen. So many wanted to 'protect' her, and keep her. One day she agreed because her children were hungry, and so was she. Soon it became her profession. She also runs a beauty parlour now, but when money is needed she accepts clients who ring her up. She feels she will have to give it up some time for her sons are growing up. Her face lights up when she says that. Her elder son asks her at times, 'Who was it on the phone?' or 'Why do you come home so late?' She has to invent reasons. But he asks with such authority! Her heart swells with pride when he speaks in that manner. She would never want her sons to know the secrets of her body.

One is reminded of a very early story by the well-known Tamil writer Jayakanthan, called 'Unnaipol Oruvan' (Someone Like You), later made into a famous film—where a small boy in a slum accuses his mother of being a wayward woman. She tells him that her life has taken this turn because there had been no one in her life like him who could be angry with her if she went wrong.

There are other mothers in similar circumstances.

The area she lived in was violent. There was not much money at home, and although she was good at studies—she went to an English medium school, in fact—she had no ambition to study and make something of herself. She knew such decisions were not for her to take. At fifteen, a marriage was arranged. She was tall and dark, with bright, sparkling eyes, and a smile that lit up her entire being. The husband was a thin, sick-looking man, and she felt repulsed by him but could not describe that feeling in words to anyone. She had to live with him for she was his wife and had no choice. Her duties as a daughter were, however, not complete. Her father was in serious debt, and her mother took her one evening to a man. She ran away in anger and frustration, without giving herself to him. Her mother denied any knowledge of the man's intentions, when she questioned her, later. In time, she began to see her body as a means of earning a living. By then she had a daughter she adored, and whom she swore to educate and make independent.

Her parents do not know what she does for a living. They think she has a job somewhere. Maybe they know, but pretend they don't. She has left her husband a long time ago, and would not like to go back to him now that she has chosen her own path. What she does for a living is not kept a secret from the daughter. Her daughter is now working in an office. She respects her mother, and recently when a boy proposed to her and told her that the only condition to the marriage would be that she would have to cut herself off from her mother, she looked straight into his eyes, with her head held high, and told him, 'That day will never come. My mother has chosen this path for me. I would never let her down.' The mother chokes, as she says this.

And there is another young girl whose child dies, vomiting, in the general ward of a government hospital, a mere skeleton in her hands.

She sits there with the dead body of her child, not knowing how to bring him back to life. She tries to put his mouth to her breast. Her little baby boy does not respond. The nurses and doctors tell her that the child is HIV positive, and that her husband, an auto rickshaw driver, must be the cause for this. He flexes his muscles and shows off his body. 'Look at my body, woman! Does it look as if I have HIV, or whatever it is they are saying? I am a man, a healthy man, and these are fake doctors,' he shouts. She believes him, for she is only sixteen. Soon, he dies a terrible death—and much to her shock she realises that she is also HIV positive. But she still feels hungry. There is no one to help. And then someone suggests a way out—she takes it. It is a secret. Her family do not know, although they know she is HIV positive, and occasionally her brother-in-law or someone makes derogatory remarks about the disease. That hurts her, and she wipes her tears talking about it. Otherwise she is known for her cheerful and fun-loving nature.

It all starts either after a broken marriage or relationship, widowhood, or poverty during childhood, where a mother herself may tell her daughter to make her body the path of her life. The girls conceal themselves with garish makeup, dark pink foundation, blood red lipstick, black painted eyes and cheap, glittering clothes, and stand apart in a crowded street. Very often there is a 'partner', a man who becomes a permanent fixture in their lives, protecting them from other ruffians, or the police, and who takes away most of their earnings. Then there are those clients with their special needs, some violent, some not so violent, and some perverted ones. The girls carry scars on their bodies—cigarette burns, knife marks, marks of other abuse—and there are times when their bodies feel like a festering wound.

The stories pour out one after the other, sounding so similar and yet so apart, for each woman is telling a story of her own. The chorus of voices infuses the room with warmth. They look like busy executives in a conference. They wear very little makeup, and are well dressed, in crisply starched cotton or flowing silk saris. There is nothing hidden in their eyes, and they are here to talk about their bodies' secrets. The confidence seems to have come from the knowledge of their bodies, of what can happen to their bodies, of working with dignity, of enabling others to do so, of facing life not as a victim—but as a contender. They are no more individuals struggling alone with their bodies, but a community of women who share their lives, and work for one another—unburdening their secrets to each other.

The NGO that these women belong to encourages them to talk, to sing, to act, to express themselves. They advise one another on many aspects of their life and work—how to deal with a stubborn customer, a violent partner, or a suspicious family; how to take care of their health; how to deal with their children. Because of this, their bodies have ceased to be mere tools of survival, and their work is no longer an act of degradation. They may have all taken a decision to make their body their capital, but it is not a body to be ashamed of. It is a body that needs to be defended againt infections, and when infected, the body needs to be medicated and cared for. It is also a body that needs to be defended against violence and misuse. It is this knowledge of the rights of their body that has given these women the confidence to speak out openly, to acknowledge facts about their life. There is no self pity, no self reproach, no guilt. They know what the risks are, and how to deal with them. That is why they can tell a customer that he may offer lakhs, but they will not agree to sex without condoms. A particularly stubborn client will not know when a condom is put on him during oral sex. No more garish makeup, or foul language. They are women who are also earning a living. They offer their services on their own terms.

Having taken their lives into their own hands, some women have told their partners to leave. They have mobiles through which they can be contacted. They have learnt to deal with the police, and live with no fear. They are clear about their work and their future. While they have no illusions, they are not without hope.

'I will work till my daughter completes her education and is well settled. After that I may do just community work,' one of them says. Another one dreams about her sons becoming professionals: 'My son wants to be a policeman, and wants to beat up his useless father,' she says. 'I know I am HIV positive, but it is only a condition, not a curse. I have the right to live a normal life,' says another. 'I feel it is my duty to tell others how to prevent it, and how to live a healthy life,' declares a young girl enthusiastically. Educating their children, looking after their family, keeping a roof above their heads— they earn for all this, and say that they will continue to work as long as they can.

In their neighbourhoods, no one knows what they do for a living; for they don't look different from the others. They are invited for family functions, and many neighbours have become close friends. They are full of ideas and plans about their work and their lives as individuals and as community members. And while they are at it, they might as well laugh; like the woman who runs a beauty parlour, who jokes with a programme officer that she would not mind giving him a head massage at a discount rate, for he is bald in any case! They coax the director of the NGO to begin the session with a song, and she readily agrees. The girl whose husband gave her HIV can still talk about meeting Kamalhasan, the actor.

'So what did you tell him?'

'You know, on the screen he looks so different. I told him, "Sir, you look so tall on screen. How come you are so short in real life, sir?"'

Laughter fills the room. Children join in, clapping and giggling. A little kid removes his mouth from his mother's breast and looks up in surprise. The children must wonder why their mothers have started smiling and laughing so much; how beautiful their mothers look when they do that.

THE HALF-WOMAN GOD
Salman Rushdie

According to Greek mythology, Hermaphroditus, the child of Hermes and Aphrodite, fell so passionately in love with a nymph named Salmacis that they beseeched Zeus to unite them for all time, and were joined in a single body in which both sexes remained manifest. The Hindu tradition contains, if anything, a more powerful version of this story, elevated to the very summit of the Hindu pantheon, and glorifying not merely the beauty of the physical union of the sexes but the union of the male and female *principles* in the universe, a metaphor reaching far beyond biology. In a cave on Elephanta Island in Bombay harbour is a sculpture of the deity named Ardhanari or Ardhanarishvara, a name composed of three elements: ardha—half, nari—woman, ishvara—god; thus Ardhanarishvara, the half-woman god. One side of the Elephanta carving is male, the other female, and it represents the coming together of Shiva and Shakti, the forces of Being and Doing, the fire and the heat, in the body of a third, double-gendered deity. A cultural history so rich in the mighty possibilities of sexual admixture ought by rights to find it easy to understand and accept not only biological hermaphrodites but also such contemporary gender benders as the hijra community. Yet hijras have always been, and still are, treated with a mixture of fascination, revulsion, and fear.

I remember feeling both fascination and fear when, as a young boy in Bombay long ago, I watched the tall, garish figure of a hijra mendicant, dressed like a queen of the sea and carrying a long, silver trident, striding proudly through the traffic on Marine Drive. And like everyone else I saw hijras performing their celebratory blessings at weddings, only half tolerated by the hosts and guests. They seemed then like visitors from a louder, harsher, brighter, more dangerous world. They seemed alien.

A part of the problem is, of course, the Operation, the reality of which, with its curved knife and long, painful aftermath, is hard to stomach. In John Irving's 1994 novel *A Son of the Circus*, there is a graphic description of what happens.

> A hijra's operation—they use the English word—is performed by other hijras. The patient stares at a portrait of the Mother Goddess Bahuchara Mata; he is advised to bite his own hair, for there's no anaesthetic, although the patient is sedated with alcohol or opium. The surgeon (who is not a surgeon) ties a string around the penis and the testicles in order to get a clean cut—for it is with one cut that both the testicles and the penis are removed. The patient is allowed to bleed freely; it's believed that maleness is a kind of poison, purged by bleeding. No stitches are made; the large, raw area is cauterized with hot oil. As the wound begins to heal, the urethra is kept open by repeated probing. The resultant puckered scar resembles a vagina.

Ouch.

Irving also says, 'Whatever one thought or said about hijras, they *were* a third gender—they were simply (or not so simply) another sex. What was also true was that, in Bombay, fewer and fewer hijras were able to support themselves by conferring blessings or by begging; more and more of them were becoming prostitutes.' Fourteen years later, these words are still accurate. And consequently the world of the hijras, already beset by the larger world's distrust, dislike, and distaste, is now also threatened by the increasing danger of HIV infection, and so of AIDS.

These are the three traditional forms of hijra work: manti (or basti), that is to say, begging; badai, the marriage celebration; and pun, the selling of sex. In today's Bombay, with its high rises, its guards at the gate, its loss of interest in hijra badai, its police force that is prepared to arrest beggars and implement the laws against manti, which impose a Rs 1200 ($30) fine for the offence, only pun now offers the chance of earning enough to survive. There is a law against begging, but there are looser laws against sex work. Yet there are other, greater risks, the risks of infection, and death.

The hijra world is remarkably structured and hierarchical. There are seven hijra gharanas in India, like the 'families' we know of from mafia movies, though far less powerful, far less ruthless, far more vulnerable. At the head of each gharana is a naik or head guru, and these are scattered across India; only one of the naiks lives in Bombay. In each gharana, there descends from the head guru a pyramid of lesser gurus and chelas, locked together in relationships of protection and exploitation. If a disciple is arrested, the guru will provide bail; if there are quarrels between hijras, and there are often quarrels, the guru will adjudicate and resolve them. It is not easy to change gurus. It is not easy to alter the hierarchy in any way. To enter the hijra community you need to be intro- duced by other hijras and given the blessings of naiks and lesser gurus. Once you are in, there is really no way out. The hijra gharana is like a family; and you can't resign from your family.

This family structure is what gives a hijra's life meaning, and constitutes its greatest appeal. This, they say, this more than the transgendering, is what draws them in. Only about 60% of Bombay hijras actually have the Operation, although, they say, 'in Gujarat it is insisted upon'. (And, by the way, *pace* John Irving, it is not always called 'the Operation' in English. The most common word for it is 'Nirvana'.) Even more surprisingly, there are female hijras, women who were born women, who are drawn into the gharanas by the attrac- tion and apparent safety of the hierarchies' substitute for family life. This, they told me over and over again, is what it means to be a hijra; to be a part of your gharana and to serve your guru. The sex thing is secondary. The family rules.

And sometimes the family can be a part of the problem. At the bottom of the gharana pyramid, a small guru will give disciples the task of bringing back a certain amount of money every day, and that guru has to pay her guru, and so on up the pyramid. The pressure to earn the daily requirement forces hijras into agreeing to five or six sex acts daily, often hurried and careless. If the client doesn't want to use a condom, sometimes there is no time to argue. And so their vulnerability increases. Those who are there to protect them are in part responsible for their exposure to deadly infection. Such is hijra family life.

Hijras exaggerate their numbers, claiming that there are 100,000 of them in Bombay alone. The real figure is probably nearer 5000 for Bombay, with 100,000 being closer to the total figure for hijras in the whole of India. They travel a great deal, moving from event to event around the country— one hijra told me she had been in Ghaziabad, Haryana, Nepal, Ajmer and Gujarat in the previous two months—and, it seems, few hijras settle in their places of origin. Only one of the hijras I met in Bombay was from Bombay, and this is not atypical. Family rejection and disapproval probably accounts for the uprooting. Having recreated themselves as beings whom their original families often reject, hijras will usually take those new identities to new places, where new families form around them and take them in.

Malwani in Malad is a rough part of town, a dumping ground for convicts half a century ago, a slum zone in which many Bombay hijras now live. Proper housing is a problem. 'In Andhra the Chief Minister gave housing to hijras, but not here.' Ration cards are a problem, and, if you can get hold of one, a treasure. And without a ration card, or an income tax card, or a voter identity card, or a bank account, you don't exist, and the state can ignore you. Not surprising, then, that hijras feel vulnerable, that they fear not only policemen but hospitals too. Doctors are often rude and unhelpful, although, I was told, there are signs of improvement, even among policemen. 'Now they call us Madam, and don't only give us galis.'

A 'gut' is a self-help group set up to combat the various risks to hijras, health risks above all. The Aastha gut in Malwani is one such group. 'It has been very successful. When 15 people go to the police station because one person has been arrested then the police behave better.' With the help of a gut, a group of hijras can become 'peer educators' and spread the word through the community. Today, there are perhaps 7000 such peer educators, each of whom 'tracks' 50 community members, and as a result more and more hijras are being made aware of, and persuaded regularly to visit, health clinics around the city, to be blood tested. Though there remains much work to be done. Condom use by hijras' clients is still low, perhaps only at 50%, and even though the fall in gonorrhoea and chlamydia infections to below 5% shows that the use of condoms is improving matters, the risks remain. The Aastha gut makes and disseminates paan-flavoured condoms, and hijras are trained (with the help of attractive wooden penises) to hold the popularly flavoured condoms in their mouths, and then apply them quickly to the client's member. (I was given a couple of impressively swift and skilful demonstrations of the technique, on, I hasten to add, the wooden members only.)

The hijras of Malwani are worried about their image—'the police have misapprehensions about us'—and they are concerned, especially, about 'those people who wear male dress at night but in the daytime, dressed as women, they rob and steal, and so hijras get a bad name'. This animosity towards the fake, the naqli hijra, was widespread. 'Of course we can all tell the naqlis. They run when they see us.' 'They smoke beedis and drink alcohol on the street.' 'When we ask them who is their guru, they cannot reply.' 'They walk like men.' 'They do not know the special language.' Hijras have a coded communication made up of words and signals that they can use, for example, to warn of danger. 'We are not bad,' they say. They concede that they are not perfect either. 'Even if a few hijras do wrong, do not judge us all by them.' 'Nobody goes to steal children from villages [to turn them into hijras]. They say it, but it doesn't happen.'

The hijras I met mostly 'became aware' around puberty; some discovered their nature a couple of years later. 'As a child I followed girlish ways and was laughed at and scolded for my girlishness.' 'I often thought I should live like a boy and I tried hard but I couldn't do it.' 'It's in the genes.' Rejection and fear followed. 'My family always knew but are still in denial.' 'Because of family izzat they cast me out.' 'My father beat me when I was at college, I said, "Hit me, what can you do?"' 'I wouldn't have stayed alive if not for the community. At home I was shouted at, sworn at, everything.' But there are rare exceptions. 'I only go at night to visit my family, but I do go.' And there are the beginnings of political conscious-ness. 'Women's rights have advocates, but we have no advo-cates, not even as "second-grade women".' 'We also are part of creation.'

Thane, the so-called City of the Lakes, is an altogether more attractive setting than the slums of Malwani, or the red light district of Kamathipura, where there is a special hijra alley. (It is said that the hijras once owned the whole of the red light district but had to sell it off, alley by alley, as the gharanas grew poorer.) I went to Thane to meet an exceptional hijra named Laxmi, a hijra of extreme articulacy and force of char-acter. By the Talao Pali Lake in Thane, Laxmi, a local star of sorts, did her 'ramp walk' every evening in the old days when she started out. Laxmi is a rarity among hijras; she lives at home, and, to avoid upsetting her parents, dresses as a man when she is with them. They call her by her male name, Laxmikant, or by her family nickname, Raju, and, as a man, she works at home as a bharatnatyam teacher. But when she leaves home, she is Laxmi, and everyone in Thane knows her. She is a voluptuous person with purple-black lips; hard to miss. Her beginnings are not unusual. 'At nine or ten, I told people I'm gay. I was called names. "Gur." "Meetha." One day, in the Maheshwari Gardens, I met Ashok. "Something is wrong with me, what should I do," I said. "The world is abnormal," he told me. "*You* are normal."'

While she was still at school, she went to gay pubs and started to dance for money. 'Then fifteen years ago I became First Drag Queen of Bombay.' Soon after that she met a woman, Gloria, who opened the door into the hijra world. 'My brother is like you,' Gloria said. Laxmi met Gloria's brother, the hijra Shabina, at a phone booth in Victoria Terminus in Bombay. 'Normally she wore saris but that day in VT she was wearing jeans.' Laxmi took Shabina to the Café Montecarlo. Shabina didn't want to go in. 'I took her by the hand. You are yourself and should enjoy yourself, I said. But in the cafe I told Shabina I used to hate hijras. Why do you clap and beg, I asked her. You should do proper work. Then Shabina explained about the structure, the gharanas. This was attractive to me. This was more than just sex talk.'

Shabina took her to meet other hijras, notably Manjula Amma, aka Fat Manjula, of the Lashkar gharana, of which Lata Naik was the head. Laxmi joined the family. 'In Byculla I entered the hijra world. Lata Naik was also there. I was sweating. An old man told me where to go. I saw Lata Naik. She was 55 but looked 45. There were six frightening hijras around her. They reminded me of Ravana. I said, "I want admission. How much fees? Donations?" Lata Naik laughed. She accepted me, for no money, orally. At that time nothing was written. Lata Naik was the one who later began the process of keeping records. She had beautiful writing; I have seen it in the hijrotic books which she now maintains.'

Before Lata Naik there was Chand Naik. Another Naik wanted to be Chand's chela, but was abusive to her, and Chand refused her. So there was a split between their two gharanas, which lasted several years, but afterwards the two houses were reunited. 'When there are such disputes, the Lashkars are always the mediators.' Then, 13 years ago, the splits began again. 'When I became a chela, it was the very day before we split. Three of the gharanas on one side, four on the other. The split lasted until just recently. So now people are very excited. There is a big change in mood. The war is over. There is no competitiveness any more.'

Laxmi's father is a 'UP Brahmin military type'. He found her transformation very hard to accept, especially as Laxmi was from the beginning a very forward sort of hijra, giving interviews to Zee News, and so on. After the Zee TV interview, her father wanted to marry her off. She fought against the marriage and in the end her father wept and gave in. 'My father, the pillar of my house. He wept.' Her mother's love was never in doubt. 'For me, my world is my mother.'

Now her parents have accepted her, even to the point of being curious about her breast implants. Once at home she sat bare-chested, having forgotten to put on a T-shirt. Her father scolded her. 'If you have made it,' he said, 'then learn to respect it.' 'Now,' Laxmi says, 'my father is my best friend.'

Laxmi is vocal, confident, self-assured. She wants to be a voice in the HIV/AIDS campaign, and to help save what she, too, calls 'the third gender of India'. 'Hijras have become more vocal,' she says, 'but the problem is that activists are trying to put us inside the MSM culture.' (MSM are Men who have Sex with Men, and they are of three kinds: Panthis, who go on top, Kothis, who go on the bottom, and Double Deckers, who need no explanation.) 'The MSM sector is getting so strong,' Laxmi says. 'But we are not simply MSMs. We are not even simply TGs [transgendered persons]. We are... hijras. I am carrying a whole culture with me. It's that collective aspect, the hijra culture, that is important. We cannot sacrifice it. We are different.'

The hijras of Bombay and the rest of India are held to be the community most at risk of HIV infection. There have been improvements in organisation, outreach, education and self help, but for many hijras, their lives continue to be characterised by mockery, humiliation, stigmatisation, fear, and danger. Laxmi of Thane and the 'peer educators' of Malwani may be success stories, hijras who have taken charge of their destinies and are trying to help their fellows, but many hijras are mired in poverty and sickness.

According to the poet saints of Shaivism, Shiva is Ammai-Appar, mother and father combined. It is said of Brahma that he created humankind by converting himself into two persons: the first male, Manu Svayambhuva, and the first female, Satarupa. India has always understood androgyny, the man in the woman's body, the woman in the man's. Yet the walking Ardhanaris among us, the third gender of India, still need our understanding, and our help.

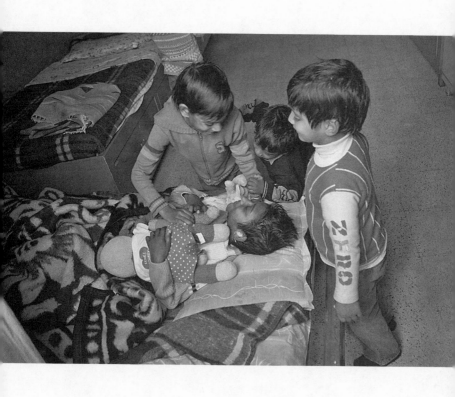

BHOOT KI KAHAANIAN
(Ghost Stories)

Jaspreet Singh

Egg curry, gobi aloo, carrots, rice, dahi and dal, in steel thalis. The children, back from school, start lunch in the kitchen-cum-dining room. There are two oblong tables. Under the watchful eyes of three grownups, the caregivers, even the little ones are well behaved. I sit down with the older kids.

'Namaste uncle,' they say.
I fold my hands.
'Namaste namaste... The subzi smells good.'
All heads turn towards me.
'Are you interested in stories?'
A hushed silence. Then a tiny spoon hits a thali.
'Uncle tells stories,' explains the caregiver.
No one utters a word.

They are aged between three and fourteen, and all of them are HIV positive. Our table is composed largely of boys. The second table is mixed, with boys and girls. The very young, those below five, are sitting on a clean chatai on the floor.
'I too am interested in stories,' says Shashank. He is around nine.
The paisley patterns on his shirt are as animated as his face. His eyes sparkle.

'What kind?' I ask.

He consults his friend.

'Should I tell him?'

'Tell him. Tell him!'

Shashank whispers something in his friend's ear.

Then:

'No,' he says. 'You tell.'

'Bhoot ki kahani,' says the friend finally.

Ghost story.

'O yes,' I say. 'Let me think... Once upon a time...'

'Keep eating,' says the caregiver to the boys.

And I think about the bhoots and prets and churails of my childhood. Vikram and Baital. Ruskin Bond's ghost stories set in the hill stations. 'Ghosts don't require passports,' wrote Mr Bond. 'They arrive unexpectedly when you least expect them.'

'Uncle, tell us a good ghost story,' requests Shashank.

I am in no mood for scary stories. But how does one explain this to children. So I ask, 'Do they really exist? The ghosts?'

Ishan raises his hand.

'I know,' he says.

Ishan is the oldest. Fourteen maybe. A fledgling moustache on his face.

'Ghosts don't exist,' he says, 'but they also exist... it is a paradox, Uncle.'

I try to divert the conversation.

'I know a tale... a man climbs Everest to measure the distance to heaven.'

'Is it scary?' they ask.

'No.'

They are not interested.

'Uncle, listen to my story, it will send a chill through your spine. You know the place where the Muslims bury their dead? Once a boy passed by the place... and a woman was standing by the gates with a lantern... He looked at her face—she had no face!'

Shashank giggles, and covers his eyes with both hands. Lunch is over. His green sweatshirt has a hood. Suddenly he decides to become a hooded creature. He picks up an apple from the bowl on the table. The hooded creature bites the apple. Then he runs towards me and holds my finger tightly. 'Let me show you upstairs, Uncle.' He guides me towards the first floor dorm. He walks fast. I slow him down. Shashank will not let go of my finger. The place feels like a cross between Harry Potter's boarding school and a very large family. On the wall by the stairwell I notice black and white photos of children—past and current residents of the children's HIV positive care home[1] where we are.

Shashank points his index finger at a boy.

'Is that you in the photo?'

'No, that's Sunil.'

Sunil died a few months ago, and was cremated in Jungpura. Shashank, it appears to me, is the same height as Sunil. Shashank doesn't tell me that he is wearing Sunil's sweatshirt and shoes.

In the photo Sunil looks happy.

Shashank opens the first floor door. The younger children are doing yoga. It is a large U-shaped room, and there are 14 or 15 beds arranged in perfect geometry. Colourful yoga mats lie on the floor.

Behind the yoga instructor I notice someone wrapped in a blanket on the bed. A thick woolen cap covers her head. The girl's eyes are wide open. She is around eight. Her arms as thin as lotus roots. Unable to do yoga, she watches everyone.

Mani. She stares at you. You talk to her, and she stares back. Mani has PML. I have never heard of PML.

Surfing through the net I read the details on a neurological website:

Progressive Multifocal Leukoencephalopathy. Caused by the reactivation of a common virus in the central nervous

---

[1] Not referred to as an orphanage.

system of immune-compromised individuals. Polyomavirus JC (often called JC virus) is carried by a majority of people, and is harmless except among those with lowered immune defenses. PML is most common among individuals with AIDS. Studies estimate that prior to effective antiretroviral therapy, as many as 5% of people with AIDS eventually developed PML. For them, the disease was most often rapidly fatal. The infection causes the loss of white matter (which is made up of myelin, a substance that surrounds and protects nerve fibers) in multiple areas of the brain. Without the protection of myelin, nerve signals can't travel successfully from the brain to the rest of the body. Typical symptoms associated with PML are diverse, since they are related to the location and amount of damage in the brain, and evolve over the course of several days to several weeks. The most prominent symptoms are clumsiness, progressive weakness, and visual, speech, and sometimes, personality changes. The progression of deficits leads to life-threatening disability and death over weeks to months.[2]

Mani joined the care home at the age of six. Mani's grandmother abandoned her outside a temple in Maharashtra. An orphanage sent her here. She made friends quickly, and joined school like the other children. She was on first line antiretroviral (ARV) medication when she started getting epileptic fits, and she quickly lost the ability to walk. Generally, ARVs are able to fight the deadly virus, slowing down the progression to AIDS. Scans confirmed the PML. All India Institute of Medical Sciences (AIIMS) agreed to admit her, but she was extremely unhappy there. The caregiver explains, 'Hospitals are the worst places for people living with HIV in this country. And Mani is a child after all. The physical discomfort of the feeding tube prompted Mani to try to pull it

---

[2] National Institute of Neurological Disorders and Stroke, www.ninds.nih.gov/.

off. So we brought her back. She likes people around her. She likes to be touched.'

By earlier estimates, India is home to the largest number of AIDS orphans in the world—anywhere between 1.5 to 2 million.[3] There is no official count indicating what percentage of these orphans are HIV positive, or if they have just lost their parent(s) to AIDS, and subsequently been abandoned by their extended family. In its latest (2006 end) HIV data release, the Government of India estimates that of the 2–3.1 million people living with HIV/AIDS in India, 3.8% are children under the age of fifteen,[4] but there exists no official estimate on the number of orphans, which is expected to be larger. The proportion of infections among children is growing every year; the worst hit by the epidemic come from low income backgrounds. Given the high levels of HIV stigma in the country, many consider a child with the virus a bad omen from which they must free themselves.

I am sitting in the Director's office in the basement. She started the care home eight years ago. Someone abandoned a positive child in her drop-in HIV clinic, and no one was willing to accept him—not even the orphanages. 'We started with one child eight years ago, and now there are 34,' she tells me. 'There are only a handful of HIV/AIDS care homes in India, they are seen as dark and dingy... this one is different. High quality care is the right of every child.' She has become one of the most vocal advocates for AIDS care in India. Behind her office chair there is a marvellous fish tank. The fish at the top are half the size of the fish at the bottom. The bubbles at the top are double the size of the bubbles in the bottom.

'20 children from the care home attend an NGO school,' she tells me. 'The headmaster knows that the kids are

---

[3] Figure cited by the World Bank and UNICEF, 2005. According to the UN, AIDS orphans are defined as those under the age of eighteen who have lost one or both parents to the disease.

[4] National AIDS Control Organisation, www.nacooline.org/Quick-Links/ HIV_Data.

"positive", but he has left it to them to reveal, or not to reveal, to others.'

Not many schools in this city are as enlightened. They throw the kids out. The virus spreads through mosquito bites, they think. By standing next to a positive person. Or by using the same toilet.

'Do the children know? What story do you tell them?'

'Those above the ages of ten know that they are positive. Before we disclose this to them, the child goes through counselling, and detailed sessions on the body, illness, disease, and children's rights. The process is not as easy as it sounds. It is difficult to explain the deadly virus to a child... social stigma... discrimination.'

'How do they respond?'

'In different ways,' the Director tells me. 'One of them said, "Introduce me to someone who is also positive." The first question he asked the other kid was, "How did you contract the virus?"'

'Some go through behavioural changes, post-traumatic stress... that is why we have a counsellor here,' the caregiver tells me. 'Some start getting poor grades at school. Others are more resilient... But after Sunil's death there were many more questions; "Does this mean I am going to die, Didi?" "What happens after death, Didi?"'

Mani is not on her bed. On the pillow, a cell phone is ringing. Where is Mani? Is she alright?

The cell phone belongs to the yoga instructor. Some kids have moved to the roof terrace to learn advanced postures. Someone installed Mani in a different bed.

'Mani is a fish,' Shashank tells me. 'She swims from one bed to the next.'

Shashank and I move towards the fish.

I sit down on the edge of Mani's new bed. Nisha tries feeding Mani a cookie, but the girl refuses it.

'Uncle, what are you writing?' asks Nisha.

She is around nine, and incredibly cheerful.

I hand her a sheet of paper. Then the boys flock around us. I hand them three or four blank sheets. The boys make planes. Nisha makes a boat. Then she sends it up in the air as if it were a plane. The boys say, 'Boats go in water only.' Nisha says, 'This is a boat that can also fly.'

Mani stares at the boat as it lands on the crib close to the green window.

Tanu has arrived. She is eleven. The moment she arrived Nisha ran away. I sense a strong rivalry between them. Mani struggles to sit in her bed. An involuntary tear rolls down her cheek. It lands on Tanu's shoe.

'Come, Uncle!' exclaims Tanu. 'We are going to practise dance downstairs. Will you join us?'

If there is one thing on this earth I can't do, it is dance. I freeze. I become conscious of my body.

On the way down, I overhear Nisha saying to the dance instructor that she doesn't want to participate. She would rather read. I was exactly like her.

A few days ago they were all strangers to me, and I was a stranger to them. And now they are becoming my friends. If I don't leave this place soon, I will end up staying here. I remember my first visit to the care home. The first time I saw Tanu dance. I didn't know anything about her then. In my mind, I'd described her as cute, chubby and sprightly. I didn't know that her platelet count drops every month. Blood clots form on her skin. She has been put on steroids. The clots have disappeared, but her face has swollen as a result.

Tanu saw her parents die. She was eight then. The extended family rejected her. She is still attached to them. She asks the caregivers to call her sister and brother-in-law. But her brother-in-law has changed his number.

'Did people treat the TB patients better?' I ask myself. Last time I visited India I had wandered into an old TB sanitarium in the hills of Kasauli, and spoken to the eighty six year old dhobi who had washed clothes at the sanitarium from 1941 to 1976. He told me that the relatives would come every three to four months, and they would stand 20 metres away from the patient, but they would at least talk to them.

I remember when I was a schoolboy in Delhi, a teacher told us that cancer spreads by touching. 'Don't wet your finger with your tongue while reading a library book,' he said. 'Never turn pages with a wet finger. God knows how many cancer patients borrowed that book before you.'

In our biology textbook there was a chapter on the human body. The teacher was so embarrassed, she chalked with a shaking hand two little organs on the blackboard, then ran out of the class. Myths about masturbation, VD, syphilis and gonorrhea floated around, and sometimes transformed into a nightmare.

Not much seems to have changed in India. Six state governments have recently banned courses on sex education in schools. Instead, they plan to teach a course on 'Indian values'.[5]

'The children are forbidden to ask honest questions,' explains the Director. 'Harsh judgements are passed on those who dare to ask. Not so long ago, I was invited by a local school to talk to thirteen and fourteen year olds about HIV basics,' says the caregiver. 'The teachers were nervous around me, one warned beforehand, "Whatever you say, don't mention condoms." During the session, the students were tongue-tied. But the moment the teachers stepped out, a dam of questions burst open: "Is it possible to contract HIV by wet kissing? By giving or receiving oral sex? By a knife or a needle? By eating food cooked by a positive person?"'

Whenever Tanu sees a plane flying, she says, 'My father is in the plane.'

She is putting on weight, and at times other kids tease her. She tries fasting. Sometimes, the caregivers discover piles of discarded dal and rice under her seat in the dining room.

---

[5] Sex Education Curriculum Angers Indian Conservatives', *International Herald Tribune*, May 24 2007, www.iht.com/articles/2007/05/24/africa/letter.php.

'What would you like to become, Tanu?'

She never answers. Other kids say, 'I want to become a nurse, or a chef, or a pilot, or a firefighter,' but Tanu never answers the question.

I say goodbye to Tanu.

I am close to the gate. The pet dog Sultan wags his tail, and jumps up to sniff me. Nisha appears out of nowhere. She tries to frighten me with her scream, and monster paws—she is wearing 'tiger' gloves.

'Bhoot aa gaya!'

I must admit a part of me did get scared.

'This is for you,' she says.

She has sketched a colourful wristwatch on the side of the paper boat.

'Thank you,' I say. 'But why does your watch have no hands?'

'Uncle, this is a ghost watch,' she says, and covers her head with the hood and runs inside laughing. 'Ghosts don't have hands, Uncle.'

The next day I don't visit the care home. I walk around in my own neighbourhood. Huge hotels and malls under construction. Bare hands at work. Flimsy scaffolding. I take pictures. No one stops me.

On the way to the market I notice a playground. It belongs to a preschool. Swings, slides and tricycles. Jhoolabari. Two boys desire the same yellow cycle, and the teacher is trying hard to solve the problem. I install myself on the bench. She has noticed me. I wave at the teacher. She walks towards me, staring at my camera. 'No, I will not take pictures,' I assure her. 'So, who gets the tricycle?' She sits next to me, and shares stories about how children solve 'big problems'.

'I am curious,' I say, 'why are there more boys than girls in the playground?'

'70% in this preschool are boys.'

'Where are the girls?'

'It is the mentality of the people here. This is a highly educated middle class neighbourhood. Despite that we have female foeticide... I am ashamed. To tell you the truth, I am ashamed of my country.'

Her sari and cardigan flutter in the wind. Delhi is cold today.

'In this preschool, is there someone who is HIV positive?' I ask.

'That thing,' she says, 'that thing is not our problem.'

'Excuse me?'

She points at the woman in the playground, by the swings.

'You see the teacher over there. That is what she believes.'

Her sari flutters in the wind.

'But,' I say, 'You seem to be so aware?'

'No,' she says, 'I am not like that.'

She plucks a blade of grass, and starts rolling it between her thumb and first finger nervously.

'Four years ago two positive kids were thrown out of a school in Kerala. This outraged me, and for the first time I started probing my own attitude towards AIDS. I was repelled by the parents who had demonstrated "non-violently"—a bit like Gandhi—outside the school. The headmaster kicked a five year old and a seven year old out of the school.'

'Ours is a very cruel country,' she says.

Today, when I arrive at the the care home, Mani is staring at the white ceiling. Her mouth half open. A volunteer from Colombia is comforting her. Her hand rests on Mani's brow. A caregiver, not far from the bed, is sorting out the freshly dried laundry. They rarely leave her alone.

I have never heard Mani utter a word—perhaps a namaste a few days ago, but I am not sure. I have never seen her smile. They tell me sometimes she laughs a belly laugh. 'Mani is a tyrant!' the caregiver tells me. 'Mani threatens! Cook tomatoes and kheer for me otherwise I will not eat! Take me to

Aunty's room in the basement, otherwise I will report you!'
Mani loves watching fish in the tank in the Director's room
in the basement. Mani is a fish. She swims from bed to bed,
from lap to lap. Her skin—the colour of cassia; the whites of
her eyes—tinged with yellow. Her hair—black and short.
Tears in her eyes. But today, even she doesn't know the
reason. The first time I saw Mani she was weeping silently,
because she felt the caregivers would not take her downstairs
to celebrate Sachin's birthday.

Sachin turned one on the 23rd of January. He is the youngest
at the care home. His age was determined the way physicists
determine the age of a star—backwards. Sachin was abandoned in a cradle outside an orphanage, in Rajasthan. The
orphanage was established to prevent female infanticide. It
has saved many girls. Ironically, it also managed to save a boy.

Tanu danced at Sachin's birthday before the huge chocolate cake was cut, and the balloons were popped. She danced
like Karishma Kapoor, like Aishwarya Rai—slow first, then
fast, improvising, switching forms, now classical, now contemporary, as if narrating a story. 'Dance,' I thought. 'Is it
possible to learn dance at my age?'

A standing ovation!

The audience showered Tanu with hugs, and praises.

Mani could not, or would not, applaud. But I noticed a
glint in her eye. She was the first one to eat the cake (because
her condition has improved, she no longer requires the feeding pipe). Quizzically, she looked at Ishan, who sang a popular song from a recent Bombay film.

Chehray pay aanay dayta nahin/ Pur dil hi dil mein
ghabrata hoon/ Tujhe sab hay pata mayree maa/ Mein
kabhi batlata nahin/ Pur andharay say darta hoon mein
mayree ma.[6]

---

[6] *Taare Zameen Par*, Aamir Khan Productions, 2007.

(I don't allow my face to reveal it/ But deep in my heart I am anxious/ You know it all, my mother/ I never say it, but really I am afraid of the dark, my mother)

Listening to the song, my mind drifts to a recent book by the writer Stephanie Nolen, *28 Stories of AIDS in Africa*. Her words fill me with hope, and then take away that hope.

More than 90% of all children with the virus contract it from mothers at birth. Those infections are easily avoided: used together, a single dose of nevirapine given to the mother in labour and baby at birth, a Caesarian delivery and formula feeding, lower the risk of passing the virus to the baby to less than 2%... Because it is so simple, fewer than 300 children were born with HIV in all rich countries combined in 2005... But less than 10% of women in poor countries get those interventions (in fact, most aren't even tested for HIV), and so thousands of children are born infected each year...

'Children have an immature immune system, which means HIV hits them harder. They need ARVs early, often as infants. But small children can't swallow pills... Pharmaceutical companies have little incentive to develop, or produce, pediatric medications because there are so few HIV positive children in the developed world—where there is a market of parents, or health systems, willing to pay high prices for drugs.

Ishan is a music prodigy. Like Sachin, he was born with the virus. He is fourteen, the oldest at the care home, and the only one on second line antiretroviral medication. First line ARVs (available free of charge in India) stop being effective after a few years. Second line medication is equivalent to a middle class salary, anywhere between Rs 5000 to15,000, per month.

Ray is on anti-depressants. But he, too, loves music.

Ishan and Ray are headed to an art school close by for music lessons. I would like to join them.

'Uncle,' they say, 'the teacher will not allow you in.'

I accompany them on a blue rickshaw anyway. It is a tight squeeze.

'Sapna kay pass,' they tell the rickshaw wallah.

He is a frail man with a shock of white hair.

'Sapna?' I ask.

'Sapna is a cinema hall.'

'Have you seen any good films of late?'

'*Taare Zameen Par*,' says Ray; the movie he has been singing from.

'What did you like about it?'

'Everything.'

'What happens?'

'There is a boy. He can't read and write. Words start dancing when he looks at a page.'

'And...'

'Only Aamir Khan understands the boy.'

'Who is he?'

'The temp teacher. He says that even Einstein had reading and writing difficulties as a child.'

'Then what?'

Ishan shrugs his shoulders.

'Uncle, you ask so many questions!'

The rickshaw wallah zigzags through the choked traffic. It occurs to me that I have not taken a rickshaw ride in many years... An old memory: I am nine or ten... we are headed home on a rickshaw after a long train journey... Father promises to buy me a musical instrument... 'If you do well in maths, we will buy you a guitar,' he tells me.

We pass by a park filled with old people. Outside the art school many parents have come to drop off their children. We disembark from the rickshaw, and enter the multi-storied yellow stucco building.

'I am worried,' says Ishan breathing heavily. 'I don't think the teacher will allow you in.'

Ishan and Ray remove their shoes, and put them on the rack.

They take me to the office. Portraits of Tagore cover the red brick wall. The woman in a kantha sari and thick glasses generously permits me to attend the class for 'five minutes only'.

Ishan and Ray run up the stairs barefoot. I remove my shoes outside the class. I feel I have entered a film. The teacher resembles a character in Satyajit Ray's *Pather Panchali*. He is a dhoti-clad Brahmin with a huge elephantine belly. A black umbrella by his side.

He is annoyed we are late.

'Who is this man with you?' he asks.

'He is our uncle,' they say.

Ray gets ready to play the tabla, and Ishan sits behind the kids practicsing the harmonium.

Sa ray ga ma pa dha ni sa
Sa ni dha pa ma ga ray sa

Ga ma ni dha
Dha ma ni dha
Ga ma ni dha...

I sit cross-legged on the chatai. The fragrance of jasmine incense floats in the room. Ray's tabla is out of tune. The teacher stops him, and tunes the drums with a hammer. Ray looks at me as if to remind me, 'Your time is up.' Then he begins:

Dha dha dhinak
Da dhinak
Dhinak dhinak da da
Dhinak
Da da dhinak...

'Who is going to sing?' asks the teacher, adjusting his dhoti.
No one seems interested.
'Jaldi.'

134

Ishan flips through his textbook (in Hindi), *Introduction to Ragas*.

'Sarasvati vandana is four lines only.' The teacher is angry. 'You can't even memorise four lines. When I was your age I would learn by heart thick books on history. Really you kids study out of fear… because you are afraid of your father and mother.'

Other kids laugh. Ishan and Ray don't join in the wave of laughter. One has seen his parents die, the other one was too young to remember when he became an orphan. It is a secret they carry inside. And what if they shared this secret with the 'normal' 'negative' children in the school? (I don't ask them. Is it possible Ishan and Ray think if the teacher, or the parents of other children, sniffed out the details, the school would burn the carpets, the chatais, the tables, and the harmoniums—all the things touched by their HIV fingers…)

'Only four lines,' says the teacher.

The tall girl in a white turtleneck raises her hand, and sings in a falsetto voice. The teacher corrects her, but her mind is elsewhere. She is definitely here because of parental pressure.

'Ishan, you move to the harmonium,' says the teacher. 'Raag Bilawal. Teen Taal.'

Ishan transforms the harmonium. He is a wonderful singer.

'Ka say kahoon… Piya baata… ka say kahoon.'
(Whom should I tell?)

I wait outside on the stairs for the class to end.

The khaki-clad watchman stares as we step out the gates of the art school, and jaywalk across the road to the cluster of rickshaws.

The world appears lighter. The rickshaw moves faster than the cars and trucks—creates its own path. Now it is their turn to ask me questions.

'Are you married?'

'I was involved with someone. It didn't work out.'

'Why?'

'Because I think both of us were afraid.'

The rickshaw goes past a stalled city bus. By the window is a young woman, peeling an orange. I notice the precise moment her eyes lock with Ishan's eyes.

'Are you afraid of something Ishan?'

'No.'

He looks in the other direction. The rickshaw moves in and out of lanes. The rickshaw never remains in one lane. There are questions I would like to ask Ishan. Where will he go after the care home? Is he keen on vocational training? Does he desire someone? But I can't bring myself to ask him so many intrusive questions. So I ask: 'What do you think of while singing? What goes on inside you while playing the harmonium?'

'Music,' he says.

Then: 'Only music.'

He says all the right things. I visit the principal of an elite school in south Delhi. 'A child with AIDS is a child with special needs,' he says. 'In our classrooms we have children with dyslexia, Down's syndrome and even leukemia.'

'But would you admit an HIV positive kid?'

He pauses to think. The cell phone in his hand emits a strange bluish light.

'It is a hard question,' he says. 'I have no problems, but I don't know how my teachers might respond.'

'But would you be bold enough to admit someone from an HIV positive care home?'

'The thing is... I don't want to treat that child like a guinea pig.'

He is right. The founding principle of all elite schools is discrimination between the rich and the poor.

'What if someone in your school, a parent, tells you that their child is positive?'

He pauses. He surveys his watch.

'Things are changing in this country,' I say. 'On the way to your school I asked the cabbie if he knew about HIV. He was very frank. "AIDS is not a choot ki bimari," he said—not a disease that spreads by touching. "60% of the people in my village are well informed about it... The same 60% have also stopped believing in caste prejudices." "But, the other 40%?" I asked. "They are different," he confessed. "For them an AIDS wallah is worse than an animal."'

The cell phone rings two or three times in the principal's hand. He shuts off the ringer.

'You want to know something?' he says.

I know whatever is going to come out of his mouth is difficult to share.

'There are two positive children in my school,' he says. 'Both contracted the virus during surgery in hospitals. Their mothers disclosed this to me. Both fathers are in complete denial. The children don't know that I know. No other parent, no other teacher in the school knows about it.'

I would like to see the children from the care home one last time. 'On Sunday,' the caregivers tell me, 'the kids are headed for a picnic to the Lodhi gardens.'

I get delayed because of a traffic jam, and I am unable to locate them in the garden. The place hums with birds, foreign languages and accents. There are other children playing not far from the 15th century Islamic ruins—not the children I am looking for.

I walk towards the crumbling monument, the sheesh gumbad. It is a wonderful structure—at once a square, and an octagon with a dome. Every single crack is filled with melancholy. Friezes of blue enamelled tiles survive only in traces. No one knows who is buried inside. Two or three drops of water fall on me. How astonished I was as a child when I heard that the pleasant smell of earth at the beginning of rain is due to actinomycetes, a fungus.

A middle aged woman, with a little dog, runs towards the swaying trees. Disappears. The trees of my childhood. Tamarind. Neem. Ashok. Gulmohar. Amaltas. Frangipani. Peepul. Fig. Under the peepul tree... And there they are, the children from the care home. They are playing.

My first impulse is to run towards them, but I don't. I am not good at farewells. So I sit down under the high arch, and watch them play; Ray who calls Jaya 'Jerry', and Kavya who calls Ishan 'Tom', like the cartoon characters. M who signs his name as Maniac, and Raunaq who refuses to say sorry for his little crimes and misdemeanours. 29 out of 34 are here. Mani and Sachin and three others are absent. 29 are here. 1.9 million are not here. Where are they? How are they? I am supposed to write about all of them. I don't even know how to begin.

'Garam cha, garam.' I buy a cup of cardamom chai. The children have formed a train. The tiny one in red pants is in the front. She is the steam engine. 'Shook, shook, shook,' she says. 'Dha dhinak dha dhinak,' she says. 'Watch out!' Her toe hits an exposed root. The caregiver picks the girl up. She whistles. She falls again. It has become a game. Then: the girl is on her own, spinning around. She separates from the rest of the group, and keeps spinning. She seems to have mastered, suddenly, the invisible centrifugal force.

The security guard taps my shoulder.

'Yes, yes, I am leaving,' I say.

A question from Kiran Desai sparks laughter among sex workers along the Kakinada Coast.
(East Godavari, Andhra Pradesh)

A client surveys a roadside 'bed' spread out by a sex worker.
(East Godavari, Andhra Pradesh)

Files from Dr Toku's popular matchmaking service for HIV positive community members.

(Chennai, Tamil Nadu)

Children huddle around Jaspreet Singh for story time at an HIV positive care home.

(New Delhi)

Salman Rushdie listens to Laxmi describe life among Bombay's hijra community.

(Bombay, Maharashtra)

Devotees carry a statue of the Goddess Yellamma to pay homage at the Saundatti Yellamma Temple.

(Bagalkot, Karnataka)

Siddhartha Deb explores a market in one of Manipur's most economically depressed districts.

(Churachandpur, Manipur)

A man injects himself in the leg at a graveyard, which also serves as a 'shooting range' for local injecting drug users.
(Ukhrul, Manipur)

Sunil Gangopadhyay talks with a group of social activists and HIV practitioners in Sonagachhi's red light district.

(Kolkata, West Bengal)

Two women pose inside in room along the famed corridors of S⟨...⟩ red light district.

(Kolkata, West Bengal)

Aman Sethi takes a chai break at a roadside dhaba with fellow truckers.
(Kishanganj, Bihar)

Mukul Kesavan learns about the many identities of India's MSM community.
(Bangalore, Karnataka)

Two MSM outreach workers share a laugh in Cubbon Park, cruising centre of Bangalore.
(Bangalore, India)

Nalini Jones spends an afternoon talking with Ashwini about work, family, and love after HIV.

(Mysore, Karnataka)

RETURN TO SONAGACHHI
Sunil Gangopadhyay

I returned to Sonagachhi after many years, nearly four and a half decades. My friends and I had spent many evenings there as young men, during the sixties. It was thus that I came to observe the prostitutes and their world very closely.

I'd heard of Sonagachhi since my childhood when we lived in the oldest neighbourhood of north Kolkata. Walking down Central Avenue as a young man, I would always pass a vast stretch of straggling houses to the right. Some 'know-alls' among my friends told me it was the largest red light area in Asia. Some people love the cities in which they live so greatly that being first in any field, even in the size of the red light area, is a matter of pride for them.

In college we, a congregation of young poets, became involved with the publication of a journal called *Krittibas*. Other interests went hand in hand with our poetry writing. One was an unlimited imbibing of liquor. Drinking was socially unacceptable in those days. Even writers and artists rarely touched spirits. And the few who did drank on the sly. The only exception was Michael Madhusudan Datta, the great Bengali poet, about whose wild drinking sprees we had heard many stories. But he wasn't of our time and class. He lived in the 19th century, had rejected Hinduism and become Christian. For us, of course, drinking was part of a youthful rebellion against Hindu society. Rebellion—but cautious and kept well within limits. Since none of us were financially independent we were still living under the rule of strict, middle class parents. There was no question of drinking within the house and we followed this rule very conscientiously. We were good boys at home—wild and bohemian outside it. And all our rebellious activities were carefully shielded from the eyes of our elders.

Many foreigners used to visit Kolkata in the sixties. I formed a close friendship with one of them, a poet called Paul Engel. He was the head of the English Department at the University of Iowa and deeply involved with their international writing programme. He visited many countries, among them India, to meet with young poets. As a farewell present before he returned to USA, he gave me two bottles of premium Scotch whisky.

That wonderful, much prized gift put me in a quandary. Scotch was rarely seen in this country at the time I speak of and we youngsters could afford nothing better than cheap country liquor from unlicensed bars. What would I do with these two unimaginably expensive bottles? There was no question of taking them home. Drinking in public parks or by the side of the Ganga could lead to trouble. We might be caught by the police and sent to the lockup. Or they might ask for a fat bribe, for which all our money pooled together would not suffice. I dared not entrust the bottles to a friend, for in matters such as this even friends were liable to turn traitor.

Around this time, the Bengal Cultural Conference was being held in Kolkata. We sat in the conference grounds, racking our brains for a solution, when an elderly writer joined our circle. 'You're looking for a place where you can sit and drink?' he asked. 'If you give me a share, I can take you to a safe and secret place. Why don't we go to some girl's room in Sonagachhi? All we have to do is make an hour's payment.'

Under the gentleman's leadership, we went to Sonagachhi. I can't say I wasn't in a moral dilemma. I was twenty three years old at the time; a schoolmaster's son. Some guilt and shame dogged me. But the heady feelings that came with breaking rules were too strong to resist.

Prostitutes of Sonagachhi charged their clients by the hour, but there were different rates for different women. If the girl was good-looking and her room had a fan or an air conditioner, the charge was pretty high. For an average looking girl in a modest room, the rate was about Rs 15 (38 cents) per hour. Now, 15 rupees, in the sixties, was quite a lot of money. Clerks and schoolmasters earned about Rs 150 ($3.75) a month.

The girl we went to was called Teri. This was not an English name. It was a nickname given to her because she was cross-eyed, 'tera' meaning crooked in Bengali. Lots of girls would have hated the name and taken another—but not she. She gave it to us quite composedly. I must say, though, that I didn't perceive her squint as a flaw. In fact, I felt it lent her face a certain attraction. She was alarmed, in the beginning, to see five men troop into her room together. But, when we explained that all we wanted was to sit in her room and drink, she relented and let us in. There was no furniture in her room—only a thick mattress on the floor spread with sheets. A few calendar pictures of gods and goddesses adorned the grimy walls. And, in a cupboard in a corner, were rows and rows of glasses. Some two or three hundred of them.

We had a good time in Teri's room. We had to pay Rs 3 (8 cents) per head, which we could afford. In return, we had the place to ourselves and an attractive young woman to pour out our drinks. What else could we wish for? And when she took a glass herself, held it aloft and cried 'Cheers!' our day was made.

After this, we started visiting Sonagachhi every now and then—a bottle wrapped in newspaper tucked securely under the armpit. We found it comfortable and far more economical than even the cheapest of bars. As soon as we arrived, scores of girls would surround us, clamouring to take us to their rooms. They had never seen customers like us. Men who wanted nothing from them except a place to sit. Who didn't abuse them verbally or hurt them physically. Who gave them a share of the liquor and treated them with respect.

And thus we came to know many of the girls. While drinking we would argue animatedly about literature—a subject with which they were totally unfamiliar. So it was a bit of a shock when one of them said suddenly, 'You guys write poetry? My mother writes poetry too.' The girl's mother, also a prostitute (in those days the term sex worker hadn't evolved) lived in the same house on the ground floor. Mother and daughter had a common profession and a common moral code which they followed religiously. They wouldn't entertain the same man. Once a client insisted on having sex with both at the same time. He begged and pleaded, offered a lot of money but couldn't get the women to agree. When he became too troublesome, they threw him out of the house.

The mother's name was Lakshmi. We saw what she had written one evening—eight notebooks full of poetry. Shy as any budding poet, she was reluctant to show it to us at first. The woman had never been to school. She had learned to read and write through her own efforts. We read her poems with interest—although the language and the sentiments were mediocre, they were clearly a great labour of love. She had never thought of publishing her work. There was no one to read it in the house either. Yet she went on writing. When we asked her why, she had no answer.

Jean Genet wrote a novel while incarcerated for life in a French prison. Jean Paul Sartre expressed surprise at it. Like him, I too expressed surprise. 'When do you write?' I asked Lakshmi. Her answer startled me. 'When I'm depressed,' she said. Jean Genet, of course, was set free and went on to become a famous writer. But such was not the case with Lakshmi. She was never liberated from her prison.

Then there was Basanti. A customer left a purse full of notes in her room one night. He must have forgotten where he had been for he didn't come back to look for it. A month

160

and a half later he came to another girl in Sonagachhi. Basanti heard his drunken laughter and recognised it. She took the purse to him and said, 'Ogo Babu. Count the money and see if it is all there.' Basanti didn't want any credit for what she had done. If anyone mentioned the subject, she lowered her eyes bashfully. Yet, the man, from what I heard, was an extremely unpleasant character. He used to beat the girls quite freely and take pleasure in it.

One evening, some friends and I were sitting in a girl's room reading our latest when we were interrupted by loud screams, sounds of running feet and cries of 'Police! Police!' A servant ran in and informed us that a girl had been murdered in the next building and the police, convinced that the murderer was hiding here, had surrounded the house. When we tried to leave, we were caught and taken to the police station along with the other inmates. A big, burly policeman started grilling us but was interrupted by some of the girls. 'Let them go sir,' they begged. 'They are boys from good families. They don't misbehave with anyone. They just sit in a room and read their poems. They are young and innocent.' The policeman wasn't paying attention to the girls at first but the phrase 'young and innocent' made him sit up in surprise. His lips curled in contempt. 'Go, go,' he waved his hand at us as if we were a swarm of troublesome flies. 'Get lost.' From the expression on his face, it was clear that he considered poets such a worthless lot that he felt a simple thing like a murder was beyond us. I would have liked the cross examination to go on for a while longer, it being a new experience for me. But I had no such luck. We were hustled out of the police station with scant ceremony.

Someone once asked William Faulkner what the ideal livelihood for aspiring writers was. 'Playing the piano in a brothel, because the hours are easy,' he replied. 'The company is nice and there is plenty of opportunity for interesting conversation.' There were no pianos in Sonagachhi. Besides, the images of brothels that we see in Hollywood movies where girls bursting with health and beauty romp, dance and sing in lavishly appointed, brilliantly lit salons, had nothing in common with the reality of Sonagachhi.

This was a dark world. There were hundreds of cell-like rooms—dim and airless; poorly ventilated. The toilets were filthy and there was scarcely any water. There were no common areas and no facilities for light amusement. Customers came for the sex alone and paid by the hour. Those who wanted to spend the whole night had to part with exorbitant sums. They were called 'whole night babus'. Very few of the girls were healthy and cheerful. Most of them looked crushed and defeated. They came from the lowest rung of society and the poorest of families. The ones who had been residents of Sonagachhi for two or three generations fared no better. There were too many exploiters. Madams, pimps and servants demanding shares of whatever the girls earned from peddling their bodies. Consequently, most of them got little to eat and looked pale and emaciated.

Their future would be even darker. When they developed a serious illness or their bodies aged and lost their attraction, they were treated like refuse to be thrown out into the street. Most had no opportunity to save for the future. Some tried to get work as maids. But that wasn't possible for long. Their pasts caught up with them and they were dismissed from service. The master of the house might have spent his evenings in Sonagachhi, but he wouldn't employ an ex-prostitute in his house. As a result, many of these women were reduced to begging in the streets. But even begging is exhausting and most lacked the energy for it.

At the time I speak of, the two deadly sexually transmitted diseases were syphilis and gonorrhea and many prostitutes fell victim to them (HIV/AIDS was still undiscovered at this time). Penicillin, newly used during the Second World War, was the treatment for these diseases, and those who had the money to obtain treatment were saved. If they didn't, their bodies rotted from the diseases and, eventually, they died.

The few girls who still had some glow in them, maybe 10% of the lot, enjoyed better facilities. Their rooms were larger and well furnished. Some even had air conditioners. Their rates were higher, some of them making as much as reputed doctors and barristers, and many of their clients were foreigners. These lucky few are called Agrawali which means that, though they have lived in Bengal for several generations, they originally hail from outside it—from Agra or Lucknow.

Rich men from all over the country had always flocked to Kolkata from its beginnings in the 18th century when the British took three tiny villages in Bengal and transformed them into their bustling capital city. Gradually, the city became divided into two distinct sections. One was the saheb para, or neighbourhood, where British, Armenian, Dutch, French and Greek, in short, white-skinned people lived. The other was the native para. The white area was neat and clean, with wide roads and smart bungalows. In comparison, the native area, towards the north of the city, was congested and unplanned. Then, slowly, sprawling, opulent mansions started raising their heads in the midst of the dirt and squalor. These were the dwellings of the nouveau riche who had made their fortunes doing business with the British and were eager to display their wealth.

In the first few decades of their rule, the British sent shiploads of gold, silk and spices to their homeland but the ships came back empty, there being nothing worthwhile in England to send back to India. But the empty ships were tossed and buffeted on the high seas and, more often than not, destroyed and sunk by storms and tempests. Then someone got the idea of weighing them down with earth. Shiploads of English earth found their way to India. This earth was dumped in a canal in central Kolkata. When the canal got filled to the brim, it was turned into a road which came to be called Chowringhee. In later years it was renamed Jawaharlal Nehru Road. It is the only road in India built entirely with English earth.

Soon afterwards the British realised that bringing back earth was a waste as it yielded no returns. Salt was a better option. It could be sold. But the natives resisted the move. They would not eat British salt. Just as the whites despised the natives for their dark skins, the latter looked down upon the 'white-skinned mlechhas' and considered them untouchable. What were the rulers to do? What was the use of bringing back salt if no one would buy it?

Fortunately for the British, there was no dearth of subservient natives ready and willing to help them. Contracts were signed with Indian agents who bought up English salt and sold it in the market without divulging the truth. And so the salt business, an enormous swindle, flourished—enabling many unscrupulous traders to amass inordinate amounts of wealth. In later years, the British tried to stifle the production of indigenous salt, with a slew of laws, so that the natives would have no option but to buy theirs. As a protest against this mode of oppression, Mahatma Gandhi led the Salt Satyagraha in the 1940s. That, of course was much later—at the height of the freedom movement

Turned affluent overnight, the salt traders started buying up estates in various parts of Bengal and became respectable. Lord Cornwallis' Sunset Law made it easy for them to acquire the properties of zamindars (landowners) who were in financial trouble. The new zamindars, eager to display their wealth, built palatial mansions for themselves, traces of which can still be found in some neighbourhoods of north Kolkata.

It was rumoured that money flew about in the air of Kolkata; money which filled the homes of the rich with furniture and paintings, cooks and servants, horses and carriages. Wine sellers brought the finest of English liquors and the best singing and dancing girls flocked to the city for the entertainment of the new babus of Kolkata. Gradually, a red light area formed itself on a piece of land adjoining Chitpur, close to the tomb of a Muslim pir, or saint, called Sona Gazi. Sona Gazi got corrupted through repeated usage and became Sonagachhi.

Some people called it 'Golden Tree', which is the literal meaning for the contemporary word, 'sona' meaning gold, 'gaach' meaning tree. There are other red light areas in Kolkata but Sonagachhi is the largest and best known.

The rich babus conscientiously spent their evenings in the company of singing and dancing girls. It was the social norm of the time. They kept a number of mistresses—each according to his status. The phrase 'kept woman' was used so often it became part of Bengali vocabulary. The babus were generous to their mistresses and showered them with gifts—carriages, jewellery, even houses. The more a man gave his mistress, the greater his prestige among his peers. When the mistress grew old and unattractive or her protector died, she often turned her home into a brothel and lived on the commissions earned from her tenants.

It's worth emphasising the way a prostitute was regarded at the time, and indeed in ancient India. If a woman was beautiful and talented; if she could sing, dance or converse intelligently, why should she waste her skills on one man alone? Why shouldn't a number of men enjoy her company? That is why a prostitute was called barnari or barangana—meaning public woman—and the source of her earnings was her skill in some performing art. Even 50 years ago a prostitute's ability to sing or dance was considered her primary asset. Now, of course, all that has passed. Prostitution has been reduced almost completely into a trading of the flesh.

The zamindars and babus of old are extinct species. And Kolkata is no longer the pivot towards which beauty and talent from all parts of India are pulled. The few who have survived, over the generations, are the first class citizens of Sonagachhi today. Their clients are underworld dons, bank dacoits and coal mafia agents. The truly affluent are no longer constrained to go to Sonagachhi to enjoy women. They have other devices. Spending a crore of rupees on securing a film star as a mistress is quite common, today, among the affluent in India.

Sonagachhi caters to a different clientele now. Many men come to Kolkata from the adjoining states in search of a livelihood. Most of them don't bring their wives. A great number of them are bachelors (whenever a census is conducted in Kolkata it yields a skewed ratio—more men than women). These men, as is inevitable, go to red light areas to satisfy their sexual urges. Unemployed youths and those who earn meagre salaries often lack the courage to marry. But they have their compulsions too.

After leaving north Kolkata I never went back to Sonagachhi. Our old gang had split up by then, and many of my friends had moved to other cities. The newspapers reported disappearances of women from the small towns and villages of Bengal, every now and then, and it was said that the women didn't always end up in Sonagachhi. Many were taken further—to Delhi, Mumbai and Saudi Arabia. Sometimes the culprits were caught and the girls brought back. But the police manipulated the cases so cleverly that many of them escaped punishment. The real perpetrators, the kingpins, didn't lose any sleep. No one could touch a hair of their heads. The girls, rejected by their parents and thus, unable to go home, were sent to women shelters, nari niketans, where the treatment meted out to them was so insensitive that many of them escaped and found their way into brothels. The government, caught up with other, more important problems, could not be bothered to waste time on these girls. All this was brought to light through the efforts of investigating journalists. These were not the only dangers to which these poor women were exposed. By the late eighties and early nineties, HIV had joined the ranks of syphilis and gonorrhea.

But times have changed. In the last 10 years or so the term 'prostitute' has been replaced by 'sex worker'. In 1995, a group of sex workers from Sonagachhi, established Durbar Mahila Samanwaya Committee (DMSC), which today is one of the most powerful social work groups in West Bengal. Started as a government public health programme in 1992, the women of Sonagachhi took over the management of DMSC a few years later. Their mission is to improve the lives and health of sex workers and their children. They hold seminars and conferences, highlight problems faced by sex workers and try to find solutions.

I'm a writer—not a social activist. This kind of work doesn't fall within my purview. But I did meet the members of Durbar through my good friends Dr and Mrs Moni Nag.

Dr Nag, an internationally renowned cultural anthropologist, taught in Columbia University for many years and is presently advisor to a number of international organisations such as the World Bank, the World Health Organization, and the Ford Foundation. He lives in New York but spends four months each year in India, mainly in Kolkata. He keeps himself engaged in research—not armchair research but fieldwork—and interacts extensively with NGOs. At his request and that of the members of Durbar, I agreed to be a delegate at a Sex Workers' Conference they had organised some years back.

On reaching the conference venue, I was amazed at its scale and size. It was being held in a huge stadium called Jubabharati, and 7000 sex workers, from all over the country, were present. It was inconceivable that such a vast public demonstration could take place in our country! Books like *Kamasutra* had been written in India at one time, but centuries of puritanical thought had dominated, between then and now, and the word sex had become taboo.

Sex workers are creatures of the dark. They exist in every society but are kept invisible. They are to be used but not talked about. This was what I had believed all these years. Suddenly I found thousands of them given voice. They were expressing their grievances; sharing their problems with others. They were talking about AIDS. They knew about the virus, that it is spreading rapidly and that they, as sex workers, in particular, are at risk.

The term sex worker is a good one for it has a special connotation. It tells us that they are workers too. A lot of women use their bodies to earn a living. They carry bricks on their heads, break stones and clear debris. And, with their labour, big houses, streets and bridges are built. Sex workers, like the others, use their bodies to feed themselves. Most villages and small towns in India lack good sanitation systems. There are septic tanks in some houses which need to be cleaned periodically. Women are employed to carry drums full of faeces and urine on their heads. Some are pickpockets. Others beg in the streets and on railway platforms, a baby straddled on one hip. Earning a livelihood by renting her body to some male, for a few hours, is surely a better option.

Like all workers, they too wanted their own organising body. In this age and time, all workers enjoy the benefits of a trade union. Why shouldn't sex workers be given the same? Their demand for security and hygienic conditions in the workplace is a legitimate demand. They need life insurance and facilities for educating their children. But they are not allowed to form unions. I don't understand why the government is withholding permission. Perhaps the men in power prefer to deny their very existence. A ration card is the poor man's identity card in this country. Even that is denied to sex workers. The only right they are given is the right to vote and political parties vie with each other to capture this votebank during election time.

Despite the presence of a red light area of the size and density of Sonagachhi, and other smaller ones in various pockets, the spread of HIV/AIDS has been fairly well contained in Kolkata. Sonagachhi has managed to keep HIV rates down far below similar brothel settings in India. This is what the statistics show.[1] But how is this possible? How much of it is truth and how much propaganda? I was curious and wanted to find out for myself. And so I went to Sonagachhi—after nearly 50 years.

---

[1] While HIV rates have hovered between 5–10% in Sonagachhi over the last decade, Bombay's red light district of Kamathipura had a 50% HIV rate among sex workers in early 2000. Sexually transmitted infections are also less frequent in Sonagachhi.

The locality, from the outside, does not seem to have changed at all. The lanes and bylanes look pretty much the same. So do the houses. The rest of Kolkata has altered drastically. Roads are wider. Old houses have been pulled down and apartment complexes built in their place. Brilliantly lit shopping malls are springing up everywhere. But Sonagachhi remains as it was.

I wondered about the women I used to know there in my youth. I saw no sign of them now. I didn't want to go from door to door in search of them. So I went and sat in the DMSC office and chatted with some of the members I had met already. The office was spacious—lodged in one of the larger houses—and had many employees. Not all were activists. Many of them were there to make a living, for the quantum of work done by DMSC has increased substantially over the years. Its involvement has spread beyond Sonagachhi to red light areas in the suburbs and other districts of Bengal. Yet a certain commitment and dedication was visible in all the workers. Many sex workers form part of the team. Some have retired from the profession. Others work here during the day and go back to their clients at night.

Though Sonagachhi looked the same, I could detect a distinct change in the psyche of the women. They don't perceive themselves as sinners and fallen women anymore. They don't claim to be victims of a cruel destiny either. They speak of their profession, quite naturally and spontaneously, as though it was one of many. One sex worker informed me that she had been in Sonagachhi for 22 years. She had looked after her aged parents and educated her three younger siblings: 'If I believed that using my body for earning a livelihood was immoral—a notion that applies only to women's bodies in this society—would I have been able to save my family? Or myself?' she asked with a proud tilt of her head.

The NGOs started with the basics, making sure women got a fair share of their earnings. But, without any laws to support them, how do these women curb the greed of pimps and madams? Yet it is happening. They are doing so by banding together. All these years they existed as islands, each responsible for herself. Now they stand by each other. When one of them is beaten or arrested without cause, others step in and protest. They are more forceful about using condoms with their clients. Strength lies in numbers and their strength is yielding them grudging but definite respect. And it is slowly eroding their own lack of self respect, which has been the real cause of their vulnerability.

Another big achievement for the NGOs is their success in opening a cooperative bank for the benefit of sex workers. Instead of frittering away their money, losing it or being cheated out of it, they invest it and look forward to a secure old age. Loans are given on the basis of their investments, at nominal interest, which they can draw upon in times of difficulty. The only option for them earlier was to go to money-lenders. These vultures in human form charged exorbitant rates of interest, sometimes 100%. That wasn't all. Prostitutes, being largely illiterate, were unable to read the terms of the contract to which they were putting their thumb marks. If 5000 was written where 500 had been borrowed the woman, unable to detect the fraud, ended up paying interest all her life. Recovering the original was a distant dream, never to be realised.

They have also set up a self regulatory board to prevent minors from being initiated into the trade. The members are drawn from the sex workers themselves on the basis of their age and experience. These women, together with a couple of representatives sent from the Labour Department, sit on the Board. Young girls are brought before them and their ages assessed. If a girl is found to be below eighteen she is rejected and sent to a government home. Homes are few in number and small in capacity. Thus no one can be kept there for more than 15 days. During this period, the members of the NGO try to locate the girl's parents and send her back to them. But, while doing so, they have to pretend that they found her wandering in the streets or crying in a public park or a railway station. For, if parents come to know that the girls were taken to a brothel, they refuse to take them back. Some girls don't want to go back home and, out of those who've been returned, many have run off again to be caught by dealers and sent to other red light areas.

Children of sex workers have shrugged off the stigma they have carried for centuries. They might be educated and working in responsible positions, but they don't deny their ancestry or place of birth. Some time back, a young man gave me a book he had written. It was a good book based on the life of a eunuch. The introduction surprised me. In it, he tells his readers, at considerable length, that he was born and nurtured in a red light area and thus has firsthand knowledge of the world he is describing. Another young man, a doctor employed by an NGO to educate sex workers in matters of health and hygiene, told me that because his mother was a sex worker, he knew the problems of these women quite intimately. 'They open up to me much more easily than they would with any other doctor,' he said.

Schools have been opened in Sonagachhi for the children of sex workers. They are not debarred from attending mainstream schools. But once their background gets exposed, they are liable to be teased and tormented by their peers. Unable to bear it, many abandon their studies halfway. Thinking of these children, I was reminded of an incident I had read about many years ago. Towards the beginning of the 19th century, a school was founded by some eminent men of Kolkata. Called Hindu School, it was an institute of great repute, churning out, year after year, students who went on to achieve great fame and prosperity. Some years after the school was founded, a prostitute named Heera Bulbul brought her son for admission but refused to give the father's name. Though this was unusual for the time, the principal, an Englishman, admitted the boy on the strength of his mother's name. But there was a great public outcry and parents and guardians started withdrawing their wards from the school.

When the school was nearly emptied of its students, the members of the board were forced to close it down. However, it was not for long. The offending boy was expelled and the other pupils trooped back in triumph. Mindsets haven't changed much since then.

I think of another girl, her name is Renu, quite often. I saw her, not in Sonagachhi but on the outskirts of an obscure village 150 miles away from Kolkata.

Eight or nine years ago, I was travelling by car to Bankura town where I had been invited to speak at a literary event. Suddenly, in the middle of nowhere, the car broke down and would not move despite all the efforts made by the driver to coax it into action. Strange sounds emerged from the engine but not one of them was the right one. The three passengers, myself included, got out and began pushing the vehicle. But though we pushed hard—the effort leaving us panting and sweating profusely—the car refused to cooperate. The nearest market was five miles away. In the hope of finding a mechanic there, the driver set off on the long walk, leaving us standing on the road.

It was the middle of June and unbearably hot. A burning wind, akin to the loo of north India, was blowing. We looked around for a tree whose shade might offer a little respite but couldn't find one. A raging thirst, intensified by the sight of the empty water bottles we carried, turned our chests and throats to dust. The minutes passed as though they were hours. Despite being so close to civilisation, we felt as though we were stranded in a trackless desert from which there was no hope of return.

Before our eyes the land stretched away, stark and barren, till it reached the skyline. Except for one tiny spot. This was a hut set on top of a mound not too far from where we stood. Two or three children playing outside the hut were staring at us with big, solemn eyes. Approaching them, I addressed the eldest, a girl of about ten. 'Khuki,' I said, 'will you give us some water?'

Her answer took me by surprise. Never, not even in my wildest dreams could I have anticipated it. 'No I won't,' she said roughly. 'We don't talk to people who ride in cars.' Putting out her tongue, she contorted her features in a grimace; her siblings followed her example. The vehemence of her reaction startled me. 'How class conscious children have become!' I thought ruefully, 'even in a remote village like this one.' Pulling myself together, I smiled at her. 'This isn't my car,' I said. 'It's a rented one in which I'm being given a lift. I'm very thirsty. Is there no water in your house?'

At this moment, a woman emerged from the hut. She was about thirty, with a pleasant face and a tight, well knit body draped in a worn and soiled sari. She was obviously the children's mother. 'Is this the way to talk?' she said, as she struck a blow on the girl's back. 'Don't you know that refusing water to anyone is a sin?' The girl, it seemed, hadn't learned that as yet. Turning to me, the mother asked hesitantly, 'Will you drink our water? We are very low caste. Untouchable.'

Entering the hut, we drank water, deliciously cool, from an earthen pot. The woman handed out pieces of jaggery along with the water and appeared crestfallen when I told her I didn't eat sweets. She looked around the hut as if wishing she could offer me something else. But I didn't need anything else. The water cooled my body and my spirits lifted. The family was, clearly, exceedingly poor. The house was not much of a shelter. It had mud walls, which would collapse with the monsoon rains, and a thatched roof wearing away in places. Yet, sitting there, my soul felt flooded with peace. It was a happy household—I was convinced of this.

The woman's name was Renu. Though her clothes were worn, poverty and deprivation had not left their marks on her. But that was not the case with her husband. He was a rickshaw puller, thin and emaciated, and he coughed incessantly.

A couple of years later, travelling along the same road, I remembered Renu and stopped the car outside her house. Though everything looked more or less the same from afar, on coming closer, I found things vastly improved. The roof had been newly thatched and the children's clothes looked fresher and cleaner. The family crowded around me, chattering excitedly. Suddenly, in the middle of it all, the rickshaw puller burst into tears. 'Babu!' he cried, 'Renu is no more.'

No more? What did that mean? Had Renu died in the interim? No, she hadn't died. I pieced together the story, bit by bit, from the rickshaw puller's laments. Some months ago, Renu's husband's cough had assumed alarming proportions and he had started throwing up blood. The doctor had diagnosed tuberculosis and prescribed expensive medicines. Weakened by the disease, he couldn't work anymore. They had no savings and no land. Starvation stared them in the face. At this point, Renu had no option but to find work and fend for the family. She was a fine looking girl with a strong, healthy body. This body was her only asset. It was also her worst enemy.

Renu found employment, first with a rich family where she was required to milk the cows and clean the stables. But she couldn't keep the job for long. The youngest son of the house cast lustful eyes on her and tried to rape her twice in succession. Next, she joined a brick kiln as a labourer. There she found that sleeping with the employers was an unwritten part of the contract. She gave up her job, but unable to see her husband wasting away and her children starving, she set out to work once more. But this time, her mind was made up. If she had to sell her body to earn money, she would insist on getting the proper price. Her husband agreed with her. Renu left for the big city and enrolled herself in one of the brothels. In this, she had her husband's full support. In fact, he went with her and settled her in her new profession.

With the money she sent every month, the condition of the family improved. The children were well fed and clothed. The husband enabled, at last, to buy the medicines he needed, was well on the road to recovery.

Renu's history set me thinking. 'There are many Renus in our country,' I said to myself. 'What can I, a single individual, do to alleviate their sufferings? But, perhaps I could take one family under my wing and work for its welfare.' I thought of ways and means. I approached an NGO whose director was known to me and asked for help. The NGO undertook to pay for the rickshaw puller's medicines, the children's school fees and also to give the family one free meal a day.

So far so good. It was time Renu was brought back home. But, upon making enquiries, I found that she had left the city. She had fallen victim to recruiters who lured women with hopes of better wages, then sold them to brothels in the Arab countries. Thus Renu was lost to her family. She had reached a point of no return.

When I hear of the improved conditions of prostitutes in our country in recent times, I feel happy. But I can't help remembering Renu. I see her face in the faces of all the others.

(Translated from the Bengali by Aruna Chakravarti.)

NOWHERE TO CALL HOME
Mukul Kesavan

Before getting to Bangalore, I assumed that I was going there to talk to a community of homosexual men through the good offices of an NGO which works amongst them to promote safe sex. MSM, or Men who have Sex with Men, seemed to me simply a roundabout way of saying gay men, but I should have been alerted by the acronym used in the literature I had been sent about the NGO's outreach work. There was a point to the careful neutrality of 'men who have sex with men' as I would discover.

I walked into a long room on the second floor of a building that houses a drop-in clinic, providing HIV counselling for MSM in a crowded, commercial part of Bangalore, KR Market. Narrow mattresses to sit on bordered the walls and there were chatais spread in front of them: it was a conference room for the poor.

The room filled with members of the community that the NGO serves; two organisers, a heavy, grey-eyed, stubbled man and a gamine young woman welcomed them in. By the time everyone sat down, there were close to 25 people in the room. Two of them were hijras in saris, there was a slender young man in trousers wearing a dupatta, and another round-faced boy in an oversized skull cap, his mouth highlighted with such thick, scarlet lipstick that he looked like a mime. The rest seemed like ordinary men, in trousers and shirts,

179

mainly young but there were two or three who looked older than forty.

Someone tried to break the silence by asking if Sharada, the gamine with close-cropped hair, would sing us a Kannada song. I didn't understand the words but a line or two into the song, I did realise from the timbre of her voice that Sharada was, very likely, a man. Sharada volunteered to sing another song, in the same Carnatic style but this time in English. It was plaintively sung: its simple English lyrics told of the torments of the MSM life, and each verse ended with a refrain that questioned the world's unthinking cruelty.

After the singing was done, there were introductions. I explained that I was there to write a piece on the MSM community for a book in which several writers were spending time with communities particularly vulnerable to HIV and AIDS. A few people nodded. It was an epidemic they lived with, one that had taken friends and partners. Telling this community of people that I had parachuted in for a couple of days for a firsthand sense of their circumstance seemed presumptuous.

But no one laughed or looked disbelieving. The devastation that had ravaged this community was too serious a matter. Nearly 20% of Bangalore's MSM community is HIV positive, which is 20 times higher than the incidence of HIV/AIDS in the general population.[1] It was a reasonable assumption that four of the 20 people in that room were likely to be HIV positive.

When I finished, the community members in the room introduced themselves. There was a practised ease to the way in which people identified themselves, a name-rank-and-serial-number fluency, which suggested they had come across inquisitive outsiders before. Each one announced his name, his sexual identity and his designation within the NGO.

---

[1] National Interim Summary Report (October 2007), Integrated Behavioural and Biological Assessment (IBBA), Round 1 (2005-07), Indian Council of Medical Research & Family Health International.

So the typical introduction went like this: Sharada, kothi, field supervisor, or, if the person introducing himself wasn't employed by the NGO, he would typically replace designation with the term 'community', a way of indicating that he was part of the MSM community: thus, Nazia, kothi, community. Of the 20 people gathered there, about five worked for the NGO, all of whom had been recruited from the community that they now served.

Kothi? I must have looked puzzled at the recurrence of the term because someone explained in English. 'Kothis,' he said, 'are those who are penetrated.' The kothi's partner is the panthi. The meaning of that seemed to follow, but someone spelt it out: 'Panthis penetrate.' And then there were double deckers, who did both. As we went round the room, a cumulative lopsidedness became apparent. Nearly everyone there, bar two, described themselves as kothis. Of the two who didn't, one described himself as bisexual and the other as a double decker. If the gathering was a representative snapshot of Bangalore's MSM community, it was a community of kothis.

By the time the meeting ended, I was trying to sort out a puzzle. It wasn't just that the majority of men present were kothis, most of them also had alternative names, women's names. Aslam was Najma, Jagadish was Sharada, Javed was Tabassum, Imran was Nazia, Aijaz was Nuzhat Bano and so on. I expected the hijras I met to have the names they did: Manju, Sree, Shahana. But in the course of talking to the community in large and small groups, I realised that nearly everyone there, regardless of costume, thought that his real self was to some degree female.

Whether they were pant-shirt kothis or satla kothis (cross-dressing kothis), whether they were wearing moustaches or lipstick, the people present had two things in common: they submitted to penetrative sex and they thought of themselves as women. I began to appreciate the ginger, tiptoeing caution of the term MSM; if anything, it didn't seem non-committal enough. The group didn't seem to me

181

to be a gathering of homosexual men; it felt more like a community of thwarted women.

Sharada's Story

Sharada, the man who I had mistaken for a girl, had begun life as P Nagaraj. She (it seems natural to say she because she presented herself as a woman) was small, just over five feet tall. She tinted her lips a little, wore studs in her ears and a long kameez over her trousers: the turnout suggested androgyny rather than the emphatic invocation of womanliness signalled by a hijra's sari. Part of the reason for the subtly femme look was that Sharada lived with her parents, who in turn were part of a large extended family. They knew about her sexual identity but didn't want her bringing it home, so she only cross-dressed at the drop in clinic.

This was true of many there: while the drop in clinic provides medical care and counselling, it also provides the community members a place where they can be themselves, in a way that is not merely metaphorical. So even as I talked to Sharada, she companionably gave Nazia's lips a fresh coat of paint and beside her Javed became Tabassum by softening the outline of her cropped hair with a skinny white dupatta.

Sharada is a field supervisor with the NGO that ran the clinic. She was at once poised and relaxed, and she had a social manner made up in equal parts of calmness, affection and a dispassionate self-awareness. I wanted to know from her how a kothi came to identify herself as a kothi and she told me without hesitation in conversations spread over two days.

In her mid twenties now, she had grown up in a neighbourhood called Chamrajpet, in a large house with 12 rooms and an extended family made up of 36 relatives. Her father worked as ground staff in the air force and she struck me as middle class if only because she spoke English fluently. She said she had felt feminine since the time she was a child. When I asked her what she meant, she said that she liked doing domestic things, washing clothes, trying to help in the kitchen, the sort of things girls did. She didn't know the term kothi then, but she did know that she was different from the boys in her neighbourhood.

We met the following day to finish Sharada's story in Cubbon Park, a cruising place for kothis where she had done sex work before joining the NGO. She had sex for the first time when she was sixteen. A neighbour of hers, Venky, four years older than her, took her to a place called Krishnagiri in Tamil Nadu for the Pongal festival. Her parents didn't object because she was a boy and he was a male friend. What they didn't know was that Venky had planned the trip so he could seduce Sharada, which he did. 'Not anal sex,' said Sharada. 'Oral.' She didn't do anal sex. It had been ten years since Krishnagiri, and she and Venky were still together.

He got married in between. 'I slapped him when he told me he was getting married,' said Sharada, smiling at the memory. 'He has a child now, but his wife knows me and she's okay about us. We meet, every fortnight on an average, for sex. On the top landing of the building's staircase, sometimes... I like him to be rough with me when we're together, be dominant. Pull my hair, force me to lie down... like, come here, you!' She ran her hands over her face and giggled at the remembered pleasure of it. 'But only during sex, okay? If he tries to be like that any other time, I'll...' I asked her if he knew about her relationships with other men. She covered her mouth in mock horror: 'No, no. He thinks I only go with him. He would go mad if he knew about the sex work.'

Sharada's circumstance is not untypical of the sexual triangles in which many kothis live: either as lovers of married men or as married men who lead parallel sexual lives with male lovers.

Given the likelihood of multiple partners because of sex work and the social disapproval that make a monogamous kothi–panthi relationship nearly impossible, kothis are at much greater risk of acquiring HIV and passing it on. Condom use is infrequent and inconsistent. Even kothis who are aware of the danger of unprotected sex are forced to submit to it if their customers insist. Their economic dependence on sex work leaves them with little or no discretion in the matter. Even in consensual sex, kothis often agree to sex without condoms if the panthi is good-looking and desirable. If he is a long-term partner, they do without protection as a token of affection and trust. And oral sex is generally performed without protection because many kothis aren't aware that HIV can also be acquired through this route. Public health workers are trying to encourage the use of protection during oral sex by distributing flavoured condoms.

In Hyderabad district in Andhra Pradesh, the state bordering Karnataka, one third of the surveyed kothi population is HIV positive. In Madurai district in Tamil Nadu, the figure for infected kothis is over one quarter of the community's population.[2]

Sharada came to sex work quite by chance. After finishing school, she had enrolled for a diploma in electronics. But the harassment at the institute was unbearable: she was called 'chakka' and 'No 9', derisive terms for homosexual. One morning, she played truant and visited Cubbon Park, where she saw kothis and hijras working the park. She had an epiphany. She wasn't a freak, there were others like her.

The first time she did sex work in Cubbon Park, her client gave her Rs 30 (75 cents). After a lifetime of unwantedness, relieved only by furtive sex with Venky (her father scalded her legs with boiling water the first time he caught her with him), the excitement of being desired by men, wanted enough that they were willing to pay for sex, was liberating. Rs 30 to 50 ($1.25) was the going rate, so she dropped out of the diploma and began working a stretch in Cubbon Park.

But she didn't just become a sex worker kothi, she became a hijra.

---

[2] National Interim Summary Report (October 2007), Integrated Behavioural and Biological Assessment (IBBA), Round 1 (2005-07), Indian Council of Medical Research & Family Health International.

The only time I had ever dealt with hijras was when they came home in Delhi immediately after my son was born. Most middle class Indians thought they were cross-dressing hermaphrodites or eunuchs, hoarse-voiced, potty-mouthed, in-your-face grotesques who made a living by shaking down people like me on occasions like a birth or a marriage or the completion of a new house.

So to hear this poised, self-aware, attractive person (who wasn't dressed in a sari or conspicuously lewd) recall how she became a hijra, was startling. Sharada wasn't castrated and didn't plan to be. Being a hijra is a cultural identity that doesn't depend on being castrated or cross-dressing, it goes far beyond this. Initiation into the community starts with being accepted as a daughter/disciple by a hijra guru. Sharada's guru was called Farida and she served as her mentor and mother figure in the community. Soon Sharada, with two other disciples, her hijra sisters, began servicing customers in their part of Cubbon Park.

On an average, she had 15 to 20 customers a day, enough to make a decent living and give her parents Rs 1200 ($30) a month. How much she charged depended on the panthi. The corporate type with his shirt tucked into his trousers was good for even Rs 200 ($5).

Sharada no longer did sex work. She stopped when she joined the NGO, and she now visited Cubbon Park to spread the good word about condoms and safe sex. It could have been very different. She sometimes thought about two male cousins in her large joint family, two boys who, like her, had felt like girls. Growing up, the three of them had shared their problems with each other, but her cousins dealt with them by leaving home. They just disappeared. No one in the family ever heard from them again.

Sharada was fortunate, it was her cousins' story that was more common. The feminised manner of most kothis makes them conspicuously vulnerable. Since they don't fit social definitions of masculinity, they are seen as weak and exploitable.

In the words of Shivananda Khan, a pioneering scholar and authority on the MSM community in India, '[S]tigmatisation around feminisation produces a range of human rights abuses, blackmail, violence and male-on-male rape by local men, thugs and beat constables.'[3]

The stigma built into their social identity limits kothis' employment options, forces them into sex work and leaves them vulnerable to coerced sex and consequently, to HIV infection, while simultaneously limiting their access to treatment and care. Government hospitals are often staffed with people who see kothis as unnatural men and know very little about the anal infections that plague them. Ignorance, prejudice and violence leave kothis demoralised and not infrequently, suicidal. This isn't the best frame of mind in which to receive advice about safe sex. Sharada's lost cousins could stand as a kind of metaphor for the precariousness of kothi existence.

Nature/Nurture

It seemed to me that poor non-straight men in Bangalore grew into a kothi identity because their material and social circumstances were so oppressive and so intolerant of sexual difference that effeminacy (which in a more hospitable environment might have grown into a spectrum of sexual behaviours), found itself channelled into the one pariah form that traditional society tolerated: the kothi/hijra. So instead of growing into a range of identities—transgender, transvestite, transsexual, some attracted to women and others to men, and gay—they all became kothis, absorbed into a kind of default identity that had traditionally received boys or young men who felt sexually out of step with their peers.

Like Sharada, every kothi I spoke to came to a sense of her sexual identity in two stages: first being drawn to girlish

---

[3] 'MSM and HIV/ AIDS in India', Shivananda Khan, Naz Foundation International, J Sreeary 2004, p 10.

things like doing housework or wearing frocks, and then being seduced by an older man. Nuzhat and Najma, aka Aijaz and Aslam, twenty three years old now, had identical sexual initiations. They were eleven years old when they were sodomised by a neighbour. This happened to both of them when they were sleeping out in the open on charpoys. It wasn't the same man but he could have been; as I spoke to the NGO's community of kothis, the predatory neighbour appeared so often that he came to seem like a stock character in a play.

Aftab was ten when he was first sexually exploited. His mother was friends with a woman in the neighbourhood and Aftab sometimes had lunch in this friend's house. One afternoon, as he was napping after lunch, the neighbour's twenty year old son slipped into bed with him. The way Aftab tells it, he woke up screaming.

In many of these cases the seduction was rape: the boys were too young to consent to sex in any meaningful way. Aftab was repeatedly sodomised by his seducer's friends. When he was fifteen, his father discovered him with five men queued up to have sex with him. I asked him how he remembered that early experience of sex. Did he recollect it as abuse or was it a good memory. Aftab was ambivalent; he had been taken against his will but there was pleasure and relief in being wanted. After years of being teased and harassed and despised, to be sexually desired, to be taken by a man was confirmation of his childhood experience of feeling feminine.

In one conversation I had, a large man with long black hair and a moustache, who didn't look like a kothi but was one, summed it up: 'When I was seven, people wanted sex with me. I was puzzled... then I realised later that they knew I was a kothi.' It wasn't the actual sex (which was often uncaring and brutal): it was the relief of being recognised.

One of the challenges that NGOs face in preaching the message and methods of safe sex is the commonness of sex between men and adolescent boys; predatory sex marked by furtiveness, ambivalence and, sometimes, violence.

The need to have her femininity confirmed was the anxiety around which the life of the kothi seemed to turn. It defined her attitude towards sex and it determined her attitude towards panthis. The kothi didn't expect sex to give her pleasure, if you defined sexual pleasure in terms of climax or orgasm. The castrated hijra literally sacrificed the possibility of orgasm at the altar of womanhood: the kothi might not have had her penis surgically removed, but she did the next best thing—she pretended that it didn't exist.

For Sharada, the point of sex was the frisson and reassurance of being desired, not some spasm of pleasure at the end. Aftab, who had had many lovers through adolescence and young adulthood, was categorical that his partners never touch his penis. It was almost as if he conducted his sex life wearing a metaphorical fig leaf that his partners knew not to disturb. Sex shored up his sense of himself as a desirable kothi. Sexual fulfilment in the narrow sense of orgasmic pleasure wasn't important. Nothing illustrates the inequality of the kothi–panthi relationship more vividly than the irrelevance of orgasm to the kothi experience of sex; in fact, the whole point of MSM sex as described by kothis, seems to be to give panthis opportunities to take their pleasure.

The Trouble with Panthis

Most kothis said that they wanted permanent, monogamous relationships. Equally, every kothi I spoke to was agreed that this was an impossible dream: panthis were either paying punters, or parasitic partners or 'husbands' who lived off the kothi. Sree, a castrated hijra who looked like a plump, plain Kannadiga housewife from her nose ring and gold chain, down to her toe rings, set it down like a natural law: 'Panthis always leave,' she said.

They leave because the world is so hostile to the idea of a man and a kothi cohabiting that the panthi, even if he loves his kothi, is worn down by the hostility. The two can't function socially as a couple and in the end the strain of living in a forbidden relationship becomes too much for him. But mainly, the 'husband' leaves because his kothi is only approximately a female (she can't have children) and so it follows that he is always on the verge of backsliding into an ordinarily heterosexual relationship with a natural born woman.

Subbu, a sturdy, moustached young man in a bright red shirt who didn't look like the stereotype of the kothi but was one, had been in a long relationship when he was twenty. Then his partner left him to get married. Subbu was so desolate that he poisoned himself and the lesson he learnt was that panthis are treacherously bisexual. He was certain that the reason kothis are promiscuous is that the pain of being abandoned is intolerable; they prefer casual sex because it leaves them less vulnerable to heartbreak. Amar said something similar: given the fragility of monogamous relationships, and the inadequacy the kothi feels after the inevitable breakup, casual sex and sex work become ways of affirming their womanliness.

The impossible strain at the heart of the kothi–panthi bond is that it calls on two biological men to conduct a heterosexual relationship. And they have to perform their roles as lovers or man and wife before a hostile audience that sees their every action together as a grotesque charade.

The panthi is less vulnerable to ridicule and hostility because he is a man playing a man's role in a masculine way. He isn't conspicuous: he doesn't sway or mince or paint his face. His job is to take his pleasure and to be dominant, thus to be a man.

The gender inequalities built into heterosexual relationships are reproduced in kothi–panthi relationships, only exaggerated by a kothi's anxiety about 'real' women. The Indian man's storied indifference to his wife's sexual fulfilment is stylised into the kothi's near-heroic rejection of her own. In this world of willed heterosexuality, the idea that some kothis and panthis could come to see each other as men who loved other men and had sex with them, whose love is, therefore, homosexual, is a contradiction in terms.

Since most panthis don't see themselves as homosexuals or even as men who have sex with men, they feel no sense of community with kothis. Consequently they are insensitive to the HIV implications of anal sex because they don't see it as homosexual activity. They are sexually defined by the fact that they penetrate women and effeminate men and, as Shivananda Khan graphically puts it, discharge semen. As purchasers of casual sex, they are indifferent to the health risk posed by unprotected, unlubricated sex with kothis, to themselves and to their wives and children. The hierarchies of power that defined male–female sexual relations in India inform their relationships with kothis in an even more unequal way.

For organisations that seek to control the HIV epidemic through programmes of prevention and risk reduction, panthis pose a peculiar challenge. Kothis are identifiable as a community; they can be gathered, counselled and organized, and my experience in the drop in centres made it obvious that they are knit by a sense of solidarity, induced by their common condition. Panthis, on the other hand, are invisible; their outward manner and appearance and their embeddedness in heterosexual family life make them hard to identify. They can't be educated in the routines of risk reduction as an accessible part of an MSM community simply because they don't see themselves as a part of it.

Sex and Circumstance

With one or two exceptions like Javed, Amar and Sharada, nearly everyone I met was drawn from the ranks of the lower middle class or the respectable poor. To be poor in India is to be dependent on family. The poor are badly educated and jobs are hard to come by; their safety net in times of unemployment is the natal home. To be poor and part of a conspicuous sexual minority is to have that dependence exaggerated. Jobs are even harder to find because employers, like everyone else in the straight world, consider feminised men unnatural and unsuitable.

Most of the kothis I met in Bangalore are employed in some way. Sharada and Shalu work for an organisation that promotes safe sex within the MSM community. Nazia works in a shop on Commercial Street that sells, in his words, fancy ladies dresses. He is occasionally harassed by his colleagues but his employer is unusually supportive because Nazia loves his job and is a good salesman. He makes some money on the side as a mehendi artist. But he lives with his parents. His father sells fruit. His parents, he said, were saddened by his sexuality but loved him so much that he couldn't think of leaving home. If they hadn't loved him as much, he would have left long ago (he is twenty five now), had himself castrated and made a life for himself amongst hijras.

But it wasn't clear to me that Nazia would take that irrevocable step. His guru, Shalu, a much older individual, considers himself a hijra, but wears trousers and shirts and a moustache and still lives with his parents. As a child, he left home with a group of hijras who promised his parents they wouldn't have him castrated. They kept their promise though the young Shalu had wanted desperately to have his nirvana, or castration, done. He travelled to Bombay and Delhi, did some sex work along the way, then returned to live with his Marathi-speaking parents in Bangalore.

What keeps Shalu, Sharada, Nazia and Najma home is, ironically, their traditional role as sons of the house. But along with this sense of what is owed their families, they are held back by the stark insecurity and precariousness of being on their own without the means to buy or rent a home. Manju and Sree, castrated hijras both, made the choice that Sharada and Shalu and Najma hadn't. They live on their own, often in squalid bath houses, making their living, more often than not, with sex work, struggling to sustain live-in relationships: they are kothis who refused the option of switching between their feminised selves in public and a feigned normalcy at home.

Stay-at-home kothis, being sons, live in the same web of familial obligation and duty that tradition, low wages and high real estate prices impose on heterosexual men. The difference is that their sexual preferences twist their filial roles into charades which are played out at a considerable cost to themselves: unstable relationships, furtive and dangerous sex, the demoralisation brought on both by the strain of pretending to be someone else and the derision provoked when they tried to be themselves. The only escape from this life (besides joining the uncertain sisterhood of hijras) is to find a home of their own. Sridhar, Tabassum and Shalu said more than once that they kept up with their families in the hope that they'd be given a share of family property so they could buy or rent the privacy they needed to live a life of their own.

The conventional understanding of a kothi's role seems closely related to class and education. For example, the kothis I spoke to believe that members of the gay community in Bangalore are socially distinct from them, that they are a different category of people: gays belong to a professional, middle class, English speaking world. Shalu was contemptuous of the gay lifestyle: he thought it was furtive and hole-in-corner compared to the way in which the kothi or the hijra flaunted her orientation for the world to see. For the same reason, Sharada thought that gay partnerships last longer than those of kothis and panthis. Gay men faced less stigma because they weren't as socially conspicuous and were better equipped, economically, to insulate themselves from social censure.

The one gay person I met in the MSM community was Amar, an Anglo-Indian man, who was a field supervisor with the NGO. Amar (the name was an alias designed to protect his family from the stigma of his homosexuality) was clear that he wasn't a kothi, that he didn't think of himself in any way as a woman and had no interest in cross-dressing. A long term relationship he had been in had broken up because his partner wanted him to dress like a woman when they had sex, to be something he wasn't.

Amar fit the kothi stereotype of the gay person: he was middle class, besides being fluent and expressive in English. His sex life was based on reciprocity: he pleasured his partners and expected to be pleasured in his turn. Like kothis, he was the one who was usually taken in the rear but unlike them he expected his lovers to be ready to reciprocate with oral sex, to be penetrated in return. And he agreed with Sharada that the gay person's ability to look straight makes for an easier life than the more conspicuous kothi persona, which is a magnet for heterosexual harassment and abuse.

But even within the kothi community, opportunity, experience and social pressure prompt redefinitions of identity and orientation. Aftab, whose coming of age in many ways closely followed the kothi archetype, had to rework his identity in adult life. Pressed by his parents to marry, he held out for a while, then tried to fashion a compromise. He would marry the girl of his parents' choice if she accepted him as he was. When a distant cousin was proposed as a bride he met her and explained to her that he had sexual relationships with men and didn't know if he was capable of heterosexual sex. Remarkably, his wife to be was impressed with his openness and agreed to marry him despite everything.

On his wedding night, the two of them sat together not knowing what to do till his bride broke the impasse; she reached out and touched him. Her touch gave him an erection and she said, 'Haan, aap mard hain' (Yes, you're a man). They had sex regularly afterwards like a normal married couple and in time Aftab had two daughters, Khusnoodah and Sakina.

Aftab's marriage was not exceptional. Many kothis get married because their families expect them to. During my first meeting with the NGO's community I met Sridhar, a middle aged man who had first had sex with a man as an adult while working the night shift as a security guard. A few years later, when he was thirty, his family married him off. Unlike Aftab, he couldn't consummate his marriage and he now lived by himself, a casualty of the Indian belief that marriage was destiny.

But in public health terms, the people most at risk from such unions are the wives and, indirectly, the children they bear. A recent study of a large sample of MSM in the state of Andhra Pradesh showed that 43% of the men surveyed were married. Just under half the MSM interviewed (45.5%) had regular female partners, and over a third had purchased sex from women. The contribution of men who have sex with men to the spread of HIV in India is often underestimated because studies don't factor in the 'bridge' role played by both panthis and kothis, in ferrying HIV infections from high risk, male on male relationships to the women they frequently have sex with inside and outside marriage, and the children they father.[4]

Aftab, like most married kothis, continued to have male relationships; in his case, his wife knew about them. He had recently fallen deeply in love with a man and pledged himself to a permanent relationship with him. He was encouraging his lover to get married too because Aftab had learnt from experience that it was impossible for kothis and panthis to live together and care for each other. They needed the support system of heterosexual marriage to sustain long-term relationships.

Aftab's choices seemed to be strategic moves to carve out a space for MSM love by making his peace with a heterosexual world; a plausible reading of his actions. But even strategic choices have unintended consequences. Aftab is fond of his wife and proud of his daughters. He doesn't live with his parents any more; he has set up house with his new family. He

---

[4] National Interim Summary Report (October 2007), Integrated Behavioural and Biological Assessment (IBBA), Round 1 (2005-07), Indian Council of Medical Research & Family Health International.

doesn't describe himself as a kothi any longer. 'I think of myself as bisexual, now,' he said. Having fathered children as a man, he finds that identity leaking into his relationship with his male lover. It's harder now for him to think of himself as a woman.

'I know what I am,' he said. 'I don't want to change my body. When my partner calls me his girl out of love, I like that, but I don't want strangers calling me a kothi. It isn't who I am anymore.'

Sharada has changed too. She has learnt a lot, she says, since she began working with the NGO. She still thinks of herself as a hijra and a kothi, but she no longer thinks of herself as a woman. She has friends who routinely inject themselves with progesterone, a hormone that helps grow breasts. Sharada doesn't want breasts. Her friends sometimes tease her because her chest is (according to them) as flat as a carrom board. She laughs along with them. No hormones, no silicon, no sex reassignment surgery for her. 'I'm not a man and I'm not a woman,' she said as we sat on a bench in Cubbon Park, watching kothis work. 'I'm intergender.'

None of us choose the worlds we're born into; we improvise our lives on the fly, making the best of what we're given. The kothis I met had less wiggle room than most people: their lives consisted of fraught families, brutal policemen, no private space, the absence of respectable work, the imminence of disease, a birth identity that didn't fit and an alternative identity that didn't always fit either. Over two days and some 20 hours of talk, they showed me how they extemporised new lines for themselves out of these thin materials and refused to be extras in a play that had no speaking parts written for their lives.

THE LOST GENERATION
OF MANIPUR
Siddhartha Deb

I had been in Ukhrul for only a few hours when I discovered that it is home to one of the rarest flowers in the world. The flower is called the Shirui lily, a small, pink bulb that comes out once a year in this hill district of Manipur. It was December, far too late in the year for me to see the flower, but David, the young Naga man accompanying me, evoked it so vividly as he pointed out the mountain where it bloomed that for a moment I thought the peak was covered in clusters of pink and that its slopes were crowded with villagers making their way up to take a look at the Shirui lily.

David and I were in an SUV bouncing along a narrow road that had been cut through the 10,000 feet high mountains that form part of the Arakan Yoma range straddling India and Burma. The road we were travelling on, National Highway 150, eventually crosses over from Manipur into Nagaland, a remote lifeline flung across two of the most isolated states in India. They lie in the country's northeastern region, a place of densely forested mountains and terraced rice fields that is home to a diversity of ethnic groups, many of them embroiled in decades of conflict with the Indian government and each other. Delhi is more than 3000 kilometres away, and although Burma is very close, just across the eastern frontiers of Manipur and Nagaland, the Burmese stretch of the Arakan Yoma mountains is even more remote, closed off for decades by a secretive, authoritarian regime. As we drove along the empty highway, the mountains and conifer forests around us interrupted only occasionally by a church spire or the tin-roofed houses of a Naga village, I felt a long way from anywhere.

It was probably an awareness of this isolation that made David speak so enthusiastically about the Shirui lily. He was a stocky, cheerful man from a well-to-do family in one of the local villages, someone who had studied in Delhi and worked for a big hotel chain in Rajasthan before returning to Manipur. He had seen enough of the other India, with its new cars, shopping malls, and businessmen thumbing their Blackberries to be aware that his home might look rather insignificant to a stranger. Throughout our two hour journey up from Imphal valley to Ukhrul town—headquarter of a district of the same name—he had been offering me little doses of information about his home. He had pointed out a building set amid the wilderness as a boarding school run according to national standards; when we came into Ukhrul town and drove through its winding streets, he stopped to show me the first church in the area, built at the turn of the last century by a Scottish missionary called Pettigrew. Like the Shirui lily, these sights were meant to emphasise that Ukhrul had a place in the world. The alternative would have been to accept that it is a forgotten place, of no consequence to anyone other than the people who live there.

Manipur wasn't an entirely new place for me. I grew up in the northeast, in a town that was a microcosm of the region in the beauty of its landscape, the diversity of its people, and the simmering ethnic conflicts that tinged everyday life with uncertainty. And I had travelled through Manipur in the past, at a time when a conflict between the Naga and Kuki tribes had led to a series of massacres in the villages and on the highways, leading to the deaths of nearly 1000 people and the destruction of thousands of houses. But that had been a decade ago, and much had changed in India in the intervening years. In Delhi, where news from the northeast was sparse and fragmentary, it was possible to think that things had changed in Manipur as well, and that perhaps some of the wealth visible in the metropolitan centres had flowed into the border state. I thought of travelling through Manipur for a couple of weeks to see if this were the case, and if life in a peripheral region was different, because India, so I was often told in Delhi, had transformed itself from a third world nation into a rising superpower.

It took me only a few hours after I flew into Imphal, the capital of Manipur, to see how wrong I had been. In the cool December afternoon, people picked their way past the refuse and rubble on the streets, surveyed at every street corner by armed soldiers and policemen. The electric supply was intermittent, and the small generators chugging away in the run-down buildings added their diesel fumes to the squalor, the grey of the streets rising to meet the grey of the sky until you could no longer see the hills surrounding Imphal valley. When dusk came, there was a final, frantic burst of activity around the marketplace, creating traffic jams all along the main avenue, but by 7 in the evening everyone was off the streets, leaving behind what looked like a ghost town.

Even by the standards of northeastern India, where the unemployment rate is twice the national average and the per capita income one third of the national average, Manipur is an especially dismal place. Its decline began with the arrival of British colonialism in the 19th century, which introduced long-lasting fissures into what until then had been an independent kingdom dominated by the Meiteis of the central Imphal valley and extending up to the tribes of the sparsely populated hills. It had possessed an eclectic culture, blending strains of Vaishnavite Hinduism from Bengal with older animist practices that looked east towards Burma and China. But Manipur became an isolated place under colonialism, and it became significant only in the dying days of the empire, when a Japanese invasion during World War II briefly turned its hills and valleys into a front line in the battle for Asia.

For the people of Manipur, the war has never quite ended. It had been administered as a princely state by the British, and its accession into independent India was a controversial measure, depending on a treaty signed in 1949 by the king while under house arrest by the Indian government. It didn't become a full-fledged state until 1972, by which time the first of Manipur's separatist struggles was already under way. The periodic infusions of cash from Delhi seemed to remain in the pockets of local politicians and bureaucrats, leaving Manipur bereft of the most rudimentary infrastructure. The neglect was accompanied by harsh authoritarianism, especially since 1980, when the central government applied the Armed Forces Special Powers Act to Manipur, which gave security forces the right to arrest and kill without having to answer to the local administration. A quarter century after the imposition of the act, Manipur remains as violent a place as ever, with at least 23 insurgent groups operating among a population of only 2.5 million people. Some of the groups claim to re-present the dominant Meitei population, while others origin-ate in the numerous hill tribes, but what they all offer is an employment opportunity for young men in a place where the options are few.

As if this mix of violence, poverty, and corruption isn't enough, Manipur has, since the eighties, been flooded by her-oin and amphetamines. The drugs come across the land bor-der with Burma, which is among the largest narcotics producers in Asia. As Burma's western neighbours like Thai-land and China have begun to close down the laboratories and warehouses operating on their borders, the trade has shifted eastwards, towards Manipur. Since the late eighties, an important point on the drug route into Manipur has been the border town of Moreh, 110 kilometres from Imphal, from where the drugs flow along the national highways through the northeast and eventually make their way to major Indian cities like Kolkata and Mumbai. The easy availability of drugs in Manipur, the lack of opportunities for the young, and the constant atmosphere of violence and uncertainty has created a significant population of drug addicts. The tendency of addicts to share needles has led, in turn, to the highest HIV concentration in India. Although Manipur's infection rate among addicts has come down in the last decade, almost one fifth are still HIV positive.[1] This amounts to an epidemic, but even that is not as awful as the fact that conditions in Manipur make no impression in India or in the West. Whether it is violence, addiction, poverty, or AIDS, these miseries seem to take place offstage, in an invisible corner of India that seems to have received nothing from modernity except drugs, guns, and draconian laws.

The village David and I were driving to that day was called Shirui, like the lily. In the bright afternoon sun, with flowers ruffled by a cool breeze, thick-coated dogs lying in front of the houses, and a group of men in their twenties playing carrom outside a cottage, Shirui displayed few signs of the poverty visible in other parts of Manipur. It was only when we came closer to the players and I saw their faces, ravaged prematurely by drug use, that it became clear that the village wasn't as protected from the larger condition of Manipur as it seemed to be at first glance. The cottage behind the carrom table was a counselling clinic for drug users, and it looked down to a valley that held the local graveyard, with tombstones displaying the names of people who had died young, either from drug use or from HIV.

The clinic in Shirui, run by a thirty two year old former addict called Jacob, was relatively new. With its clapboard

---

[1] Technical Report on HIV Estimates in India, National AIDS Control Organisation, 2006.

walls, small rooms, and a poster that said, 'I am hooked/ Release me pliz/ I am too young to go 6 feet deep,' it had a makeshift, homey atmosphere, but this was part of its appeal to the young men who gathered there. The clinic offered medical checkups, free disposable syringes, condoms, and counselling sessions where addicts were nudged towards a proper effort at kicking their habit, and all this happened in an atmosphere of openness and camaraderie relatively unusual in Manipur. When the state's first HIV case was discovered in 1990, it resulted in an immediate targeting of addicts by state authorities and local volunteer groups. The addicts were often arrested and thrown into prisons to undergo forced withdrawal. Pharmacies were pressured to stop selling needles to addicts, which led to needle sharing and increased the rate of infections.

In Ukhrul, it had been common for local youths and volunteer groups to frisk addicts for drugs. Sometimes, the addicts would be caned in public or locked up for a night as punishment. They would be forced to give the names and addresses of their dealers, whose houses would then be raided by the local groups. The National Socialist Council of Nagaland (NSCN, Isaac-Muivah), an insurgent group that more or less runs a parallel government in Nagaland and the Naga districts of Manipur, took even more stringent measures. The NSCN cadres often seized addicts and imprisoned them in their jungle camps, holding them for a couple of weeks at a time and whipping them with cables to enforce obedience. Like many of the insurgent groups in Manipur, the NSCN was demonstrating its power while also attempting to address a genuine social problem, and like other insurgent outfits, it ended up focusing on rather hapless individuals even while maintaining close links with the narco-traffickers based in Burma, where the NSCN and many of the insurgent groups maintain guerrilla camps.

Jacob was among the addicts in Ukhrul who experienced some of these forceful interventions by the NSCN. A handsome man with a stylish bandanna and soulful eyes, he had something of the performer in the ease with which he told me his story. His addiction began when he was sent to school in Shillong, a northeastern town in a neighbouring state. It happens to be where I grew up, and although I had left Shillong by the time Jacob landed up there, I was familiar with the streets and neighbourhoods he had operated in, and I understood the wildness and the freedom in which he had revelled. He had begun drinking in his teens and gradually moved to marijuana and cough syrup. The switch to injectable drugs came when he was twenty one. 'It happened all of a sudden,' Jacob said. 'I used to have booze with my cousin. A friend of his came and asked for cash to buy some SP, and I wanted to try the stuff.''

Jacob was talking about Spasmoproxyvon, a painkiller widely available in pharmacies at the time, and he was quite willing to demonstrate the process of injecting SP. He dropped to his knees, shouting out for a disposable syringe to be handed to him and grabbed the cap off a Pepsi bottle. The process involved emptying out capsule powder into a 'cooker'—the bottle cap, adding 1 ml of water with a syringe, and then grinding the paste with the back of the syringe for a couple of minutes. This was followed by placing a piece of cotton wool on the needle as a filter and drawing the solution into the syringe. 'Then you look for a vein where you can inject, but it gets hard to find a vein after some time. You start getting abscesses everywhere. Here, see my arms and legs,' he said.

'Look how his hands are shaking,' David said.

The drugs had been part of something larger, of a life in Shillong that had seemed free, full of possibilities, where nothing was likely go wrong. 'I still miss those days,' Jacob said. He had had three girlfriends at the same time, and his only worry at the time had been that he might get one of them pregnant. He hadn't known anything about HIV, and he had been too shy to use a condom. Jacob had gone on trips to Shillong Peak with bottles of White Mischief vodka and injected SP inside a car with dark windows that belonged to an older man who hung out with his gang. He had beaten up people during the regular bouts of ethnic violence that broke out in Shillong, and had on occasion sold heroin procured by a friend from Ukhrul, mixing in flour when their supply started running low.

Jacob made all of it sound perfectly normal, even innocent, and he didn't lose that sense of innocence even when his story shifted gears and took us into harder terrain. After returning from Shillong, he had it easy for a while. His father got him a job working at a pharmacy in Ukhrul town, which gave him easy access to SP. There were also plenty of women in the locality to replace his string of girlfriends in Shillong. But Jacob's dosage had gone up; he had begun by injecting once a day, but he now had to take six or seven doses daily. He started getting abscesses where he injected and began losing weight, while around him, the environment became difficult for an addict.

In Shillong, Jacob had been an easygoing, anonymous Naga, but in Ukhrul he was one of the tribe. At home, his parents knew of his addiction and began putting pressure on him, while on the streets he and his friends began to be targeted by local groups and NSCN cadres. 'The NSCN would put us in a cell for two weeks without medication,' he said. 'We'd be given food, the kind of horrible food the NSCN people are used to eating, one meal at 6 in the morning and another at 3 in the afternoon. They would sometimes pull us out of the cells and tell us to give up our addiction. We couldn't argue with them because they had guns, but this method was no good. This is not the way to cure addicts, to shout at them and beat them up.' His life had been transformed in other ways as well. He had married one of his girlfriends, become a father, and changed jobs. He became so fed up with his addiction that he tried to detox himself by cutting back on the doses. He sometimes managed to stay clean for six months at a time, but then the habit would creep up on him again. He began working for a local youth group, but he was alarmed when this same group decided to cure addicts by locking them up in an isolated place for three months. 'They asked our parents for money to pay for the costs, and we protested that this wasn't the right way to help us.' It was at this point that Jacob and some of the addicts began demanding a proper detox camp. When this was finally organised, Jacob managed to kick his habit.

Even though Jacob had started drinking heavily since quitting drugs—those trembling hands David had pointed out were caused as much by this as by his old drug habit—he was in most ways quite lucky. His parents had built him the house we were sitting in, part of which he used for the clinic, and he seemed happy and involved in the work of trying to help other addicts. The workers at the clinic and the addicts looked up to him, and after all his wandering, he was a man very much at home, at peace with his surroundings.

The surroundings were part of the problem, I realised when I went back into the town of Ukhrul. There, at another clinic, bigger and better equipped, I met a group of men in their twenties who sat around me in a circle. They had the young-old faces common to heroin users, and they were nervous about talking to me. Looking shabby and hunted, they gave off a far greater sense of humiliation than Jacob. They talked about not having anywhere to gather except in the clinic, and not only because they faced harassment as addicts but because there wasn't anything to do in the town.

When I walked around Ukhrul later in the evening, I saw what they had been talking about. Without a regular supply of electricity, and in an atmosphere of fear created by skirmishes between insurgents and security forces, the town shut down after sunset. A few lights flickered through shuttered windows, and as the wind blew furiously along the dark streets, restless bands of young men walked up and down the main avenue, trying to salvage some sense of pleasure from the deserted landscape. There are no cinema halls, no bookshops, no restaurants in Ukhrul. It has received nothing from India other than army camps, government offices, and the dingy shops of small traders. If there is anything like a cultural life here, it is offered by the churches. But the churches, partly in response to the patronising Indian state, and partly under the influence of American evangelism, speak the language of abstinence and purity, with posters announcing the coming of the Rapture. They are suspicious of the idea of pleasure, and they feel that the condoms and needles distributed at the clinics encourage promiscuity and addiction.

The language of abstinence might have influence on American youth who have had the opportunity to become jaded by consumerism, but it is likely to have limited appeal here, among young people so uncertain of who they are. They feel their isolation keenly, especially because they are too far removed from the rural background of their forefathers to be content with the simple life. And because they feel themselves stranded in the backwaters, the modern world glimpsed through television, music, and even foreign missionaries, seems particularly attractive. Many of the men sitting around me at the clinic in Ukhrul picked up their habit in Shillong. They were dazzled by the sophistication of the bigger town, and because they thought this was their only chance at experiencing such a place, they tried all the pleasures that came their way.

It was easy to see with these young men in Ukhrul town, in a way it hadn't been with Jacob, their naiveté about the world. Even when they talked about the future, when they would be drug free, they made the future seem shapeless. 'I believe my uncle will get me a government job if I manage to be cured,' one of them said, speaking with great effort and staring at the wall. Some of the others said they wanted vocational training, or that they wanted to help addicts. They spoke in clichés, but they couldn't help that because there wasn't much else on offer around them. When these men had returned to Ukhrul, their youthful holidays in Dimapur or Shillong over, they had suddenly faced the lack of opportunity, the possibilities limited to government jobs, small businesses, daily wage labour, or membership in an insurgent group. Most of them had tried to ignore this shrinking of the horizon and had kept going with their addiction, sometimes stealing to supply their habit, sometimes being beaten up, until they began visiting the counselling centres, where, along with treatment for their addiction, something like a community was available. 'There's nothing else here,' a young man called John said. 'There's only this clinic. These are the only friends I have. This is the only place where I can meet them.'

The lack of opportunity partly explains why Manipur is full of NGOs and youth groups and social organisations, all of which are ways of doing something. They offer the basic structural blocks of life—an office, a job, a desk, an occupation, colleagues—that we take for granted. This was one of the reasons why those young men who weren't addicts were often out in the streets trying to cure addicts, whether through NGOs or through more coercive voluntary groups, and why so many of the recovered addicts seemed grateful to find work as counsellors. The same confused ideas about doing something leads young men to hand out business cards displaying addresses of nonprofits in Europe or North America. When I spoke to them, I discovered that most of them had never visited the addresses printed on the cards. They had made contact with these organisations on the internet, communicated with them by email and in chat rooms, and now they were waiting for some mysterious event that would convert their virtual relationship into a real one, sending them to Amsterdam or New York, out of Manipur.

Even the business cards displayed a form of social mobility that was rare in Manipur. In districts other than Ukhrul, poverty was more virulent, visible in the shabby clothes on people, in the children affected by malnutrition, and in the cheap goods displayed in the small shops. A few days after returning to Imphal from Ukhrul, I headed out again on National Highway 150, but this time in the opposite direction. I was travelling to the hill district of Churachandpur, where the population includes a mix of people from the Zomi tribe as well as valley Meiteis. Among the poorest districts in Manipur, Churachandpur has one of the highest HIV concentrations in the state and was, in the late nineties, the centre of some of the most violent clashes between the Kukis and Nagas.

For a while, we drove along the flat plains of Imphal valley, the road built along an embankment cutting through paddy fields. There wasn't much traffic on the highway apart from paramilitary patrols, long convoys of trucks from which soldiers in black bandannas stared out at the countryside. The road was narrow, with barely enough room for vehicles to pass, and we had to slow down when we came to a village and found a car parked in front of us. A few scruffy young boys, not more than eleven or twelve, were gathered around the driver's window, while another boy straddled a wooden bench that had been placed on the road as a barrier. My driver understood instantly what was going on and decided that he could squeeze past the barrier while the boys were busy with the other vehicle. He accelerated, but the bench shot out in front of us, neatly cutting off the slender gap that had been available, and the boy sat back down again on the bench, his hard gaze meeting ours. The driver sighed and reached for his wallet.

We reached the hills after an hour, stopping at the town of Churachandpur, the district headquarter. It was built on a slope, a crowded settlement of rundown, two-storied buildings and tin-roofed bungalows, connected to each other by a tangled network of electric wires and narrow alleyways. Many of the shops along the main avenue were selling wrinkled, secondhand clothes, and it was amid these shops, in a warren of rooms connected by narrow staircases, that a local group ran a centre for drug users and sex workers.

The combination of poverty, violence, and drugs has driven women throughout Manipur into prostitution, which is particularly depressing because women from the hill tribes as well as the valley have traditionally possessed far greater autonomy than those in the rest of the subcontinent. Some of the women have taken to prostitution because they are widows of drug addicts, left infected by their husbands and without any conventional ways of earning a living. Others turn to sex work to feed their own drug habit, while some find that their lives as sex workers leads to a dependency on drugs, feedback loops that have resulted in 20% of sex workers in Manipur being drug addicts,[2] a proportion far higher than among similar groups in the rest of India.

The overwhelming state of disintegration in Manipur has made the position of sex workers especially vulnerable. They are among the most invisible groups in this already invisible state, but they are also subject to pressure from the authorities, churches, insurgents and local groups. In Ukhrul, I found it impossible to find a woman who would feel safe enough to talk about her life as a sex worker, and although it was easier to do so in Churachandpur, here too the sex workers were used to threats and violence.

The counselling centre in Churachandpur town had set up a daycare room partly in response to the pressures felt by the sex workers, to give them a place where they could feel safe. 'If there's trouble from some local group, even the pimps come running here, following the women into the shelter,' the worker who showed me around said. On normal days, the women came to the daycare room to drop off their children, collect condoms, and spend time together. It was a small room with green walls and windows looking down to the bus station where the women often found their clients, and it

---

[2] 'Progress Report on the Declaration of Commitment on HIV/AIDS', UNGASS India Report, UNAIDS, 2005–06.

seemed a lively place, with tea being made on a small stove in one corner and a couple of women sitting near the window smoking cigarettes.

I sat against a wall that held posters of Norah Jones and Jesus, facing a twenty three year old sex worker called Siami. She had straight hair down to her shoulders, a snub nose, and large eyes. Although it wasn't very cold, she stayed huddled in a shawl while I talked to her, her face displaying the wariness of someone far older. She was one of countless young women who had drifted towards an urban centre because its vague sense of possibility seemed better than the utter absence of choice in the village.

Siami had left home, a village 150 miles from Chura-chandpur town, at the age of fifteen. Her parents were sep-arated when she was small, and she went to Aizawl, in the neighbouring state of Mizoram, to look for her father. She found him after a year, working as a maid in the meantime, and discovered that he had married again. He had other chil-dren from this marriage and he was unwilling to have any-thing to do with Siami. She left Aizawl and went to a village in Manipur where she worked in the rice fields, eventually marrying a farmer and having a daughter with him. Her hus-band turned out to be an alcoholic and beat her frequently, so Siami ran away to Churachandpur town, where her maternal grandparents lived. In Churachandpur, living with her elderly grandparents and working as a maid, Siami found a kind of liberation in people her own age. Like her, many of them were struggling through poorly paid, unskilled work, with little in the way of family or education to give them hope for the future. Some of Siami's friends were heroin addicts, and she picked up the habit quickly. She found she needed to spend Rs 200 ($5) daily for her four doses, and this led her into prostitution, her first client acquired for her by one of her friends.

In spite of the slightly guarded look with which Siami told me her story, she seemed disinclined to blame anybody for her life. Had she been disappointed with the father she had tried so hard to find? 'He was very happy to see me,' she said. 'It's just that he couldn't make room for me. He had a wife, other children. He didn't want to tell me to leave and so he left a note for me saying I couldn't stay with him.' She hadn't seen her mother again, or her daughter. She had been outside the northeast only once, when a Christian organisation took her and other heroin addicts to Delhi for a detox programme. I asked her what it had been like to travel out of the region. Siami laughed and said that she had seen nothing. 'I was suffering from withdrawal all the way to Delhi, and I was curled up on my bunk in the train. Once I got to Delhi, we were kept inside the centre, so I didn't see what the city was like.'

The limits within which Siami lived became even clearer when I asked her to join me and some of the staff at the centre for lunch. There is only one restaurant in Churachandpur, a large, airy place called 'Fat Jame's' [sic] that offers a wonderful view of the tin roofs of the town and the surrounding hills. In spite of having lived in Churachandpur town for a number of years, Siami had never been to the restaurant. Towards the end of our conversation in the daycare room, she had begun to relax a little—feeling sufficiently at ease to begin rolling cigarettes as we talked—but she became taciturn when we headed out for lunch. She seemed nervous as we went up the narrow stairs of the restaurant and walked past the modern-looking kitchen, and when all of us sat down at the table to wait for lunch, she wandered off on her own to the balcony and stood with her back to us.

After lunch, Fat James came up to me as we were settling the bill. He had lived in Delhi, he said, where he had trained as a chef, and he wanted to know what I thought of his restaurant. Apart from our group, the restaurant had been empty, and what I had liked most about it was its homeliness—the gospel and country music CDs lying in front of the music system in the dining hall; the simple food of rice and vegetables; and the ease of the staff, who seemed to be related to Fat James. But I understood Fat James' anxiety, that he wanted me to see his restaurant as a result of the higher knowledge and sophisticated standards he had acquired by going to Delhi. He wanted to make it clear to me that he had seen progress and brought some of it back to Manipur. In some ways, Siami had said something similar when she told me that her Indian clients, mostly soldiers, paid more generously and were more willing to use condoms. It was the people who came from the rural areas who were poor and backward, who often had no idea what HIV was and didn't want to use condoms.

Siami had agreed during lunch to show me where she worked, and after we left Fat James', we walked back past the clinic, entering an alley that led towards the bus station. We went through a small market, crowded with stalls selling plastic trinkets, dolls, and shiny chains, with flies swarming in a deserted butcher's stall. There are no red light areas in Manipur, and sex workers practise their trade in houses and hotels, often waiting near paan shops on the highway to pick up their clients. Siami worked at what she called a 'wine store', a stall selling locally brewed liquor, and she led me towards this along a little side street near the market.

The wine store was a stunted little shack, and I waited outside while Siami went in to ask if I could take a look around. I had been thinking about her pimp, imagining the kind of villainous figure one sees slashing women in Bollywood films. But the man who came out, his sweater full of holes and his aggression shot through with anxiety, was the same age as Siami. He said he would get into trouble if I mentioned his business in a local paper, but when I told him that I was writing about it in a book unlikely to ever make its way into Churachandpur, he became friendly, inviting me in with an eagerness that was all the more surprising because of the squalor of the shack.

It was a dark, low-roofed room cobbled out of plastic sheets, bamboo matting, wood and tin, with a couple of benches and tables pushed against the walls. A few bottles sat on the rough dirt floor, next to an aluminium pot. It was still early in the afternoon and business was slow, although a policeman had come in just a little while ago, threatening to arrest a solitary client until he was paid off. A few women sat at the benches, looking tired, one of them no older than fifteen. Siami led me out through the back and up rickety stairs to the room where she met her clients. It was bleakly functional, with four beds in the room, each separated from the other by curtains, and the sheets on the rough wooden cots were old and stained.

There wasn't enough room between the beds to walk around, and I didn't do much more than stand in one spot and look at everything, trying to understand the lives that converged in this space. It seemed to me that I had been travelling in Manipur for a very long time, even though I had been there only for a couple of weeks, and that Manipur had been shrinking around me with each successive site I visited. Here, in this room, it became abundantly clear that there are outsiders and insiders, those who are visitors and those who make their homes and their lives out of their rough, unforgiving circumstances. Siami had stood by and let me look around, but after a while she suggested that we go down. It was the week of Christmas, a busy time for her, and her clients would be coming in even as I took the highway back to Imphal.

THE DAUGHTERS OF YELLAMMA
William Dalrymple

'Of course, there are times when there is pleasure,' said Rani Bai. 'Who does not like to make love? A handsome young man, one who is gentle…'

She paused for a moment, looking out over the lake, smiling to herself. Then her face clouded over: 'But mostly it is horrible. The farmers here, they are not like the boys of Bombay.'

'And eight of them every day,' said her friend Kaveri. 'Sometimes ten. Unknown people. What kind of life is that?'

'We have a song,' said Rani. ' "Everyone sleeps with us, but no one marries us. Many embrace us, but no one protects." '

'Every day my children ask: who is my father? They do not like having a mother who is in this business.'

'Once I tried to open a bank account with my son,' said Rani. 'We went to fill in the form, and the manager asked: "Father's name?" After that, my son was angry. He said I should not have brought him into the world like this.'

'We are sorry we have to do this work. But what is the alternative?'

'Who will give us jobs? We are all illiterate.'

'And the future,' said Kaveri. 'What have we to look forward to?'

'When we are not beautiful, when our bodies become ugly, then we will be all alone.'

'If we live long enough to be old and to be ugly,' said Kaveri. 'So many are dying.'

'One of our community died last week. Two others last month.'

'In my village, four younger girls have died,' said Kaveri. 'My own brother has the disease. He used to be a truck driver, and knew all the girls along the roads. Now he just lies at home drinking, saying: "What difference does it make? I will die anyway."'

She turned to face me: 'He drinks anything he can get,' she said. 'If someone told him his own urine had alcohol in it, he would drink that too.'

'That can't be easy to live with.'

Kaveri laughed harshly: 'If I were to sit under a tree and tell you the sadness we have to suffer,' she said, 'the leaves of that tree would fall like tears. My brother is totally bedridden now. He has fevers and diarrhoea.' She paused: 'He used to be such a handsome man, with a fine face and large eyes. Now those eyes are closed, and his face is covered in boils and lesions.'

'Yellamma never wanted it to be like this,' said Rani.

'The Goddess is sitting silently,' said Kaveri. 'We don't know what feelings she has about us. Who really knows what she is thinking?'

'No,' said Rani, firmly shaking her head: 'The Goddess looks after us. When we are in distress, she comes to us. Sometimes in our dreams. Sometimes in the form of one of her children.'

'It is not the Goddess' doing.'

'The world has made it like this.'

'The world, and the disease.'

'The Goddess dries our tears,' said Rani. 'If you come to her with a pure heart, she will take away your sadness and your sorrows. What more can she do?'

It was the Goddess we had come to Saundatti to see—Rani Bai, Kaveri and me. We had driven over that morning from

Belgaum, through the rolling green plains of Deccani cotton country in northern Karnataka. The girls normally took the old slow bus to visit their mother's temple, so they had jumped at the chance to make the journey to go and see her in the comfort of a taxi.

It was hot and muggy, not long after the end of the rains, and the sky was bright and cloudless. The road led through long avenues of ancient banyan trees, each with an intricate lattice of aerial roots. These were cut into an arch over the tarmac so that at times the road seemed to pass through a long dark wooden tunnel, with the roots rising above and to either side of the road, like flying buttresses flanking the long nave of a gothic cathedral.

As we neared Saundatti, however, the green tunnel came to an end, and the fields on either side gave way to drier, dustier, poorer country. The trees, the cane breaks and the cotton fields were replaced by dry strips of sunflowers. Goats picked wearily through dusty stubble. Women in ragged clothing sold onions laid out on palm-weave mats placed along the side of the road. Existence here felt more marginal, more tenacious.

After some time, a long redstone ridge appeared out of the heat haze. The ridge resolved itself into the great hogsback of Saundatti, and at the top, rising up from near-vertical cliffs, was the silhouette of the temple of Yellamma. Below, and to one side, stretched a lake of almost unearthly blue.

It was here, according to the legend, that the story had begun. Yellamma was the wife of the powerful rishi Jamadagni, who was himself an incarnation of the god Shiva—he had arisen out of the ritual fire while his father, the king of Kashmir, was performing a mahayagna, or great sacrifice. The couple, and their four sons, lived in a simple wooden hermitage by the lake. Here, Jamadagni punished his body and performed great feats of austerity. After the birth of his fourth child, these included a vow of complete chastity. Every day Yellamma served her husband, and fetched water

221

from the river for her husband's rituals. For this, she used a pot made of sand, and carried it home in the coils of a live snake.

One day, as Yellamma was fetching water, she saw a heavenly being, a gandharva, making love to his consort by the banks of the river. It was many years since Yellamma had enjoyed the pleasures of love, and the sight attracted her. Watching from behind a rock, hearing the lovers' cries of pleasure, she found herself longing to take the place of the beloved.

This sudden rush of desire destroyed her composure. When she crept away to get water for her husband as usual, she found to her horror she could no longer create a pot from sand, and that her yogic powers of concentration had vanished. When she returned home without the water, Jamadagni immediately guessed what had happened. In his rage, he cursed his wife. In seconds, Yellamma became sickly and ugly, covered in boils and festering sores. She was turned out of her home, cursed to wander the roads of the Deccan, begging for alms. No one recognised her as the once beautiful wife of Jamadagni.

Later, when she returned home and asked for forgiveness, Jamadagni was angrier still. Disturbed from completing his great sacrifice, he ordered each of his four sons to behead their outcaste mother. The first three refused to do so, but the youngest and most powerful, Parashurama, finally agreed; he cut his mother's head off with a single stroke. Pleased with such obedience, Jamadagni gave Parashurama a boon: whatever he asked would be done.

Parashurama, however, was not just an obedient son; he was also a loving one, and without hesitation he asked for Jamadagni to revive his mother. The sage had no choice but to fulfil his promise, and he did as Parashurama had asked.

Still Jamadagni would not be appeased. He vowed never to look at Yellamma's face again, and went off to continue his feats of asceticism in a cave high in the Himalayas. There, he was later joined by his Parusharama, whose story is told in the *Mahabharata,* where he appears as the teacher of powerful mantras and secret weapons to another wandering outcaste, Karna.

The story is a harsh and violent one, and Jamadagni belongs to that class of irascible holy men who fill Sanskrit literature with their fiery and unforgiving anger. In contrast, the Goddess Yellamma, like Sita in the *Ramayana,* is a victim, wrongly suspected of infidelities she never actually committed. Though she had been a good wife, her husband threw her out, disfigured her beauty, and cursed her to beg for a living. She was rejected by all.

Though the story is full of sadness and injustice, devadasis like Rani Bai like to tell the tale as they believe that it shows how their Goddess is uniquely sympathetic to their fate. After all, their lives are little better than hers: cursed for crimes of love outside the bonds of marriage, rejected by their children, condemned like Yellamma to live on the roads, begging for favours, disfigured by sadness, and without the protection of a husband.

I got a little glimpse of the tensions in the devadasi's life on arrival in Saundatti. There we had gone to a teashop near the lake, at my suggestion. It was a bad idea. Devadasis are a common sight in Saundatti, where they often beg in the bazaars on Yellamma's holy days of Tuesday and Friday, and during her month-long festival, holding small statues of the Goddess on their heads. But they don't usually brave the teashops on the main street, at least not if they are as striking as Rani Bai.

Long before the glasses of hot sweet chai had arrived, the farmers at the other tables had started pointing at Rani Bai, and gossiping. They were in high spirits, in from their villages to sell their cotton at the market, and having got a good price, were now in a boisterous mood. Although both Kaveri and Rani Bai had the red tikka of married woman on their foreheads, Rani Bai's muttu—her devadasi necklace of red and white beads—and her jewellery, her painted face and her overly dressy silk sari had all given her away. Kaveri was almost an old woman now, or at least looked like one—in fact she was only a few years older than me, in her late forties. Though you could see that she had once been beautiful, the harshness of her life, and the many sadnesses she had suffered, had turned her prematurely half-way to a matron, and she no longer attracted attention.

But Rani Bai was different. She was at least ten years younger than Kaveri, in her late thirties, and was still, undeniably, tall, long-limbed and lovely. She had a big, painted mouth, full lips, a firm brown body and an attractively bawdy and energetic manner. She did not keep her gaze down, as Hindu women are supposed to in the villages; instead, she spoke with a loud voice and every time she gesticulated about something—and her hands were constantly dancing about as she talked—her bracelets rattled. She wore a bright lavender silk sari, and had rings sparkling on each of her toes and up the curve of each ear. So the farmers in their cotton dhotis with walrus moustaches sat there as we sipped our tea together, looking greedily at her and undressing her with their eyes. Before long, they were loudly speculating at the relationship she might have with me, the firangi, her cost, what she would and would not do, the pros and cons of her figure, wondering where she worked, and whether she gave discounts.

Rani had been telling me in the car about the privileges of being a devadasi, about the way people respected her, how she was regarded as auspicious and was called even to upper caste weddings to give her blessings. So the incident, and the open disrespect she had been shown, had particularly upset her. When we finally fled the chai shop, to a chorus of laughter and bawdy remarks from the farmers, her mood changed. No longer was she in feisty holiday spirits, and as she sat under a banyan tree beside the lake at the edge of the town, she became melancholy.

It was then that she told me how she had come to this life.

'I was only six when my parents dedicated me,' she said. 'I had no feelings at the time, except wondering: why have they done this? We were very poor and had many debts. My father was desperate for money as he had drunk and gambled away all that he had earned and more, and he said, "This thing will make us rich, it will make us live decently."

'At that age, I had no devotional feelings for the Goddess, and dreamt only of having more money and living a luxurious life in a pucca house with a tile roof and concrete walls. So I was happy with this idea, though I still didn't understand where the money would come from, or what I would have to do to get it.

'Soon after I had had my first period, my father sold me to a shepherd in a neighbouring village for Rs 500 [$12.50], a silk sari and a bag of millet. By that stage, I knew a little of what might lie ahead for I had seen other neighbours who had done this to their daughters, and saw people coming and going from their houses. I had asked my parents all these questions, and repeated over and again that I did not want to do sex work. They had nodded, and I thought they had agreed.

'But, one day, they took me to another village on the pretext of looking after my sister's newborn baby, and there I was forcibly offered to the shepherd. I was only fourteen years old.

'It happened like this. The night we arrived with my sister, they killed a chicken and we had a great feast with rotis and rice—all the luxuries even the rich could dream of. Then my mother went home to her village, and I went to sleep with my aunt. I was asleep when the man came, around nine. It was all pre-planned.

'I realised something was going to happen and started crying. But my aunt, who was also a devadasi, said, "You should not cry. This is your dharma, your duty, your work. It is inauspicious to cry." The man was about twenty two, and very strong. My aunt left the house, and I tried to kick him and scratch him, but he took me by force. After that, he cheated me and never gave the full 500 rupees he had promised my father. Though I had given my body to him, he used me, and then cheated me.

'The next morning, I shouted at my aunt. I said, "You are a whore and you have made me into a whore." She just laughed at me. Often, I still curse my mother. Because of that woman, my life has been wrecked. For two years, I was very upset, and we did not talk. During that time, I refused to do any sex work. Instead, I worked in the onion fields here, earning 8 annas, 50 paise [2 cents] a day.

'Eventually, I went to Bombay with my devadasi aunt, who had promised to show me the city. We went by train and I was very excited as it was my first visit. I did not know that I would be tricked again. But when we arrived, she took me straight in a rickshaw to a brothel. There she handed me over to a gharwalli—the madam, who was a friend of hers.

'The gharwalli was very sly. She did not force me, and she was very nice to me. She gave me lots of sweets and chocolates, and introduced me to all the other girls. They were all dressed up in fine clothes and good saris with amazing jewellery on their wrists: I had never seen so much gold or so much silk! In fact, I had never seen anything like this on any woman in Belgaum. I thought this was the good life. The gharwalli offered my aunt Rs 2000 [$50] for me, as I was very good-looking; but she did not ask me to do any dhanda [sex work] at first, and let me take my own time. That first month, all I had to do was to help cook and clean the house, and I was happy with that. I liked Bombay. I ate fabulous biryani at the Sagar Hotel and once when I was in the streets I saw Amitabh Bachchan pass by in his car.

'Before long, a rich man came and saw me at my duties, cleaning the house. He refused all the other girls and just demanded to have me. I was scared as he was very hefty, very fat. Much fatter even than you. So, instead, the gharwalli, who was very clever, sent some younger boys to me. They were lean and good-looking, and a nice match for me.

Eventually, I agreed to sleep with one of them. They were very sensitive with me, not like the men here. We didn't use a condom—I didn't know about them in those days.

'Eventually, I agreed to take the big man. He offered Rs 5000 [$125] for me, and the gharwalli gave me half. 2500 rupees! It would have taken me 20 years to earn that picking onions in my village, and I wasn't even a virgin—I was already used goods. So I stayed, and even though I got some diseases that first year, I remained in that house for four years.

'By that time, I had had my first two children—a daughter and a son—and it was partly for them that I went back to my village. I lived with my mother, and for the last eighteen years, I have done dhanda in our house in the village. After some time, I got a lover—a big man locally. He has a family—a wife, two sons and two daughters—and used to give me money. With him, I had a second daughter. He wanted more children by me, and I didn't. That was how we eventually parted, even though we had been happy together.

'Because I am still good-looking, I have been lucky and I've made good money. I can still earn Rs 200 to 300 [$5–7.50] from a single client. It's true that I sometimes feel this is not dignified work. There is a lot of insecurity. But I have looked after and married off my sister, I feed my mother and my son, and I now have eight acres of land with the money I have earned. On it, we keep four buffaloes and four bullocks. Thanks to the generosity of the Goddess, I will escape this work when I have saved some more, and live by selling the milk and curd from the animals.'

It was only when I specifically asked about her daughters that Rani told me what had happened to them.

'One was a singer. She eloped when she was fourteen. She came back a year later, but no one would marry her. So she became a devadasi.'

'And the other?'

'The other had some skin disease and had white patches on her thighs. We went to many doctors but they could not cure it. Like her sister, she found it hard to get married, so I had to dedicate her too.'

'But how could you do that when you were so angry with your own mother for dedicating you? You just said yourself this is undignified work.'

'My daughters scolded me,' admitted Rani Bai, 'just like I scolded my mother.'

'Didn't you feel guilty?'

'I didn't like it,' said Rani. 'But there was no alternative.'

'So where are they now?' I asked. 'Here? Or in Bombay?'

There was a long pause when I asked this. Then Rani said, simply: 'I have lost them.'

'What do you mean?' I asked.

'Both have passed away. Maybe it was because of some sins in a past life that the Goddess cursed me in this way. One lost weight and died of a stomach disease. The other had fevers.'

Rani didn't say so explicitly at the time, but I later learned that both her daughters had died of AIDS. One had died less than a year ago, aged only fifteen. The other was seventeen, and had died six months later.

The devadasis stand in the direct line of one of the oldest professions in India. The word comes from Sanskrit: 'deva' means God and 'dasi' means slave. At the heart of the institution lies the idea of a woman entering for life the service of the Goddess. The nature of that servitude has changed through time; only recently have almost all the devadasis come to be working principally in the sex trade.

What is arguably the most ancient extant piece of Indian art, the famous small bronze of a naked dancing girl from Mohenjo-daro, dating to around 2500 BC, is believed by some archaeologists to depict an ancient devadasi. By the time of Ashoka in the 3rd century BC, a piece of graffiti in a cave in the Vindhya hills of central India recalls the love of Devadinna, a painter, who had fallen for 'Sutanuka, the slave girl of the God'. There are large numbers of images of temple dancing girls from the early centuries AD onwards, and detailed inscriptions and literary references from the 6th century AD. The poetry of the 9th century Shaivite saint Manikkavacakar, for example, describes adolescent temple girls 'with auspicious eyes', 'rows of bracelets', 'heaving bosoms adorned with pearls and shoulders shining with ashes' as they adorn the temple in preparation for a festival.[1]

Several of these early inscriptions are from the area immediately around Saundatti: one from 1113 AD can be found at Alanahalli, only a few miles from Yellamma's temple, which is one of the very earliest to use the word devadasi. Another at Virupaksha near Bijapur records a devadasi gifting her temple a horse, an elephant and a chariot. The largest collection of inscriptions, however, come from the Chola temples around Tanjore in Tamil Nadu where the great Chola kings of the twelfth and thirteenth centuries boast of gifting thousands of devadasis or tevaratiyars to the temples they founded. These royal temples were conceived as palaces of the gods, and just as the Chola king was attended on by 10,000 dancing girls— they worked in rotation, according to the Chinese traveller Chau Ju-Kua, so that 3000 attended him at any given time— so the gods also had their due share of devoted attendants. The vast entourages added to the status of rulers, whether heavenly or terrestrial, and was believed to surround both with a luminous and auspicious female presence.

Not all the 2000 or 3000 'temple women' referred to in such inscriptions were necessarily dancing girls, courtesans or concubines, as has sometimes been assumed: some of them seem to have been more like nuns, busy with their devotions and temple cleaning duties. Others appear to have been domestic and personal servants of the temple Brahmins. A few had honoured and important roles in the temple rituals,

---

[1] RK Gupta, *Changing Status of Devdasis in India,* New Delhi, 2007, pp155–160; Saskia C. Kersenboom, *Nityasumangali: Devadasi Tradition in South India,* New Delhi, 1987, p 22.

keeping the images of the deities free of flies, fanning the idols, honouring them with sandalpaste and jasmine garlands, 'carrying pots of water in the divine presence', delivering prayers and food for the deity, singing and playing music in the sanctuary, and replenishing the temple lamps.[2]

By the 16th century, however, when Portuguese traders from Goa began to visit the great Hindu capital of Vijaya-nagara in southern India, there are fuller and more explicitly sensual descriptions of temple women who,

> feed the idol every day, for they say that he eats; and when he eats women dance before him who belong to that pagoda, and they give him food and all that is necessary, and all girls born to these women belong to the temple. These women are of loose character, and they live in the best streets that there are in the city; it is the same in all cities, their streets have the best rows of houses. They are very much esteemed, and are classed amongst those honoured ones who are the mistresses of the captains; any respectable man may go to their houses without any blame attracting thereto.[3]

If the partially sexualised nature of the temple women is described by the early Portuguese sources, the same is evident in the great profusion of images of the voluptuous temple dancing girls that cover the pillars of so many temples in the south—Tiruvanamalai alone has several hundred. These highly suggestive images seem to hint that the modern confusion and embarrassment at the idea of troops of young girls being kept to entertain the gods, and the priests who attended

---

[2] This argument is made at length in Leslie C Orr, *Donors, Devotees, and Daughters,* New York, 2000. For a critique of this position see Daud Ali, 'War, Servitude and the Imperial Household: A Study of Palace Women in the Chola Period' in Indrani Chatterjee and Richard M. Eaton, *Slavery and South Asian History.*

[3] Quoted in R Sewell, *A Forgotten Empire,* New Delhi, 1980, pp 240–242.

upon them, was clearly not shared by the kings and merchants who built and patronised the great temples of medieval south India.

There is, moreover, a whole body of explicitly sexual poetry from early historic south India in which the love of a devotee for the deity is envisaged as being akin to the love of a temple dancing girl for her client. Some of the most famous of these were discovered carved in an early form of Telugu on copper plates and kept in a locked room in the temple of Tirupathi. Although the copper plates were first brought to the attention of scholars in the early 1920s, it is only in the last decade that they have been translated into English by the poet AK Ramanujan.[4] In most, the God, usually a form of Krishna, has the upper hand: he is a good-looking and desirable, but thoroughly unreliable lover who plays games that drive his devotees to despair. In some cases, the courtesans clearly don't fully realise who their client is:

> You are handsome, aren't you,
> Adivaraha,
> And quite skilled at it, too.

> Stop these foolish games.
> You think there are no other men in these parts?
> Asking for me on credit,
> Adivaraha?
> I told you even then
> I won't stand for your lies.

> *Handsome, aren't you?*

> Prince of playboys, you may be,
> But is it fair

---

[4] AK Ramanujan, Velcheru Narayana Rao and David Shulman, *When God is a Customer: Telugu Courtesan Songs by Ksetrayya and Others,* California, 1994.

To ask me to forget the money?
I earned it, after all,
By spending time with you.
Stop this trickery at once.
Put up the gold you owe me
And then you can talk,
Adivaraha.

Handsome, aren't you?

Young man:
Why are you trying to talk big,
As if you were Muvva Gopala [Krishna]?
You can make love like no one else,
But just don't make promises
You can't keep.
Pay up,
Its wrong to break your word.

Handsome, aren't you?[5]

In other later poems, however, it is sometimes the devadasi
who has the upper hand:

I am not like the others.
You may enter my house,
but only if you have the money.

If you don't have as much as I ask,
A little less would do.
But I will not accept very little,
Lord Konkanesvara.

To step across the threshold
Of my main door,

---

[5] Ramanujan, et al, pp 69–70.

It'll cost you a hundred in gold.
For two hundred you can see my bedroom,
My bed of silk,
And climb into it.

Only if you have the money.

To sit by my side
And to put your hand
Boldly into my sari:
That will cost ten thousand.

And seventy thousand
Will get you a touch
Of my full round breasts.

Three crores to bring
Your mouth close to mine,
Touch my lips and kiss.
To hug me tight,
To touch my place of love,
And get to total union,

Listen well,
You must bathe me
In a shower of gold.

But only if you have the money.[6]

Partly—like the erotic sculptures which fill the walls of temples such as Khajuraho and Konarak—these poems of union and separation may be read as metaphors for the longing of the soul for the divine, and of the devotee for God. Yet they are also clearly an expression of unembarrassed joy at sexuality, part of a complex cultural tradition in pre-colonial India where the devotional, metaphysical and the sexual are

---

[6] Ramanujan, et al, pp 145–6.

not regarded as being in any way opposed; on the contrary, the two were seen to be closely linked. Because of their fertility, the temple girls were auspicious. This auspiciousness is emphasised by many sources such as the early 19th century French traveller, the Abbé Dubois: 'The arti is one of the commonest of their religious practices,' he wrote, describing the evening ceremony at a temple when a lamp is waved gently in front of the deity to remove evil influences:

It is performed daily, and often several times a day, over persons of high rank such as rajahs, governors of provinces, generals and distinguished members of society. Whenever people in these positions have been obliged to show themselves in public, or to speak to strangers, they invariably call for the courtesans or dancing girls from the temples to perform this ceremony over them, and so avert unpleasant consequences that might arise from the baleful glances to which they have been exposed. Kings and princes often have dancing girls who do nothing else but perform this ceremony. The arti is performed also for idols. After the dancing girls have finished all their other duties in the temple, they never fail to perform this ceremony twice daily over the images of the Gods to whom their services are dedicated. It is performed with even more solemnity when these idols have been carried through the streets so as to turn aside the malignant influences to which the Gods are susceptible as any ordinary mortal.[7]

The devadasis still retain this auspiciousness in Karnataka today, and for exactly the same reason: they are seen as symbols of fertility. This is the reason that they are, for example, often invited to attend and bless upper caste weddings.

There is, however, an almost unimaginable gulf separating the devadasis of ancient poems and inscriptions, and the lives lived by girls like Rani Bai today. In the middle ages, the

---

[7] Quoted in Kersenboom, p 46.

devadasis were drawn from the grandest families in the realm—among them princesses of the Chola royal family—as well as from slaves captured in war. Many were literate and some were highly accomplished poets; indeed at the time they seem to have been almost the only literate women in the region. Their confidence and self-possession is evident in much of the poetry, while their wealth is displayed in the inscriptions recording their generous gifts to their temples. Today, however, the devadasis are drawn exclusively from the lowest castes—usually from the dalit Madar caste—and are almost entirely illiterate. Around a quarter come from families where there are already devadasis among their immediate relations, and in some of these families there is a tradition that one girl in every generation should be dedicated to the Goddess.

While many medieval temple women had honoured positions within the temple hierarchy, the overwhelming majority of modern devadasis are straightforward sex workers; the devadasis I talked to themselves estimated that only about one out of 20 of those dedicated as children manage to escape into other careers—not least because almost all of them begin work soon after puberty, and so leave school long before they can get any qualifications that might open up other opportunities. They usually work from home rather than brothels or on the streets, and tend to start younger, and to take marginally more clients per week than commercial sex workers. Maybe partly because of this larger number, the infection rate of devadasis is also slightly higher than that of other sex workers: 39.6% as opposed to 34.4% for commercial sex workers.[8] Nevertheless, the main outlines of their working lives are in reality little different from those of other workers in the sex trade. This does not, however, stop the devadasis from drawing elaborate distinctions between their

---

[8] Integrated Biological and Behavioural Assessment Among Female Sex Workers in District Belgaum, Karnataka: A Report, p 56.

sacred vocation and the work of their straightforwardly commercial sisters, which they take great pleasure in looking
down upon.

Ironically, it was partly well-meaning social reformers who
contributed to this marked drop in status. In the 19th century,
Hindu reformers reacting to the taunts of Victorian missionaries, began to attack the institution of temple dancers and
sacred prostitution. Successive waves of colonial and post-
colonial legislation slowly broke the ancient links that existed
between the devadasis and the temples, driving them out of
the temple precincts and eroding their social, economic and
spiritual position. Most recently, the 1982 Karnataka Bill on
the Prohibition of Devadasis drove the practice completely
underground, outlawing the dedication of young girls and
threatening any priest who assisted in such ceremonies with
years of harsh imprisonment. All around the lake, and on the
road up to the temple, the government has now put up huge
warning signs:

DO NOT DEDICATE YOUR DAUGHTER

THERE ARE OTHER WAYS OF SHOWING YOUR DEVOTION

and:

DEDICATING YOUR DAUGHTER

IS UNCIVILISED BEHAVIOUR.

For all their efforts, however, the reformers have not
succeeded in ending the institution, only demeaning and
criminalising it: there are currently estimated to be around
quarter of a million devadasis in Maharashtra and Karnataka,
about half of them living around Belgaum. Every year, several
thousand are added to their number—estimates range widely
from 1000 to 10,000 dedications annually—and they still make
up around a quarter of the total sex workers in Karnataka. For

the very poor, and the very pious, the devadasi system is still seen as providing a way out of poverty while gaining access to the blessings of the gods, the two things the poor most desperately crave.[9]

This is why a few thousand girls, usually aged between about six and nine years old, continue to be dedicated to the Goddess annually. Today, the dedication ceremony tends to happen at night, in small village temples, and sometimes without the presence of brahmins. When brahmins do consent to attend, they charge as much as Rs 5000 ($125) to the parents of the girl, because of the risk they now have to take in doing so. A feast is thrown, prayers said, then the young devadasi is presented with her necklace, or muttu, which represents her badge of office as a sacred prostitute. Her duties and privileges are explained to her. If the girls are dedicated when they are very young, as is usually the case, they then return to a normal childhood. Only when they hit puberty are they wrenched from the lives they have led, and offered out for their first night to be deflowered by the highest bidder in the village, usually for sums ranging from Rs 50,000–100,000 ($1250–2500).

Later that day, I visited the Yellamma temple with Rani Bai and Kaveri. It was a fine 9th century building, packed with pilgrims from across the state, and we had to queue for some time to get darshan of the Goddess. Ahead of us were a party of excitable eunuchs from Bijapur. The girls had recovered

---

[9] For figures and statistical details concerning the modern devadasis, see 'Dhanda, Dharma and Disease: Traditional Sex Work and HIV/AIDS in Rural India', John O'Neil, Treena Orchard, RC Swarankar, James F Blanchard, Kaveri Gurav and Stephen Moses, *Social Science and Medicine 59*, 2004, pp 851–60, and by the same authors, 'Understanding the Social and Cultural Contexts of Female Sex Workers in Karnataka, India: Implications for the Prevention of HIV Infection', *The Journal of Infectious Diseases,* 2005, p 191 (suppl 1): S139–46. See also 'Girl, Woman, Lover, Mother: Towards a New Understanding of Child Prostitution Among Young Devadasis in Rural Karnataka, India', Treena Rae Orchard, *Social Science and Medicine 64,* 2007, pp 2379–2390.

their spirits and now chatted away with the eunuchs as they waited. They were clearly happy to be in the home of their protectress.

'I feel very devotional whenever I am here,' said Rani.

'You feel her presence so strongly in her temple,' said Kaveri.

'She is very near,' said Rani.

'How do you know?' I asked.

'Its like electricity,' she replied. 'You can't see it, but you know its there, and you can see its effects.'

When we arrived before the idol, the priests blessed us with a camphor lamp and Kaveri explained that the image of the Goddess had emerged from the hillside: 'No one made it,' she whispered.

Having bowed before the deity and made an offering, I asked one of the Brahmins whether they still performed devadasi dedications. The priest looked cagey.

'What do we know of these women?' he said, looking around for support to his fellow pundits.

'We used to bless their necklaces,' said one of the older priests. 'Then give them back to them. But now that is illegal.'

'That was our only role.'

'What they do is their own business,' said the first. 'This is nothing to do with us.'

That evening, after we had dropped off Kaveri in Belgaum, I drove Rani Bai back to the house where she lived and worked in a nearby town. This was located in Mudhol, in a back alley of the town where the devadasis have come to collect. Over a hundred worked here in a small warren of streets off the main highway heading to Bangalore.

It was a dark lane, lit by a single, dim street light. Dogs sat next to open gutters, while half-naked children played in the side alleys. It was perhaps the depressing nature of her surroundings that led Rani—always the optimist, always the survivor—to talk up the positive side of her career.

'We still have many privileges,' she said as we approached her house on foot—the lanes were too narrow here for the car. 'If a buffalo has a calf, the first milk after the birth is brought to the devadasis to say thank you to the Goddess. During the festival of Yellamma, the people bring five new saris to us as gifts. Every full moon we are called to the houses of brahmins and they feed us. They touch our feet and pray to us because they believe we are the incarnation of the Goddess.'

'Still this goes on?' I asked, thinking of the attitude of the Brahmins at the temple.

'Still,' said Rani. 'When we are called for pujas like this, we feel very proud.'

'I can imagine.'

'There are so many things like this,' she continued. 'When a child is born, they make a cap for the baby from one of our old saris. They hope then that the love of Yellamma will be on that child. If a girl is getting married, they take a piece of coral from us devadasis and they put it in the girl's mangalsutra [wedding necklace]. If they do this, they believe the woman will experience long life and never suffer widowhood.'

'Also,' she continued, 'unlike other women, we can inherit our father's property. No one ever dare curse us. And when we die, the brahmins give us a special cremation ceremony.'

We stepped over a dog, sleeping, half in, half out of an open sewer.

'You see, we are not like the ordinary whores,' said Rani, as we finally approached her house. 'We have some dignity. We don't pick people up from the side of roads. We don't go behind bushes or anything like that. We spend time with our clients and talk to them. We are always decently dressed— always wear good silk saris. Never T-shirts or those mini-skirts the other women wear in Bombay.'

We had arrived at her door now. Outside, suspended on the wall of the house was a small cubby hole stall selling cigarettes and paan. Here sat her younger sister, squatting down and handing out individual beedis and cigarettes to passers by. The sisters greeted each other, and I was formally introduced. As Rani led the way in, she continued: 'You see, we live together as a community and all this gives us some protection. If any client tries to burn us with a cigarette, or tries to force himself on us without wearing a condom, we can shout and everyone comes running.'

Inside, in contrast to the street, everything was immaculately clean. The space inside was divided in two by a large cupboard which almost touched the shack's roof. The front half of the room was dominated by the large bed where Rani plied her trade. To one side, on a shelf, were several calendar pictures of the Goddess. At the back half of the room was a second bed—the one Rani slept in. Here were all her beautifully clean pots and pans, stacked neatly in racks, and below was her kerosene burner for cooking. Above all these, on a cupboard, were a large mirror and Rani's family photos: pictures of her son and her old boyfriend—a handsome man with a Bollywood film star moustache and dark glasses. Beside that were small passport size shots of her two dead daughters. Both were pretty girls, shot smiling when they were around twelve or thirteen, full of youth and hope.

Rani took the photos from my hand, and replaced them on the cupboard. Then led me back to the front half of the room and indicated that I should sit on the bed. Perhaps prompted by the association, I asked her whether her auspicious status made any difference to her clients when they came to be entertained here.

'No,' she said. 'There is no devotional feeling in bed. Fucking is fucking. There I am just another woman. Just another whore.'

'And do you feel safe from the disease here?' I asked. 'Are you confident that the condoms can protect you?'

'No,' she said. 'There is always fear. We know that even if you persuade all your clients to wear a condom, one broken one can infect us. And once we are infected there is no cure. We will die—if not today, then tomorrow. '

She paused: 'You see, I know what it's like. I watched both my daughters die, as well as at least six of my friends. I nursed many of them. Some lost their hair. Some had skin diseases. Some just became very, very thin and wasted away. One or two of the most beautiful girls became so repulsive that even I did not want to touch them.'

She shivered, almost imperceptibly: 'Of course we feel very scared,' she said. 'But we must continue this work if we are to eat. We have a lot of misery to bear. But that is our tradition. That is our karma. We try to show our happy side to the clients to keep attracting them, and put all our efforts into doing a good job.'

'So do you have any hopes for the future?'

'I am saving,' she said. 'As I told you: I have bought a little land, and one day I hope if I can get some more buffaloes and a few goats, maybe I can save enough to retire there and live by selling the milk and curds. Yellamma will look after me.'

'You know that?'

'Of course. If it wasn't for her, how could an illiterate woman like me earn Rs 2000 in a day? Yellamma is a very practical Goddess. I feel she is very near. She is with us in good times and bad.'

We parted soon after, and I drove back to Belgaum. Later, I asked one of the project managers of the NGO working there with the devadasis about AIDS and how their families reacted to infection.

'It's terrible,' she said. 'The families are happy to live off them and use the money they earn. But as soon as they become infected, or at least become bedridden and sick, they are just dumped in a ditch—sometimes literally. Just abandoned. We had a case before Christmas with one girl. She was taken to a private hospital in Bijapur after she had complained of severe headaches. The hospital ran some tests and found she was HIV positive and on top of that had a brain tumour. She began treatment, but her family checked her out because of the expense and took her home. When we tried to find her, the family gave several conflicting accounts of where she was—different family members said she was in different hospitals. In fact, she had been taken home, thrown in a corner, and left to starve to death. We found her in a semi-comatose state, completely untended by the same family members she had been supporting for years. She wasn't even being given water. We took her straight back to the hospital ourselves, but it was too late. She died two weeks later.'

'Then it's a good job Rani will be retiring before too long,' I said.

'That is what she told you?'

'She said she would get some land and some buffaloes and try and make a living from that.'

'Rani Bai?'

'Yes.'

'I shouldn't really be telling you this,' she said. 'But Rani is infected—she's been HIV positive for eighteen months now. I've seen the tests.'

'Does she know this?'

'Of course,' she said. 'It's not full blown AIDS, at least not yet. The medicines can delay the onset of the worst symptoms. But they can't cure her.'

She shrugged her shoulders: 'Either way, its highly unlikely she'll ever retire to that farm,' she said. 'It's the same as her daughters. It's too late to save her.'

WHEN AIDS CAME HOME
Shobhaa De

It started with mysterious and monstrous boils. They popped up all over Shankar's scalp, virtually overnight. Of course, I didn't notice them for a while—but that's understandable. Shankar was our children's driver, and I met him briefly each morning to talk about the day's logistics—which kid to be dropped off, which collected, from where and when etc. Standard mommie instructions, often delivered on auto pilot without even making any eye contact with him. It sounds horrible, but that's how it is—at least in urban middle class India. People who work in our homes, and who are an integral part of our lives, become almost invisible—their presence reduced to a shadowy figure at which we shout daily orders. 'Go here. Get that. Be back on time. Don't forget to pick up the laundry. Did you pay that old bill? The dog needs a vet visit. Why has the petrol bill gone up this month? So you need leave? Again? Didn't you just take a day off last fortnight? Why does there seem to be a weekly emergency in your village? How many times do your cousins die?' All this is said briskly, everybody is so damn busy, so preoccupied. There are a thousand things to do. Who on earth looks up to notice boils on their driver's scalp?

But one morning, during our briefing, Shankar accidentally dropped a small parcel he was holding and bent down to pick it up. That's when I noticed the boils. I stopped mid-sentence and a small gasp involuntarily escaped my lips. 'Oh my God! What has happened to your head? When did you get those boils? Have you been to a doctor?' Shankar looked deeply embarrassed and tried to shrug it off by saying, 'It's nothing. It's the heat. I think they are heat boils.' I stared at them as closely as is politely acceptable and said firmly, 'No, they are not. This does not look like prickly heat to me. Which doctor did you go to?' He mumbled something about a 'vaid' who sat under a tree near his humble living quarters. A village quack, no doubt, parading as a traditional doctor and charging a small fee for spurious consultations. The vaid had told Shankar it was the soaring summer temperatures that were causing a vicious outbreak of boils across the city. 'You need to cool down the system, and they'll automatically disappear,' the man had advised, listing dos and don'ts that should be applied to Shankar's diet: 'No "heaty" foods, no spices, no garlic, no pickles, lots of buttermilk and rice.' Had this helped?

Shankar shook his head sadly before saying, apologetically, 'Please don't worry, I'll wear a cap from tomorrow.' Sweet, silly, ignorant Shankar. He thought it was his appearance and those ugly boils that were bothering me. 'It isn't about a cap,' I said, somewhat sharply. I went into my room and came back with some cash. 'Here. Go and see a proper doctor, and find out what exactly is causing these boils.'

Shankar left the house quickly, as if he was embarrassed by all the attention. 'Funny,' I thought to myself, 'Shankar has been with us for such a long time, and yet I know so little about him—not even his age.' It was on his driver's licence, but why would I ever ask to see that? Was he in his thirties or forties? It was so hard to tell. Shankar looked middle aged because of his girth. Our bond was Marathi—his mother tongue and mine; the two other drivers were from different states, Kerala and Bihar. As my kids went to his home during all the major Hindu festivals, I was aware of Shankar's living conditions. His mother frequently sent me my favourite

Maharashtrian snacks neatly packed in stainless steel dabbas. His father was retired, formerly a lowly government employee who had served under the British—a fact he was very proud of. Shankar was consistently affable and chatty, often engaging me in long conversations about local politics and popular Bollywood films. Unlike the other drivers, who hated to work overtime on Sundays, he would report uncomplainingly at 8 am, on the dot, cheerfully proclaiming that he'd rather be busy than watching TV with his cronies back at his chawl. His cronies were beer drinking chaps who occasionally dragged him off to picnics over long weekends. After these 'picnics' Shankar would show up for duty bleary-eyed and goofy, but raring to go. The kids would later tell me that they'd found him snoring in the car—conveniently parked outside their school, under a shady tree. Those were the only binges we were aware of.

Outside of these outings, Shankar appeared to be a lazy family man, hanging around in a lungi and a baniyan that stretched tightly across his gigantic paunch. My husband, a fitness freak, would berate Shankar for allowing himself to blimp out and make him run around the block. 'You are too young to have such a huge belly. You might drop dead,' he'd scold. Shankar, being the good natured sort, would huff and puff around our complex before collapsing in the drivers' room. How long ago this already seems. Eight years this May. Shankar had been with us for ten years before that. He had seen the children grow from toddlers to young adults, and ferried them to play school and discos. Shankar was their confidante, their banker—often giving them small loans for a snack or a soft drink—and their guardian, as he negotiated Mumbai's hideous traffic and managed to get them to their destinations safely and on time.

That long, hot summer, Shankar battled with his boils by using a variety of ointments ranging from antibiotics to an ayurvedic concoction made of ground neem leaves and eucalyptus oil. Nothing helped. He took to wearing baseball caps, and was clearly embarrassed by the eyesores the oozing boils had become. I noticed that he had also started to lose hair rapidly, as well as a lot of weight. A few months ago, the kids had teased him mercilessly about his potbelly. 'Go for a daily run,' I'd scold Shankar. He would grin and insist he hardly ate. 'No rice, just chapattis!' Now, in a few swift months, his frame had shrunk to half its original size, and that potbelly was gone. His shoulders stooped, and his eyes had sunk into their sockets.

We were very worried, and told him as much. 'What could be making him lose so much weight all of a sudden?' I asked the family doctor. He shrugged and said it could be one of many things—tuberculosis, for example; or, perhaps Shankar was finally trying to shed those extra kilos. 'Ask him to get a blood test,' the doctor suggested. I did, but forgot to follow it up and Shankar didn't bother to have one done. The maids started to whisper amongst themselves. They teased him about his new, slim silhouette, saying, 'Kyon hero, are you joining movies or what?' 'It is nothing,' Shankar would say, blaming the advice of a neighbour who had recommended an oil-free diet as a solution to his problems. He looked nervous as he made his excuses—almost as if he knew I'd seen through them.

A few weeks later, I remembered once again what the doctor had advised and summoned Shankar. He came into my room looking sheepish—even scared. He shook his head and said he hadn't had the time to get the test done, but that some new tonic he'd been taking was helping him. He mumbled something about worms affecting his digestion. 'Rubbish,' I snapped, still thinking it was tuberculosis. 'Go get it done immediately.' Perhaps, just perhaps, Shankar may have known, even at that point, that he was seriously sick—maybe even the truth. Or else why the stricken look in his eyes? I called up my doctor to make the appointment. He advised a comprehensive blood test, done on an empty stomach. But Shankar was extremely reluctant, pleading over and over again that this wasn't necessary. He'd been told by his village doctor that he was suffering from a persistent skin allergy which would eventually subside. I shook my head adamantly. He had no option but to go.

You can guess the rest. I received a call from the doctor's clinic late the next afternoon. His voice was grim as he informed me that Shankar had tested positive for HIV. My first reaction? Impossible! Shankar and AIDS? How? Shankar? Had the doctor told him? 'Not yet, I thought I'd tell you first,' the doctor said soberly.

My mind was racing. I looked back on Shankar's life over the past few years. I recalled his wedding. He'd gotten married—an arranged match. Just a year ago, had he known then? I remembered his excitement at the prospect of bringing his pretty bride home. She was a fiery little wench, that one. Better looking and better educated than our Shankar. He'd hired a camera man to record the ceremony and put together a big fat album crammed with his wife's pictures. 'Strange,' I'd thought. 'He must adore the girl, there are hardly any pictures of himself, but over 200 of her.' On the cover was a lurid—and heartbreaking—photograph of the two of them, placed inside a plastic heart, along with the words 'Shankar loves Prerna'. The marriage hadn't worked out, and the bride had fled within a few months—leaving Shankar a broken man. Did she know? Did his ageing parents? Shankar later said he'd made the wrong choice, that he had fallen for the girl's looks, that she was too modern for his family. 'She refused to look after my sick mother, or cook for my old father. She didn't want to wash my clothes. All she liked to do was watch TV and go shopping with her friends,' he'd explained, when it was all over. Was that the truth?

I was confused and disturbed by what the doctor had told me. Angry, too. Irrationally so. I didn't know how I would react when I met Shankar the next morning. I didn't want to sound accusing; neither did I want to make any judgements. Yet I felt repulsed. This man? The same man my children spent so much time with? I had never imagined that I would have to deal with such a situation, or such a person some day. Mostly, I was astonished; I pride myself on being a pretty good judge of character. This disease happened to debauched people, not to God-fearing simpletons like Shankar. There had to have been a mistake.

That night, I battled with my demons. I imagined all kinds of unpleasant things. He must have gotten the virus from visiting prostitutes after his wife left him. Maybe he was gay, and had multiple relationships? Had he tricked his wife into marrying him? Had she found out he preferred men? One part of me wanted to say to him, 'Get out, you filthy swine. Just get the hell out.' The other part of me questioned my baser instincts. Where was my liberal self when I needed it most? My stated stand on the HIV affected? Was I too a hypocrite, saying politically correct things in public and then turning my back on the very people I claimed to support? I could either abandon this man, who had served my family faithfully and well for so many years, or I could help him. Should I tell my husband? Would he understand, or would he fire Shankar? And the children? Did they need to know? It was one of the longest, most difficult nights of my life.

Shankar refused to look me in the eye the next morning. He stood there, a terrified expression on his face, and kept saying, 'I am sorry, I am so sorry… I feel so ashamed.' His medical reports in my hand, I wondered what to say to him in front of all the other domestic help; I couldn't let them know the seriousness of his illness. They believed he was a victim of black magic, and that his ex-wife's family had cast an evil spell on him. When the young maids were in the kitchen, out of earshot, I leaned forward and said urgently, 'Shankar, you need to know the truth about your condition. Don't run away from it. We will find a solution.' Shankar folded his hands and fell at my feet. He was sweating profusely and repeated over and over again, 'I swear to you, I have not done anything wrong. It must be infected blood that has done this to me. You remember I'd gone for a small operation last year? It was for piles. Instead of going to a good government hospital, I tried to save money and got myself admitted to a private clinic in the suburbs. The doctor there recommended a blood transfusion, I am sure I picked up the virus there. God is punishing me. But I beg of you, don't let my parents know about this. It will kill them. I am their sole provider. If anything happens to me, where will the old folks go? Who'll look after them? I don't want to live, my life is over.' I told him gently that he owed me no explanation; I wanted him to receive the best possible treatment, and for him not to give up so easily. Shankar broke down and started to weep.

The maids rushed out of the kitchen, wondering what had happened. One of them tactlessly asked, 'Is it very serious? Will he die soon?' I was at a loss for words. What was I supposed to say to a man who had given up all hope—given up on himself? I patted him on his back and told him not to despair. We'd find the right doctor, and make sure he was in competent hands. We also mutually decided to refer to his illness as tuberculosis.

The two other drivers had joined us, and shook their heads in sympathy. Shankar was a popular, mild-mannered guy, with several friends in our residential complex. But I felt protective about him, and worried. I could imagine his friends' response if they were to find out what was really ailing him. Society was alarmingly cruel towards his disease. The chances of Shankar being forced out of his home by neighbours and not being allowed to fill drinking water from the community tap, were exceedingly high. Perhaps members of our own building society would issue a notice preventing him from entering the premises. He'd certainly be turned away by the handcart owners who sold cheap street food to the area's many drivers. I still don't know if I made the right decision, but I felt that tuberculosis sounded better. This way, Shankar might not be shunned or made to feel completely wretched. I stuck to the story with my family, too. It was going to take me a while as well, to come to terms with Shankar's condition, and to figure out how to work around it.

I suggested long leave with full pay, and made arrangements with a public hospital close by to look after his medical needs. The hospital was near Mumbai's famous Dhobi Talao, and it had a special ward for patients who'd tested positive for HIV. I went there and met its young doctors, who were wonderfully aware and accepting. After scrutinising Shankar's papers they told me, upfront and matter of factly, that the picture was pretty grim. Shankar's systems were packing up. He had no will to live, had given up the fight. 'Does that mean...?' They nodded, and promised to make his last days as comfortable as possible.

The next few months moved with the speed of the inevitable. Shankar waited in his hospital bed to die and faded a little more each day. Soon he had shrunk to a fraction of his original size. He was almost unrecognisable as he lay on his cot, staring expressionlessly at the ceiling, especially to the children, who couldn't cope with seeing their beloved driver in this miserable state. Each time he saw me, he'd raise his hand by way of a greeting and ask hoarsely if he could get coconut water for me. That was Shankar—generous and kind till the end. I remembered all the times he'd bought sweets for my kids with his own money because I'd refused to indulge them. He'd taken them to his humble home during festivals and treated them to soft drinks and chocolates, after entreating them to keep it from me as I was against their having fizzy drinks. The kids adored him, and I knew he loved them from the bottom of his heart.

They had gone for his wedding, and admired his pretty bride—the same flighty girl who'd deserted him. I wondered about her. What if? Was it not my duty to inform her about her ex-husband's condition? There was no way to track her down, though. I asked Shankar's parents, but they had turned their backs on the girl who had abandoned their much-loved son. I never did manage to find her.

Late one evening as I was hovering near his bed, trying to ignore the low moans and howls of grief from patients on adjoining cots, there appeared, from nowhere, as it were, Shankar's sister. She marched up to me with a sheaf of papers which she wanted Shankar to sign. He was refusing to do so, she told me in an impatient, angry voice, and she wanted me to intervene. I looked at the documents and felt intensely sad. The sister had discovered that Shankar was dying. She wanted to grab the two rooms he occupied, and whatever else he'd be leaving behind—his bank deposits, his pension and his savings. I saw her husband lurking in the background and summoned him. 'Aren't you ashamed of yourselves?' I began by asking them, then decided to save my breath. 'Shankar isn't dead yet,' I pointed out. They looked at each other and then she hissed, 'But soon he will be. You think we don't know what he's suffering from? We may not be educated, but we know what AIDS is, and we know that he is in an AIDS ward. The doctors have told us he will go soon. What is wrong in asking him to sign these papers? After all, I am his only sister. If he doesn't sign, we'll waste years in court claiming all this. Our parents will be gone by then. And everything will be grabbed by his ex-wife. That whore who left him. Well, why blame her? Any other woman would have left him, too. He is an immoral, diseased man who used to visit brothels regularly. He couldn't have told you that, could he? But that's the truth. And that's why God has his own way of dealing with such wicked people. We want what is ours, that's all.'

I told the two of them to get out of there immediately, and leave their brother alone. They scuttled away, but I saw them hanging around in the corridor, waiting for me to leave.

Shankar, who was out of earshot but aware of their presence, summoned me with a weak wave of his free hand. The other one had an IV drip attached to it. The nurse had told me how difficult it had been to find a vein in his bone-thin arm—punctured as it was, all over, with countless needle pricks. When I leaned close to ask him what he wanted to say to me, Shankar managed to croak, 'I will not sign those papers. Tell them to go away and leave me alone.' For a brief moment his voice rose in agitation and his eyes flashed fire. I reassured him and told him not to worry. 'I'll deal with them. Try and get some rest.' He smiled wanly and replied, 'I know my time is up. My guarantee period is over.' He died peacefully, a few hours later.

It's been years now, and yet whenever I hear the doorbell ring in a particular way I think it must be Shankar at the door. His sad, unexpected death and the manner in which he died shook me up. Although they are such an intimate part of our lives, how little we really know about people who work for us. Until tragedy strikes, we take their presence and services entirely for granted. It took Shankar's death for me to see him as human—with his own heartaches, secrets, and a body that could give way. Who knows how he picked up the disease, if his sister indeed told me the truth, or if it was he who was right? I felt too embarrassed to probe into my driver's sexual life, and I am glad I didn't. It wasn't my place and now, more than ever, it feels besides the point. Instead, I think how things could have been different. Had I been better informed, more tuned in, would I have recognised the early signals sooner? Would timely detection have extended his life?

I finally told my children the truth about Shankar's death last year. Well… a version of the truth. Here is a confession: I told them Shankar contracted AIDS through an infected needle during a blood transfusion. I knew they would be shocked at the possibility of their trusted driver visiting brothels. Call it my last lie for Shankar, but I wanted him to be remembered differently. The kids and I still reminisce about his small eccentricities and endearing quirks. Just the other day, when passing The Pavement Club, a charity that teaches street children and where my children used to volunteer, we remembered how Shankar referred to it as 'The Tablecloth Club'. We laugh fondly at such memories, and hope Shankar is happy and free, wherever he is.

HEALING

Amit Chaudhuri

Celebrate Bandra, an agglomeration of events around and about the magical suburb, is what took me to Bombay about four years ago. My credentials: I'd once lived for a year in Bandra, in the last years of its pastoral, slow-stirring incarnation, between returning from England with a degree and leaving for England again. My parents, too, after my father's retirement, had lived here in the eighties, on St Cyril Road.

And now, this area—with its 'East Indian' cheer and abandonment, its cottages waiting to be sold, its new, unaffordable restaurants and teeming film stars' houses—seemed irrevocably altered. I was here to read from my works and even to make music. As I walked with streams of happy people on Perry and Carter Roads, I sensed again this city's reserves of optimism, which makes it so unique among the world's cities: but was reminded, too, from my own life here, of what I'd forgotten—its infantilism, its susceptibility to charm and excitement, a susceptibility that, in the early 21st century, has its own unforgiving momentum. Three friends came to my 'event' that evening: a journalist, whom I knew from my one year at Elphinstone College in 1978; a scientist and writer with whom I became friends in Oxford; and a friend from school—one of the two friends from school I still keep in touch with, a man who'd been a longstanding but half-hearted 'smack' addict (but who'd told me he'd been 'clean' for a year and a half at that time).

After the show, the friend from Oxford and the school friend and I walked to Pali Hill to have dinner at a small and noisy seafood restaurant, loud with karaoke music and videos. Later, we went in different directions: I towards my hotel in Bandra, the scientist towards Powai, and my school friend, whom I'll call Vijay, towards Bandra station, to catch a train to Churchgate, and return from there to Colaba, where he lives. The next morning, I moved to his side of the city, to the Yacht Club. From there (since we'd decided to meet), I called his number several times during the day, each time having perplexing conversations with the maid, who spoke no language but Marathi. I gathered from her words that both Vijay and his father (his mother had died in an accident a few years ago) had gone to the hospital. I was a little worried: had his father (who was in his seventies) taken ill? A relative was ill, perhaps? Vijay had no mobile phone.

It was only in the evening that I spoke to his father, and pieced the story together. Vijay hadn't returned home from the performance the previous night. Instead, after getting off at Churchgate Station, he'd gone to the Prince of Wales Museum, just outside which is a thoroughfare populated, especially at night, by junkies and pushers; there, probably at 1 or 2 am, he'd overdosed on heroin and lost consciousness. Vijay (in school, a good-looking but oddly introspective boxer and gymnast, always faring poorly in his studies; now a somewhat overweight, respectable looking man, losing hair, unfailingly dressed in tailored trousers) however, had no clear memory of what happened. At 3, he had been picked up from the pavement by a nameless constable and taken to the nearest police station: there, in his wallet, they discovered a number—a friend's, it turned out. Waking up the friend in the early hours of the morning, they got from him Vijay's father's number: this tall, exasperated Kannadiga, constantly, over the years, moved to despair and affection by his son, then set out, partly on foot (it was difficult to find a taxi at this time of the night), towards the GT Hospital, where his son had been put into the Intensive Care Unit.

It was there that I found Vijay in the morning, after having taken a detour into another wing of the ICU on the opposite side. He looked shell-shocked, but was otherwise unharmed. He told me many times that his blood pressure had fallen to zero when he'd been admitted to the ICU, and that really, he should have been dead. In his hands, he held a section of the *Bombay Times*, which had a small interview with me, and a picture. When Dr Shailendra, a dark, pleasant-looking, bespectacled man came in, he confirmed Vijay's low-voiced account: 'It is a miracle he survived.' Then—another reason for an intake of breath—Vijay told me he'd had an HIV test, whose result was negative. Dr Shailendra spoke to me about the ICU wing I'd almost strayed into, a wing that seemed, in retrospect, somehow more secluded than this one. A woman was dying there, he said, of AIDS, a widow who'd lost her husband to the disease, and whose children were infected. 'These women,' said the doctor, 'get the disease from husbands who are migrant workers, who live away from home and contract HIV from sex workers.' 'Don't they use condoms?' I asked, appalled. 'A condom is no guarantee,' he said. 'Some men even use two condoms, and still get infected.' Dr Shailendra was a man of genuine humility and conviction: he calmed you strangely. A small town man, in the stereotypical doctor's outfit—a long white jacket and a stethoscope slung round his neck—he was himself a 'migrant', posted at GT, but soon to move on, no doubt.

I remember those two days as a time of discovery. Firstly, of the GT (Gokuldas Tejpal) Hospital, of whose existence, in all my years in Bombay, I'd been unaware. This isn't unusual: people have a very special, discriminatory knowledge of the cities in which they grow up—secondly, the GT Hospital is a government institution, outside of the purview of private health care that 'people like us' are used to (except in the case of an exigency like the one that occurred in Vijay's life). The hospital buildings comprise an extraordinary colonial relic, without any of the functionality of much of post-Independence architecture, and, that morning, I think I saw it with eyes as new as Vijay's after his uncharted journey. Then there were the clusters of humanity—the word has a pure but double register for me in the context of these public hospitals, containing within it at once the sense of a quality as well as of a collectivity—the people you see on roads and at work, here to have recourse to the hospital's facilities; you could see visitors running up and down the stairs, glimpse the patients waiting patiently for food, and I noticed a quiet young girl in a salwaar kameez outside the ICU, with the Bible open to a page in Samuel. And there was Dr Shailendra, the stethoscope round his neck, and the reassurance he gave out unknowingly, something that transcended, subtly, his being a doctor and whatever expertise he had.

The word 'migrant', too, and its historical and emotional layers: I began to become more aware of them after speaking with the doctor. I may be wrong, but it seems that India is among the few countries that use the word for their local populations (China, I recently discovered, might be another). Is someone who moves from Nevada to New York, or Leipzig to Stuttgart, a migrant? In many ways, the Indian use of the word expresses definitions and allegiances that pre-date the nation state; that are inherited, at least partly, from a time when 'des' was not 'country' but 'familiar landscape' and 'home territory', and 'vides' primarily meant 'elsewhere'. Post nation, the term 'emigration' has been recently replaced, for the middle class, with 'diaspora', which suggests a figurative 'moving ahead', a literal betterment. 'Migrant', in its Indian usage, probably also implies, unobtrusively, people who don't own property; not settlers, but wage earners with no guaranteed income, address, or situation.

In Bombay, a few months ago, in an uncommonly chilly (for this city) January, readying myself to interview a series of doctors for this piece, I thought again of that night when Vijay didn't go home, and of the following bright morning, when I visited him at the ICU.

Now I was making my way towards JJ Hospital, a renowned government institution which I'd heard of but—for familiar reasons—never seen. 'JJ' is Sir Jamsetjee Jeejebhoy, who helped fund a gamut of hospitals in Bombay, including GT Hospital and JJ Hospital. Sir Jamsetjee, according to Wikipedia, offered, in 1838, a donation of one lakh rupees ($2500) 'for building a new general hospital with natives'. Should that be 'with' or 'for'? The other institution to which the abbreviation JJ is appended famously is the School of Art, which produced, in the sixties, probably independent India's finest alumni of painters.

The JJ Hospital is in the central (once industrial) part of the city, a part no longer deniable or ignorable; since Bombay has grown not only outwards, but in a manner that connects—sometimes enforces connections between—one section and another, in ways that weren't possible before. For instance, the near extinction of the old textile industry has converted the mills into spaces—adjoining new malls, spawning showrooms, restaurants, bars—for the young, the well-to-do, not to mention the unembarrassedly and vulgarly rich. Besides, the traffic on the major arterial routes—Peddar Road, Haji Ali, Worli—is now so foul that, with relatively new flyovers on Tulsi Pipe Road, the middle class will take routes they rejected in the sixties and seventies. JJ Hospital, in the 19th century, was surrounded by space, like a sanatorium; as our car entered it through an entrance on the side, it opened up from within: absences and trees, small, winding driveways, seemingly aimless passers-by, the old, perennial buildings, the deceptive air of tranquillity great hospitals have. We parked before what was the hub: two tall, handsome buildings, which must have long ago looked futuristic.

My first interviewee was Dr Alka Deshpande, a severe, bespectacled, but not unkind-looking woman who occupies a spacious office on the first floor, and runs the hospital's health care for HIV patients. Like some of the other doctors I'd meet in the next few hours, the bulk of her career is more or less coterminous with that of HIV's in this country. She joined the faculty in 1974. In the early to mid eighties, when she was Associate Professor at the Department of Medicine (JJ is a teaching hospital), she and her colleagues began to read about this new disease in medical journals: thinking of it, as many of us had at the time, as mainly a gay ailment in America. (I went to England in 1983, but learnt of the mysterious illness in India from *Time* magazine: the strange, disturbing signs, the unspeakable outcome. The troubling ambiguity of sex through history—the fact that it bestows life and pleasure, and also, in a way that can't be entirely explained by morality, confuses and shames—had converged in a new way upon this disease.)

Since homosexuality itself, at the time, was as good as invisible in this country, there was an innocent belief (so thinks Dr Deshpande with hindsight) that HIV wouldn't come to India. But she recalled that in 1986, Dr Jacob John of the Christian Medical College in Vellore in Tamil Nadu, acquired a testing kit and began to use it; and found out before long that two sex workers in Madras were HIV positive. (Without too many people knowing it—testimony to the uneven publicity that AIDS has received in India—Bombay and Madras emerged as the two 'epicentres' of the disease.)

Dr Deshpande didn't mention the name of Suniti Solomon, who's recognised as having documented the first case of AIDS in India, in Madras. But both the passion and the occasional provisionality of her account, with rapid to and fro transitions from year to year, locale to locale (this was information I had to sort out later), seemed to be a reliving of the unpredictable way the history had unfolded. Sixty two years old, she is very erect and straight; and, as she spoke, I could almost imagine the younger woman who, in some ways, had had to harden herself, and in other ways be content to work

262

without resolution. 'Once an ayurvedic doctor asked me if I was an HIV doctor or an HIV patient,' she said; and when I pursued this, she dismissed the anecdote, laughing briefly: 'No, no, it's just that I had to face all kinds of quacks in those days.'

In the early part of her story, the name of Dr Gilada kept coming up, someone who'd once been a burr in her side; a junior medical officer at this hospital, it turned out, and then an AIDS activist who worked with prostitutes for an NGO, and also, perhaps, a sensationalist and competitor who had broken rank. He belonged to the past, to 15 or more years ago; but she still disapproved of him having once constantly made the issue public. I could see that, as a relatively young doctor dealing with the first outbreak of the disease, but also with the press and a person like Dr Gilada (who was not shy of the print media), she would have been the moral and deeply serious and private person she is now; and that this seriousness and sense of privacy must have shaped the way she'd set the parameters for what would become, in a small but absolute way, her terrain.

Touch, or touching, was of great importance: the doctors who dealt with early HIV cases in these public hospitals were often reluctant to touch the patient. 'I did not *choose* to become an AIDS specialist,' she said, emphasising that one word slightly. 'But, in those days, I decided I would not hesitate to touch the patient. I was working in a government hospital, after all, and I must take up the responsibilities that came my way. Besides,' and this seemed important to her, 'I was a professor, the head of my department. I had to set an example.'

Although the first impression I received after my various conversations that day and the next one was that it was the working and the 'migrant' classes that had borne the brunt of the disease, I sensed also that not only had it been an occasional middle class affliction, but that it had, unsurprisingly, reached the affluent (though the affluent, naturally, were better equipped to keep it secret). But, in 1986, when Dr John discovered the virus in the blood of two sex workers, a rich businessman admitted to Jaslok Hospital with pneumonia turned out to have AIDS: this news the result of sending a blood sample 'abroad' for testing. He'd probably contracted the disease abroad himself; seven or eight years ago, he'd had bypass surgery in Houston. 'The businessman died,' said Dr Deshpande matter-of-factly, before continuing with her story.

Whenever I asked the doctors I met that afternoon about the incidence of HIV today amongst the affluent, I was told that it was relatively low, but by no means unknown. Of course, the rich or even the middle class do not come for treatment to these public hospitals, except in emergencies like the one that involved Vijay. 'But there are even famous film stars who are supposed to have the disease,' I was told at one point, with large-eyed conviction, 'and they are treated privately.' This might well be true; but I encountered nothing in my conversations about the rich except apocrypha and hunches: as if the subject was never thought about clearly, or was taboo.

The first signs of an unknown disease, as it makes its appearance in a country, must be as bewildering, and, on the level of the everyday, as much begrudged, as when it strikes a particular body, an individual. In both cases, and in somewhat different senses, the consequences of the event have to gauged; and there's relatively little to go on. Secondly, there's hasty mobilisation; internally, as far as the body's concerned, and visibly, amongst those who are on the scene almost by accident—the individual, families, the people in health care: for, as with all at first obscure diseases, there's an element of chance governing who contracts the disease and who's attending to it. As with all infections, the body (and here I mean an array of psychological and physical responses by that word), in reply, cultivates optimism, besides mobilising; in the case of AIDS in the eighties, the body's optimism was ridiculously short-lived. In what we call our 'country', this couldn't be allowed to be so; optimism had to be translated into a form of idealism. At least, that's what I understood speaking with Dr Deshpande that afternoon at the JJ Hospital.

Cups of tea arrived in Dr Deshpande's office. She watched me drink while telling me, essentially, the story of what it meant to become gradually conscious, as an Indian doctor, of the fact—indeed, the inevitability—of AIDS. 'Sero-surveillance', or the planned testing of donors' blood for the virus, began in the Department of Medicine of the hospital in the late eighties, after news began to come in from France that the incidence of the virus in such blood was high: especially as there were addicts among the donors. Not until 1990 did the Government of India officially admit that AIDS was also an Indian problem. Till then, in fact, discreet sero-surveillance was the strategy adopted by the Indian Council of Medical Research to ascertain the presence of HIV in the country; in JJ itself, there was little activity to do with the disease.

1990 was a year in which a number of things occurred. That year, the Head of the Department at the time, Dr Gupte, a few senior doctors, and physicians from other parts of India went to Australia for three months to educate themselves in the nature and treatment of the disease. Not long after their return, the idea of an AIDS ward or centre was discussed at the first post excursion meeting on HIV. It was decided that it was time to open an outpatients' department at JJ Hospital for HIV positive people: the first such outpatients' department, as it turned out, in the country.

So, in October 1990 (around the time Dr Deshpande took over as Head), once a week, on Mondays, HIV patients began to come to this department: it's now an extraordinarily busy—to the visitor, probably the busiest—section of the hospital, on the ground floor of a building behind the one in which Dr Deshpande has her office, milling with seemingly healthy people. In 1990, though, hardly anyone knew clearly the difference between HIV and AIDS, that one is the infection, the other the disease, and families would insist on having relatives who were HIV positive admitted into the hospital, such demands leading, sometimes, to confrontation. This was also a time when microbiologists were reluctant to collect blood samples and even to test them; it was left to doctors to collect blood, and hope the sample wouldn't be rejected by the microbiologist if it were sent in for an HIV test. Gloves were introduced, used, washed, and reused; disposable gloves and, importantly, in microbiology, the micropipette (with which there was no risk of accidentally sucking in the blood), were introduced in 1992, leading to a relaxation, if that's the word, of the prejudice against testing.

Earlier, in 1990, HIV counselling (which Dr Deshpande referred to as 'advocacy') had been made part of the treatment at JJ: a new notion at the time in India, according to her. And, the following year, significantly—indicating the sort of mental and emotional exploration involved in configuring the place of the disease in the lives of people and the life of the hospital—the ward meant specially for AIDS patients was closed on the grounds that it was discriminatory, and such patients, for the first time, began to be admitted into the general ward.

Interestingly, when I pressed Dr Deshpande on this— 'Were the patients unhappy to be in a separate ward?'—the name of Gilada came up again, reminding me how entangled histories can be, and how you have to be cautious when assigning praise or blame. No, she said, the patients weren't aware of the anomaly; it was Gilada who'd gone to the press about the special ward, saying it constituted a breach in confidentiality. It was then that she, as Head, decided to solve this once and for all by opening the general ward to people with HIV.

Now, in her large office, Dr Deshpande looked busy—spotless and focussed in her sari and glasses, mildly and immovably at the centre of things—but in control; as if a problem had become recognisable, and thereby changed into something you could do business with. *This* was her world: the clean, spacious office, with, intriguingly, the portraits of spiritual figures on the wall: Aurobindo; his French wife, the Mother; a figurine of the ubiquitous—and omnipotent, at least in globalised India—Ganesh; another of the goddess beloved amongst academics and artists, Saraswati; and a large photograph of a young woman in audience with a former President of India. When asked, she told me shyly, but not without pride, that this was she herself, receiving the Padma Shree, that prestigious civilian award granted by the government. It was with that same hurried shyness that she said (in answer to the gauche question I asked her two days later: 'Are you married, Dr Deshpande?'): 'No, I am single.' She is a patient, but not a *comfortable*, interlocutor; she is—this is the impression I got when I saw her with her patients—most herself at her work. In 1992, the HIV Outpatients' Department received about 6000–7000 people annually; in 1998–99, the figure was around 20,000 a year. But the expected AIDS epidemic in India hasn't happened yet; the figures to do with the spread of the disease are substantially lower than had been presumed a few years ago. The disease, too, though not curable, had become more containable, especially with treatment at JJ and other centres moving on from dealing with opportunistic infections (mostly tuberculosis in India) to the introduction of ART (antiretroviral therapy) in 1996. The latter comprises the famous cocktail of drugs that can give the patient a lease of life—sometimes 15 or 20 years, I was told by a couple of doctors and health workers that day; though (having compared that estimate to other sources) those figures appear to hint at these doctors' residual conservatism: these are not people from a world given to celebrating unduly.

But the figures are also a reminder of their realism. During a phone conversation I had with Dr Deshpande recently, more than two months after I first met her, I asked her if antiretroviral therapy had made her more hopeful. 'Not hopeful, I am very happy,' she said, suddenly sounding refulgent. 'Today I saw a patient I had seen for the first time with full-blown AIDS four years ago, on April 1ˢᵗ 2004.' She is not always so precise with dates; this one must represent a turning point. 'Two patients, including her, came to me at that time, both in a very bad way. We put them on the first line of ART. Both of them are alive.'

'How was the patient you saw today?' 'She is very well!' she said, with some excitement—an instant of release, of self-indulgence—in her voice. 'Her CD4 cell count'—the cells that, she explained, are primarily attacked by the virus—'was 15 at that time. Very low. Now it is 700! That is a normal CD4 cell count.' And yet, when I asked her if this woman could have a more or less normal lifespan, she became cautious, predicting that ART could certainly give her 'a few more years'. When, disappointed and strangely enmeshed in this oscillation of emotion, I asked her, 'Why only a few more years?', she told me what I should have known: that the poor—often for no good reason—will discontinue their own treatment once they feel better; or will have no access to medication during the long trips they make to family in villages (UP and Bihar, those two standard archetypes for the backward north Indian state, were mentioned by Dr Deshpande).

Affordability is no longer really the principal issue. It was in 2004—when the patient whose good health today made Dr Deshpande so happy, had been brought into the hospital 'on a stretcher' at that time—that JJ became the first centre to offer free ART. Before then, the first line of treatment cost Rs 800 ($20) per month per person; and, for a small working class family—a father, mother, and child with HIV—medicines worth Rs 2400 ($60) monthly were out of reach. Now, the government offers both the first and second line of treatment for free.

There was much to fit into one afternoon; our next stop was Sion's Lokmanya Tilak Hospital. Yet the two remaining meetings were, in comparison, brief stopovers, in which the interviewees largely confirmed, or, at most, slightly contradicted, what Dr Deshpande had already told me. Sion, too, is a venerable area, a place with a history. Chain store gentrification has been slow to come to it. Nevertheless, I'd stopped breathlessly, on the way, at a small anonymous shopping arcade and smuggled a Domino's pizza into the car as a belated lunch or snack: cheese and pepperoni. The Lokmanya Tilak Hospital has, in comparison to the GT and JJ Hospitals, an identifiably post Independence municipal air: functional rectangles; rudimentary windows; long-lasting facades; a hint, within, of dampness. Although we were late—it was almost quarter past 4—Dr Mamta Manglani had had the good grace to wait for us. A paediatric physician, she has been with the hospital since 1987. She was about to leave, but decided to give us 15 or 20 minutes. Our visit was almost sociable, despite the context, but unlike with Dr Deshpande, I wasn't in the presence of the humbling force of personality. Her room is a small one; identical in proportion, one might safely guess, to the other rooms on the left side of that corridor, whose floor, as we walked in, was being relaid by labourers.

None of the doctors I met that day had, initially, been trained to face the disease. What they were *now* was shaped by it; and HIV had first confronted each in a slightly different incarnation—a rumour; a makeshift pedagogy; a death. Dr Manglani first saw it in the form of a four year old child, in 1994. Neither parent of the boy was HIV positive; on further investigation, it turned out he'd been a victim of sexual abuse. When he was first admitted to the hospital, it didn't have a clinic for children with HIV—this was to be opened only in 1997. He was examined in the haematology clinic; he'd come in with thrombocytopenia, or a low platelet count. Once diagnosed with HIV, splenectomy seemed the best option; it was a way of raising the count. But then the idea was vetoed: probably because the boy had the disease, thinks Dr Manglani,

269

and few knew how to deal with this fact at the time. He was moved to another hospital, to have his spleen irradiated—a non-invasive procedure. Again, the anaesthetist, once he knew the boy was HIV positive, refused to cooperate. Despite all this, he was put on steroids and other forms of 'medical management' and, in 1996, on ART; he is alive today, a seventeen year old studying in Bombay.

In 1997, the Lokmanya Tilak Hospital opened its special paediatric clinic for HIV positive children, with 12 patients to begin with; in 2005, its ART clinic, offering free antiretroviral drugs, came into existence. Between 1997 and 2005, the clinic admitted about 650 children, of whom, says Dr Manglani, 'we lost more than half'. Why? Partly because, without recourse to ART drugs, the disease had advanced too far in the first batch of children for effective treatment; partly because the working-class families they came from—though many were orphans, anyway—couldn't afford the drugs. Since 2005, though, the number of children in the clinic has gone up to 700, with only 22 deaths—those because (as with Dr Deshpande's adults) families would stop the treatment when symptoms receded.

The story I heard more or less followed a familiar pattern: the beginnings marked by ignorance; the reluctance of hired—not regular—nurses to attend to the sick child; a feeling of 'burn out' (Dr Manglani's term) among doctors and carers, a special despondency arising inevitably from dealing with terminally ill children, until, that is, ART was introduced. ART brought into being not only a new, workable medical regime and some realisable ambitions, but a calm; I had sensed that calm in Dr Deshpande's office. ART is incomplete but, as of now, indispensable knowledge, and it partly removes HIV from the hysteria that surrounded it in the eighties and nineties.

'I not only feel hopeful, I feel fulfilled,' Dr Manglani told me. 'The children are getting better. They are putting on weight. I believe they will live to see the day when there is a cure.'

'Do you really believe that?' I asked.

'I do,' she said; and one presumes a doctor speaks not from faith in providence, but in medical research.

Dr Manglani lost her own child early (she didn't specify how), but she has an adopted daughter, now twenty two years old, who's a paediatric counsellor herself, though not for HIV positive cases. Her husband is an engineer, and apparently a great support, involved in awareness campaigns for the disease.

It was early evening, 5 approximately, when we left Dr Manglani for Dadar, for our last appointment of the day. Dr Saple is one of the senior most consultants of the 'Skin' (which covers sexually transmitted diseases) Department of the GT Hospital, and has been intimately and influentially involved with it for decades. My reason for wanting to meet him in his 'chamber' had to do with the GT connection—Vijay waking up from his coma to a new life; the woman with AIDS in the adjoining ICU wing; Dr Shailendra, the stethoscope hung round his neck.

I was early; or Dr Saple was late, as he'd warned me he would be—he was good enough to promise to make time for me before attending to his patients. Charts to do with antiretroviral treatment hung from a wall; Dr Saple, once he arrived, offered me familiar, potent, milky tea and Good Day biscuits. He is a small man, with hazel, light-coloured eyes; the kind of man, you feel, who wants to get on with his work, unnoticed, but is not entirely indifferent to being caught in the cross-currents of medical history. 'Please take,' he insisted, pushing the plate of biscuits towards me. About history itself, he had a quibble. The treatment of AIDS in Bombay (and perhaps India) started first in GT, and not in JJ, according to Dr Saple—of course, he has nothing but regard for Dr Deshpande's achievements. But, in the early days (in the eighties), GT was a sort of dumping ground for HIV patients who other hospitals wouldn't touch. People with sexually transmitted diseases were naturally referred to Dr Saple's department (Skin); and, in the mid eighties, he began to have their blood tested for HIV.

'But why did you do that?' I asked him; it suddenly seemed odd to me that an Indian doctor, in 1986, should, without precedent, begin to think along these lines.

'We were in touch with the Chelsea and Westminster Hospital in London,' said Dr Saple, hardly aware of the bizarreness of these juxtapositions and connections. 'Dr Hawkins advised us to go in for testing.' Watching me scribble, he said, 'Dr David Hawkins.'

Who was Dr Hawkins? I didn't ask. Dr Saple looks very much like a man of his environment; he exudes pragmatism: a quality that's of paramount use, surely, in negotiating this disease. One may not think him as well travelled as he obviously is. In July 1996, for instance, he was, almost in the same week, attending to a patient in India (a Delhi businessman who was paying up to Rs 80,000 ($2000) a month for his treatment), and presenting a paper on HIV related tuberculosis at Vancouver in Canada; picking up there, too, the latest developments in antiretroviral therapy; bringing these technologies and methods back to his patient the following week. The businessman, however, in spite of this back and forth of information, died in 1997 of toxicity.

As I flitted that afternoon between JJ Hospital and Sion and Dadar, I was both struck and moved by the improvisatory sketchiness with which this project (acknowledging, then battling, HIV) had taken shape. Neither extraordinary resources nor great scientific minds were at the core of the story; instead, there had been an air of provisionality, of a willingness to work with the means at hand, of experiment— not in the grand sense, but in an openness to new methods, to the possibility of error. Then there was the undeniable fact of movement: not only of workers and people, not only of the virus itself, arriving upon the scene like some new technology or fresh incursion of capital that would render certain livelihoods quite obsolete, but, in almost immediate response, that of information and ideas, a frantic but agile regrouping.

In some ways, this sketchy but exploratory pedagogy of treatment is not unlike a political movement; not political in the way we anymore understand that word, but because of its (the enterprise's) sheer semi-visible, tentative, hidden quality (for these doctors were people on the cusp of the immense but little known world of public health care and a rapidly, simultaneously, privatising and globalising nation), silent at first, gradually gaining confidence, still, in important ways, unacknowledged.

Two short narratives round off the larger one. The next morning, I made a trip to Falklands Road, which is in the red light district generically known as Kamathipura. Bombay, with a zoological garden of no particular renown, and only a passable museum, has, however, a prostitutes' quarter that was once frenetically, alarmingly active. I had been there before—three decades ago, as a teenager, to check out the prostitutes standing on raised platforms before their barred cubicles—the 'cages'. Desire, even if it was momentarily kindled, was swiftly dampened by the strong stench everywhere. It suggested the old, historical demons, gonorrhoea and syphilis. Both the number of sex workers and the number of customers have now fallen sharply, as has, I hear, the number of HIV infections.

The condom is part of everyday propaganda in the area. A bit of street theatre was underway at the end of Falklands Road I arrived at; and a decent sized circle of loiterers had gathered to watch the tamasha on this vacant weekday morning. Two men and a woman were demonstrating, with a mixture of humour, exaggeration, and didacticism, the fatal stupidity of visiting a sex worker without a condom and then having intercourse with your wife. Not far away, but removed from the audience, stood a solitary woman, almost unnoticed; from her clothes and style, a sex worker; but alone—

there were no cages here. A little group of musicians stood to one side, accompanying the players, shouting out, to the tune of old Hindi film songs, their warnings to the spectators, who smiled grudgingly.

The show over, I spoke with some of the members of that audience before it dispersed completely. No one was unfriendly; no one was forthcoming either. Representation and reality, anyway, could hardly have been more proximate and, in a sense, dissimilar; there, a mere three minutes' stroll away, was the taboo but workaday world they were being instructed to be careful of. One was a married man from Rajasthan who'd lived in Bombay for six years and unfailingly, he claimed, used the condom. Another young man came from Uttar Pradesh and had lived for 12 years in this city; slow to admitting having anything to do with sex workers at first, he ended up saying he did visit them irregularly. Another man had just arrived from Jharkhand, and had been in Bombay for a little over two weeks, having left wife and children in their hometown; he was a 'master', he said, in gold jewellery.

A 'master' in gold jewellery—some trades and skills are old, and find fresh interpretations, fresh justification; some journeys are archaic, but might be at the heart of our shopping malls, our expanded airports, the construction and reconstruction of our cities. Milieus are devastated; human beings, full of optimism, move on. The patterns that separate and bring together the old and new worlds repeat themselves constantly. I'm thinking of Tagore's story from about a century ago, 'Kabuliwala', about the eponymous migrant, a seller of wares, who becomes, for a while, an object of wonder for the girl child of a bhadralok (the Bengali word for bourgeois; literally, 'civil folk') family, and who carries in his pocket a talisman; the print, upon a piece of paper, of his daughter's hand. The bhadralok family must have been to the late 19th century what the intricately networked metropolis is to our own era: something unfathomable, at the centre of, and absorbing, many journeys. The Afghan, I now realise, has long been the archetype of the traveller, a person with no enduring abode, a seller of wares, or, often, a daily wage-earner and labourer, but large-bodied and large-hearted, inhabiting so much of the history of labour; it's in this guise—hapless, possessed of providential patience and energy—that we find him, for instance, in the Iranian cinema of Mohsen Makhmalbaf and Abbas Kiarostami, in *Taste of Cherry* and *The Bicyclist*, both contemporary parables, set in the world we know but don't properly notice, of travel, death, regeneration.

A few minutes' walk took me to the 'cages', where, at a small 'wellness' centre called Sadhan Clinic, supported by the Big Lottery Fund, I encountered a situation that both echoed and parodied Tagore's tale. I was told by the doctor and the counsellor in attendance that 39% of sex workers in Falkland Road were HIV positive; but the figure was decreasing. Many of them, I was informed—and this provoked a strange curiosity in me, tinged, maybe, with a brief homesickness—were from Bengal; not the Bengal I knew, it turned out, but Bangladesh. 'How do they cope in this new environment?' I asked; because the women were exiles in a double sense—displaced once by marriage, as almost all women in the subcontinent are, transplanted into their husband's home; and displaced again, into an alien habitat, a strange trade. These husbands don't necessarily abandon their wives; the women are a source of income, the husband is happy to look after the cooking and the children.

On asking to be introduced to a sex worker, I was taken to the tiny, frail woman who'd been sitting absently near the clinic's entrance with her child as we'd entered, in a state of waif-like dishevelment, and who'd flashed me a guileless smile—not a premeditated inviting smile, but a generously welcoming one. Sitting opposite her across a table, with only the counsellor and the restless infant for company, I soon discovered why she was in this spontaneous, unprofessional mood. She was in semi-retirement; and she was at something of a crossroads. Behind the smile was a self-reflexive tentativeness, the instinct towards self-protection, a tendency to at once be in denial and to take stock. She had been spared the infection. *That* was not one of her worries. But her husband, Akash Singh, a Nepali, had gone back home, promising to return to take her and their child back with him in a month's time. She was—she tried not to show it—nervous.

Her name was Rokeya, and she was from Phulpur in Bangladesh. She told me, in a mixture of Bengali and Hindi—she seemed to have largely forgotten Bengali, so deeply and invisibly had she settled into her life here, so integrally is forgetting a part of our identity—that she used to knit sweaters in Chittagong and make about Rs 9000 ($225) a month. A dozen such girls, including her, were sold into prostitution in Kashmir; moved by her tears, a Bengali mali who worked where she lived briefly gave her money and helped her escape. She travelled without a ticket, made friends with a woman, Brishti (the Bengali word for rain), who brought her to Bombay, introduced her to domestic work, and then sold her to a gharwalli or madam for Rs 10,000 ($250).

The story is as worn and intricate as an old rupee note: it's been so long in currency it's almost lost its denominational value. What can one do with it but keep it? Its broken telling was interrupted, occasionally, by the child: the irrepressible little Kamala. She threatened to dislodge the empty tumbler on the table.

Her father, whom Rokeya had married at some unspecified point in the narrative, was a nice man, but, she conceded, a 'ziddi'—stubborn one. (Later, the counsellor told me that the word was, in this case, as it often is, a euphemism for a violent temperament.) Akash Singh is her second husband, and the couple visited the clinic for the first time when she was pregnant. Rokeya had worked her way out of prostitution; but, if her husband didn't reappear soon, she would have to put Kamala in a free orphanage. Her present earnings, from doing domestic work, were between Rs 4000 and 5000 ($100–125) a month; her room rent was Rs 35 (88 cents) a day.

'He will come,' she reassured me.

Soon

I shall die soon, I know.
This thing is in my blood.
It will not let me go.
It saps my cells for food.

It soaks my nights in sweat
And breaks my days in pain.
No hand or drug can treat
These limbs for love or gain.

Love was the strange first cause
That bred grief in its seed,
And gain knew its own laws—
To fix its place and breed.

He whom I love, thank God,
Won't speak of hope or cure.
It would not do me good.
He sees that I am sure.

He knows what I have read
And will not bring me lies.
He sees that I am dead.
I read it in his eyes.

How am I to go on—
How will I bear this taste,
My throat cased in white spawn—
These hands that shake and waste?

Stay by my steel ward bed
And hold me where I lie.
Love me when I am dead
And do not let me die.

Vikram Seth

A POEM ABOUT AIDS
Vikram Seth

I wrote this poem about a man dying of AIDS many years ago, and it is difficult for me to remember now the exact circumstances that made me write it. I will try to recall them as well as I can.

I was at Stanford University in California between 1975 and 1986 as a graduate student in the Department of Economics. Midway during this period I spent two years in China doing research for my dissertation. Before I left for China I am sure I had not heard of AIDS. After I returned, in the autumn of 1982, there was a great deal of news about it. The disease was first officially reported in June 1981. Within a year it had become apparent that a deadly and hitherto unknown disease was about, and that many of its victims were gay men. There seemed to be neither cure nor proven cause.

I remember first reading about the disease in the San Francisco newspapers; it seemed that the incubation period was long, and that it was possible to have contracted it years before the symptoms appeared. About a year after I got back, I decided to get myself checked. I had been relatively chaste in China, but it was possible that someone I had slept with there, or in my more promiscuous years before, might have slept with someone who might have slept with someone who… It was a vague but persistent anxiety. I went to a clinic and gave a blood sample. Two weeks later I got my results. I went in person; the clinic insisted on this—both for privacy and for possible counselling if the result came out positive.

Some years earlier, I had had a biopsy done on a freckle that a doctor had feared might be a melanoma. I remembered the bizarre philosophical calm that had descended on me as I prepared to hear the report. Now, once again, I tried to prepare myself for the result of a troubling lottery. Once again, it turned out to be negative. As I left, I looked around the waiting room and wondered if everyone there would be equally lucky.

San Francisco is less than an hour away from Stanford, and many of those affected by the disease lived in the city—not just those who contracted the disease, but their lovers, their families, their friends. The breakdown of the immune system, the taking over of the body by opportunistic infections, the exhaustion, the wasting away, the disfiguring blemishes, the collapse of the body's systems, the pain, the hopelessness and the final end often brought forth the best that friendship and family feeling can give: loyalty, care, courage, comfort, love. But there were many cases where those who contracted AIDS were shunned by their families—families who might have learned for the first time that they were gay. Nor was there a shortage of religious bigots who triumphantly proclaimed that what was happening was in the fitness of things: sinners and perverts were being struck down and eradicated by a vengeful and purifying God. There was a great deal of this frothing reported in the media. But AIDS had also become a matter of general discussion and fear. One of my friends, in general a very liberal man, said that until the method of transmission could be ascertained, AIDS patients should be completely isolated, if necessary on an island, on public health grounds. What if the disease were airborne?

Around that time, having been diverted from my economics dissertation, I had begun writing a novel in verse, *The Golden Gate*. I notice that there is only one mention of AIDS in the book, though it contains, among its various threads, a gay love affair. I did not know anyone who had AIDS, but by this time—in response to the storm around me—I had trained myself to take the accepted precautions, and have done so ever since. In retrospect, it is surprising to me how automatic this became—not quite like putting on a seatbelt, but almost as casual. A wry smile, a raised eyebrow, a brief interruption of the quickly renewed excitement—the etiquette of contraceptive sex had now been generalised to all sex. But I never really thought about the possible proximity of death when all this was going on—rather, about how irksome the packaging of condoms could be.

It was now clear that AIDS was a disease that was transmissible not through the air or through general human contact but specifically through bodily fluids. As time passed, more and more cases came to light of people getting AIDS through straight sex or through the sharing of needles or through blood transfusion or by birth or by breastfeeding from an infected mother. It also began making its way from North America to other parts of the world, where all these methods of transmission, together with a greater lack of information about its prevention, helped it spread—though at first its progress was slow.

I had returned to Delhi, meanwhile, and had begun gathering thoughts and ideas for *A Suitable Boy*. The centre of my world had moved from California in the 1980s to north India in the 1950s. But this shift of focus was interrupted when I accepted a residency for a few weeks at the Djerassi Foundation in the hills not far from Stanford. Once again I became aware of what was happening in the San Francisco Bay Area, where cases of AIDS were rife. I wrote a number of poems during my stay there. And I am almost certain that this short poem was one of them.

At this point I will quote a few forceful and frustrated lines from a friend and editor who read the last paragraph and found it wanting. She writes: 'V, I would love to hear more about the poem. Did you write it very quickly? Did you by this point know anyone, even distantly, who had the disease? The poem, it seems to me, has a great deal of fear in it—the voice of the narrator alternates between acceptance and resignation and then panic. "He whom I love, thank God/ Won't speak of hope or cure/ It would not do me good/ He sees that I am sure" and then "How am I to go on—/ How will I bear this taste". The last verse captures this yo-yoing best I think, the paradox and pain of it: "Love me when I am dead/ And do not let me die." Do you want to say something about this, about what you were trying to do in the poem? I am interested in that tone of panic.'

I too sense the tone of panic—among others. I am equally frustrated. How could I not remember what made me write it and what I was trying to 'do'? I cannot visualise myself writing it—quickly or otherwise. But this is the case with many, perhaps most, of my poems. Unless I can find some jottings from that particular period, I doubt I'll ever be able to recall the immediate stimulus. Since I didn't at the time know anyone who had AIDS, I must have been affected by something specific that I had read or seen. But what? My imagination draws up several alternative scenarios—which is as bad as having none. Besides, the chances of my finding any independent notes from the time are remote, since a poem is itself a sort of note.

But though I can't recall with certainty why I put pen to paper, I can clearly recall two events related to the poem that happened at about that time. The first was at a bookstore in Berkeley where I did a reading from *The Golden Gate* and later also read this poem. It is monosyllabic, and I read it quietly. I can still recall the silence as I read it and which followed it. I imagine that, by that time, there was hardly anyone actually living in the Bay Area who did not know someone who had been afflicted with AIDS. The second was when I showed a sheaf of poems, which included 'Soon', to a friend at the foundation. She came up to me later in the evening, her face white with shock, put her hand on my arm and began commiserating with me.

I told her at once that it had been written as an act of imagination rather than experience, and that I was not the protagonist. However, her reaction made it clear to me that if 'Soon' were to be included in any collection, I would have to handle things with some care. I couldn't very well insert a footnote dissociating myself from the first person of the poem without in some sense dissociating myself from those who had the disease. On the other hand, I didn't want my friends and family to panic or grieve on my behalf. Eventually, when it was published in my collection *All You Who Sleep Tonight*, I included it in a section of dramatic monologues and translations entitled 'In Other Voices'. This reduced but did not eliminate the misunderstandings—which are exacerbated by the fact that whenever the poem is anthologised there is no such implicit explanation.

I wrote 'Soon' two decades ago. Things have changed since then. Not only do we now know how AIDS is transmitted, but we know, scientifically and medically, what its original genesis might have been, the virus that causes it, the actions that can prevent it, and, if contracted, the treatment that can restrain, reduce and even almost eliminate it. The physical fear of the narrator in the poem, bound by tubes to his steel ward bed, his hands shaking and wasting away, is an image of its time. He is a man attacked, as it were, by a scourge. If I were to write a poem about the disease today, I might perhaps imagine a different scene. And yet, for various reasons, our increased knowledge and more effective drugs have not been accompanied by a reduction in the numbers of those with AIDS. Quite the opposite—the disease has spread rapidly and dangerously throughout the world, particularly in India and Africa. In the case of India, the whole matter is exacerbated by our ignorance and shame about sex. We simply don't like to talk about it—even to impart or receive essential, life-saving information.

When I read the poem now, which is not often, the grief and fear and hopelessness of the narrator still affect me. This is odd, because many writers, myself included, become somewhat inured to their own works once they have been published and become public property. There is something about the poem which seems mysteriously to come from outside myself as much as from inside—and I wish I were capable, more often than I am, of recreating its tension and its sense of (or, at least, hope for) fellow-feeling.

THE LAST OF THE USTAADS
Aman Sethi

Slow and fast, up and down, broad and narrow; seen through the oversized windscreen of the Tata 2516, National Highway (NH) 31 flickers past—bobbing up and down like a bad home video. Cycle rickshaws skitter out of the way, overpowered sedans overtake from the left and then from the right, crater-like potholes loom in the middle distance, but the rust-leaf coloured truck nimbly steps out of the way. At its helm, the giant steering wheel wedged between his splayed out legs, sits Sanjay Kumar; an awe inspiring, beedi smoking, frenetically gesturing, constantly abusing, bear of a man who, at times, appears to be a caricature of a calmer, quieter self that he left behind in his village, in Uttar Pradesh. Still only thirty five, but with salt and pepper hair and a grizzled countenance, he belongs to that type which makes the abrupt transition from looking wise beyond their years, to appearing old before their time. He retains his boyish grin, only partially masked by the corpulence brought on by too much alcohol. Nicotine and alcohol addictions usually have contradictory manifestations—cigarettes and beedis make your face shrivel up like a prune, while alcohol imparts a genial puffiness about the cheeks. Theoretically, an artful balance of both should leave one looking perfectly toned. Looking at Sanjay's face, I deduce that he drinks more than smokes. A surmise he hotly denies; 'I do both in equal measure.'

The second driver, Kamlesh, is a quiet, angular Bihari; a skinny boy who wears baggy clothes in an attempt to disguise his slightness, but only ends up looking even more waif-like. Only nineteen, he is yet to start drinking, but smokes incessantly. Painfully quiet, with an air of gently fermenting melancholy, Kamlesh often goes for hours without speaking a word—staring blankly at the highway that stretches out ahead him. The few times that I do get him to speak, his words are invariably drowned out by the roar of the engine—prompting me to stick my ear out at him like one of those deaf old men in the movies whose entire role seems to involve stroking their beards and saying, 'Wassat?'

'He has a problem with his volume,' explains Sanjay, his hand leaving the steering to turn an imaginary dial. Sanjay, on the other hand, has a voice like a foghorn, which he uses to great effect. He takes his eyes off the road for a second, and bellows into my ear.

'So you want to know about sex, eh?'

Stretching from Barhi, just short of Patna, the capital city of Bihar, to Guwahati, the commercial capital of Assam, NH 31 runs from the eastern edge of the vast Indo-Gangetic plain up into India's isolated northeast region. The dense network of national and state highways comes to an abrupt halt near the Darjeeling–Bagdogra chicken neck where NH 57 and NH 34 flow into NH 31, making it the sole gateway into the northeast. Through its length, NH 31 traverses the flat plains of Bihar up towards the mountain passes in Sikkim, skirting past the Bangladesh border on one side and the Indo-China border on the other. I hopped onto Sanjay's truck at Siliguri—a small town, almost 600 kilometres north of Calcutta, that serves as a four-way transit for trucks moving east–west from eastern Bengal to north and central India, and those moving north–south along the Nepal–Bangladesh axis. The traffic is tremendous, and Siliguri feels more of a truck depot than a town, but the locals assure me that it is a wonderful place to live, with a laidback pace of life and balmy 25°C weather year round.

I am hitching a ride with Sanjay and Kamlesh as they travel from Siliguri to Delhi. I plan to get off near Patna, a journey of about 450 kilometres that will take us nearly 20 hours. Having been told that unsafe sexual interaction between truck drivers and sex workers is one of the main routes of HIV transmission, I have asked Sanjay to serve as my able guide through the labyrinthine network of truck drivers, sex workers, pimps and roadside eatery owners—a role that he has kindly assented to take on.

Our vehicle is a triple axle truck carrying 25 tonnes of candle wax that has been securely loaded, tied down and tarpaulined along the length of the truck. In the front, all four of us have squeezed into the six feet by four feet by five feet cab—a space we shall share with the truck's 6000 cc engine, which sits in the middle with thermally insulated casing; a bench and shelf arrangement at the back that serves as a bunk bed for the drivers; a tiny cooking stove, assorted clothes, a tiny statue of Lord Shiva with a red light bulb suspended over it, and a strangely shaped sack which, when dropped, makes a metallic clang that suggests cooking utensils. A mild fragrance of boiled cabbage hangs about the air; I suspect it emanates from one of the three pairs of worn out shoes jammed under the driver's seat.

I check the time as we cram into the back bench, and Sanjay and Kamlesh sit in the driver's and passenger's seats. 8 pm: only 20 more hours to go. I smile at Sanjay and take out my audio recorder and notebook. I don't really need both, but I have found that far from inhibiting a person, the notebook actually encourages conversation. By the end of the journey my notebook will be covered, margin to margin, with doodles of cubes balanced in precarious stacks, as Sanjay has the tendency to clam up the moment he feels I have stopped writing.

He tells me about his first (and he claims only) encounter with a sex worker.

'I must have been seventeen, eighteen. Had just started working in the truck business. I was even younger than Kamlesh here. Not a wisp of hair on my face. I was working as a second driver with a senior ustaad.'

Back then, Sanjay explained, first drivers called themselves ustaads. Certain working class professions require a fair degree of craft, and the people who take them up are thus regarded as craftsmen or karigars. Anyone aspiring to be a karigar must first find themselves an ustaad: i.e. a karigar who is good enough to pass on his craft to the next generation. However, only certain trades, like those of carpenters, cooks, butchers and tailors, follow this hierarchy; the assumption being that such trades require a skill that can only be learnt through prolonged apprenticeship. Other trades like manual work, rickshaw pulling, the carrying of loads, are assumed to require strength, not skill. Hence the karigar professions command higher prices, as they charge a premium for their expertise—which cannot be replaced easily.

Truck driving has occupied a fluid position in this order of professions. When Sanjay began driving in the early nineties, many truck fleets still used updated versions of the Tata 1210 semi-forward—perhaps the most distinctive truck on Indian roads—which drivers tell me required a great amount of practice to master. Power steering, now a standard accessory in the smallest of passenger cars, came to trucks only in 2000. Brakes in the old trucks were based on hydraulic pump action, which slowed down the braking time and lengthened distances. The double clutch gearshift required considerable skill to change gears, and the lack of power steering made manoeuvring a risky and imprecise business. Truck owners often opted for making the driver's cabin cheaply, from a local manufacturer, which could be dangerous in the event of an accident. Driving these unwieldy vehicles required skill. Thus, truck drivers were classified as karigars, and the profession upheld a similar tradition; where a newcomer first worked as the understudy of an ustaad, and took to the wheel only after a few years of apprenticeship.

Most trucking crews consisted of an ustaad, or primary driver, who took responsibility for the truck and consignment and piloted his craft through the trickier stretches of the highway; a second driver, who functioned as an understudy and rode out the long hours of the night; and a khallasi, or helper, who served as a liaison between the mothership and the alien lands she encountered. On board, the ustaad actually did the least work, sleeping through most of the ride, and waking only to deal with policemen, checkposts and densely populated stretches of city. He was, however, responsible for any pilferage and delays in shipping, and for this he was rewarded with three things: a fixed salary of about Rs 3500 ($88) per month, an expense account, and the pleasure of lording over his second driver and helper.

The second driver was paid a flat sum per trip of about Rs 1000 ($25) for a two week round trip, and was expected to handle the truck while the ustaad stretched out in the back of the cab; his only distraction was the luxury of ordering around the helper or khallasi. Usually the youngest member of the crew, the khallasi was tolerated only so long as he never made the mistake of appearing unoccupied. An understudy of the second driver, he had no fixed salary, surviving solely on the good humour of his ustaad and second. He washed, cleaned and maintained the truck; changed tyres, cooked food on tiny gas burners, and jumped out at checkposts to hand over bribes and documents. At short stops he scurried out in search of alcohol for the drivers, and occasionally found himself the object of his ustaad's sexual desire; a suggestion that Sanjay hedges with a non-committal, 'Maybe, maybe not.'

Today, the intense competition in the trucking business has severely compromised the transporters' margins. A World Bank report[1] suggests that despite the inefficiencies that arise from poor road infrastructure, and smaller and less powerful

---

[1] 'India's Transport Sector', Vol 1 and 2—World Bank, 2002.

vehicles, India's surface transport sector has among the lowest average costs per tonne kilometre—between $0.019 and $0.027—in the world, as compared to, say, China, which has costs of between $0.04 and $0.06 per tonne kilometre. This means that trucking business costs in India are among the lowest in the world. The industry is also largely informal in nature, with no powerful unions, standardised work hours or working conditions.

Sanjay explained to me that the dropping margins have meant that most crews have been pared down to two members, with the second driver absorbing most of the duties of the khallasi. The improvement in road conditions and truck technology has demystified driving, making it a far easier skill to master. The new trucks, like the 2516 that we are travelling in, have company made cabins, power assisted steering, improved brakes, and synchromesh gearboxes which make gearshifts far easier. The ustaad is no more a skilled navigator of troubled waters; he has been demoted to the position of 'first driver'—first among equals perhaps, but a driver nonetheless. Better trucks have also reduced the need for a prolonged apprenticeship to learn driving. Driving is now viewed as a profession that no longer requires the skill that was expected of a first class ustaad.

That fateful day in 1993, Sanjay and his ustaad were driving, without a khallasi, along NH 87 from Haldwani, Uttar Pradesh, down towards Delhi, when they decided to stop at Rampur for the night.

'Maybe I imagine it now, but when he stopped the truck near the railway crossing, I thought I saw a glint in his eyes. He smiled, handed me a hundred rupee note [$2.50], and sent me off to the wine shop. I bought him some countrymade liquor—deshi, we call it—and he pulled out two steel glasses and handed me one.'

At this point, I sat up a little straighter and pushed my recorder closer to Sanjay. He continued weaving expertly through the congested stretches along the highway. Truck drivers 'who consume alcohol are 2.71 times more likely to visit a commercial sex worker than those who do not', says a study[2] I looked at before embarking on this trip. Clearly, I was on the threshold of a high risk behaviour case study.

'So then?' I ask.

'So then what? I looked at him and said "Ustaadji, I ate solid food for the first time when I was thirteen years old. Till then I had grown up on just two things—my mother's milk, and ghee from our very own buffalo. I had milk five times a day. No one in my family had ever as much as touched a drop of alcohol. My father didn't even smoke!"'

'You had mother's milk till you were thirteen?'

'Well maybe not thirteen, but you get the picture. For some reason, the motherfucker ustaad was in no mood to listen that night. "You drink this glass," he said, "Or I'll never let you touch the steering wheel again." Now, I was just a poor second. I had dreams of becoming an ustaad very soon. If he didn't teach me, I was fucked. So I pleaded once more, and when he refused to yield, I put it to my lips and knocked it back in one shot!'

'The whole glass?'

'The whole glass. It went down like molten metal, burning everything on its way until it hit the bottom of my stomach with a dull thud. I sat still for a moment, and then it seemed like the truck had tripped over and fallen on its side. I lay there for maybe half an hour, puking every two minutes. My ustaad threw me back into the truck, and I vomited all the way to Meerut.

'At Meerut, he realised that he still had some money left over from his expenses, and the horny old goat decided to pick up a whore on the way. I was just happy that the truck had stopped moving, and I jumped out and lay by the roadside—puking quietly to myself, minding my own business,

---

[2] 'Sexual Behaviour Among Long Distance Truck Drivers', S Chaturvedi, Z Singh, A Banerjee, A Khera, RK Joshi, D Dhrubajyoti, *Indian Journal of Community Medicine*, Vol 31, No 3, July–September 2006.

not saying anything to anybody, while he had loud noisy sex in the truck cab; and then he said "Chottu, you ever fucked a whore before?" And I said "No Ustaadji, but I don't want to." But he refused to listen.'

'So he forced you to do it?'

'Well he gave me a choice. The whore or another glass full of deshi. I considered it briefly, but the thought of throwing up for another 12 hours was too much to bear. I mouthed a quiet prayer and jumped onto her.'

'So how was it?'

'Awful, and what's worse is that she had an upset stomach and was running a high fever. I was scared, she was ill, my ustaad was drunk. It was terrible.'

'So did you use a condom?'

'No; and sure enough I fell ill a day later. High fever, diarrhoea, headache, the works. By the time I got home to Ghaziabad, I could barely walk. En route, we stopped at Dr Tomar's clinic on Maula Road in Meerut; my ustaad was finally feeling some remorse—especially since he was completely unaffected—and I was convinced that I had AIDS. I got two injections, Rs. 70 [$1.75] each.'

'What for?'

'I think it was just a general tonic. But I was ill for almost six months. I got myself tested for HIV twice in that time, and both times the tests came back negative. I even paid Rs 350 [$8.75] for the tests each time—but the tests said I was fine.'

'So what was it?'

'It took some time, but they figured it out. I had a severe stomach infection. My doctor said it was from the liquor. Strangely, even after finding out the reasons for my illness, I never went back to a whore again—but I started drinking a whole lot more.'

Statistics belie Sanjay's story. A study[3] published in 2004 on HIV infection among transport workers along the

[3] 'HIV Infection Among Transport Workers Operating Through Siliguri-Guwahati National Highway', India, Baishali Bal, Syed Iftikar Ahmed et al. J Int Assoc Physicians AIDS Care (Chic Ill) 2007; 6; 56, DOI: 10.

Siliguri–Guwahati stretch of NH 31 suggests that 67% of participants interviewed said they visited sex workers, of which a little over half (58%) said they used condoms. In a concentrated HIV epidemic, such as the case is in India, HIV/AIDS tends to be largely prevalent among 'high-risk groups'; ie population groups that statistically show greater prevalence of HIV/AIDS than the rest of the population. The reasons for higher prevalence could be due to the nature of their profession—as in the case of commercial sex workers—or due to certain practices that could prove risky, such as sharing needles among drug users. Truck drivers are considered to be bridge populations that serve as a conduit between high-risk groups like sex workers and the general population. The most commonly understood pathway for the virus being that of the truck driver acquiring the virus from a sex worker at one stop along the highway, and passing it on to other sex workers and his wife back home. A recent study suggests that 3–7% of truck drivers in India have HIV/ AIDS[4], as compared to the national average of 0.43% among adult males, and yet HIV prevalence was highest among women whose spouses were employed in the transport industry[5].

It is now 10:30 at night; we have been on the road for two and a half hours—with one quick stop, where Sanjay pulled over at one of the small bazaars just outside Siliguri to try on a pair of track pants, and look for something for his son. 'He's twelve now, hating every minute of school, but I've told him he has to finish.' Sanjay's elder brother works as a minor clerk in a government office in Ghaziabad; Sanjay was supposed to join the police. 'I didn't want to sit for the exams,' he grins. 'But my son will have to do something with his life.' Given Siliguri's proximity to Darjeeling—a scenic hill station

---

[4] Integrated Behavioural and Biological Assessment (2005-07), Indian Council of Medical Research.
[5] National Institute of Health and Family Welfare (NIHFW), National AIDS Control Organisation (NACO), India Annual HIV Sentinel Surveillance Country Report, 2006.

inundated with Bengali tourists—Sanjay's son often asks his father if he can ride with him from Ghaziabad to Siliguri, and then press on to Darjeeling for a family holiday. 'But I say no! Trucking is a very risky business. What if we have an accident?'

Our present stop is at a roadside dhaba, or diner, about two hours from the Bengal–Bihar border. The mist, which had made a brief appearance earlier in the evening, has congealed into a thick fog that makes the tiny, well-lit shack appear far more inviting than it is. A group of truck drivers and their helpers sprawl on a series of chairs and low couches arranged around a TV set showing *Bhagam Bhag*—a 'suspense comedy' starring Govinda, Akshay Kumar, and Paresh Rawal. A young boy scurries around taking orders, serving hot rotis and putting the volume up or down as per the wishes of each table. 'Watch TV. That's all everyone tells us to do,' remarks Sanjay. 'We're sitting at the transporter's office, waiting for a shipment, what to do? Watch TV. I'm at home, my wife is busy bustling about the house, my son is at school. There is only so much I can sleep. So I watch TV. I stop by the roadside for dinner, I travel with Kamlesh for two weeks of every month—so I'm sick of talking to him; I watch TV. Trucks and TV; TV and trucks.'

The TV is a welcome distraction from the road. I take a seat, and am transfixed by the antics on screen. A boy comes and places a beer by my side. Sanjay and Kamlesh face each other on the same couch, a huge plate placed between them. Dal, two types of vegetables and a large slab of butter are mixed together into a wholesome gruel, which they spoon into their mouths with hot rotis. Sanjay asks for a Sprite with Shot 70, a colourless liquor sold in clear plastic bags; Kamlesh has a cup of hot tea. We smoke a few cigarettes and watch some more TV. I am happy sitting here, watching TV, smoking the odd cigarette and exchanging desultory notes about Bollywood. It's a little nippy, but we're out in the open—a relief after the truck's claustrophobic cabin. We laze around for as long as we can. On his way out, Sanjay quickly knocks back another Shot 70, clambers into the cabin, stretches out in the back seat, pulls a blanket over his head, and promptly falls asleep. Kamlesh smiles genially, lights his nth beedi, and starts up the truck. It is time for the second driver to take over.

The fog hasn't lifted yet, so Kamlesh restricts himself to third gear, rarely crossing 35 kilometres per hour. I sit on the edge of the bench, nodding off to sleep. Two hours later, we are at Dhalkola—the final checkpoint before we cross into Purnia, the eastern most district of the state of Bihar.

I jolt out of my nap when I hear the sudden noise of some-one loudly rapping on the truck door. It's the police, I sup-pose, and nothing more. I try to move my head, but stop as I nearly impale my eye on the indicator lever. I am stretched out with my head on the driver's seat, my lower back on the engine casing, and my feet on the window ledge of the pas-senger side. Near my hip, the gear stick presses against my side, uncomfortably close to my groin. It's 3 in the morning. I am not happy; I do not like gear sticks uncomfortably close to my groin.

An hour ago, Kamlesh pulled over to the side of the road and climbed into the tiny shelf above the bench at the back of the cabin and curled up into a foetal ball. 'Why have we stopped?' I asked before he passed out.

'Checkpoint,' he replied.

'So why don't we cross it?'

'It is not yet time,' he replied cryptically, and pulled the blanket over his head to pre-empt any further questions.

Behind me Sanjay snores on, cocooned in his blanket. The knocking is getting louder. Someone is shouting, 'Sanjay, Sanjay, the border is clear. It's time, let's go.'

I sit up and peer out of the window; the fog has lifted. I notice we aren't very far from Panjipara, once a favoured stop for sex work on NH 31. But, when I had visited two days ago, the once busy village stood silent, enveloped in the slightly tragic aura of a poorly attended farewell party. Sex workers sat playing with their children, pimps lazed around on the steps of roadside eateries.

'Sex work tends to be available in stretches,' said Pinkie, a sex worker who has worked out of Panjipara for more than fifteen years. 'Earlier it was the Panjipara–Harda area, but now it seems to have shifted towards Islampur, on the Siliguri (Bengal) side, Gulab Bagh in the Purnia (Bihar) side, and up beyond Tamkoi and Gorakhpur in the Uttar Pradesh area.' While the routes remain the same, many factors can affect business in an area. In Panjipara for instance, the police are proving to be a real threat. 'We are raided practically every day,' rued Pinkie, 'and that too at any hour of the day and night.' It wasn't the frequency of the raids that unsettled the sex workers, as much as the absence of any pattern in their execution. 'We have had cases of policemen arresting clients in the midst of sex with one of the girls; why would anyone come here again?

The newly broadened stretch of highway adjoining the village seems to be another reason for dipping business. Traversing India's highways is often a staccato of inching painfully along single lane streets, followed by bursts of speed along newly broadened highways. Life springs up around bottlenecks and border crossings to provide sex and sustenance to the serpentine queues of trucks waiting to get their papers cleared. Drivers tend to plan their stops around the quality of roads and checkpoints they expect to encounter; heavily loaded trucks tend to take time to pick up speed, so few stop along broad, well surfaced roads, breaking for meals only at points where they are required to stop anyway.

Long waits at checkpoints are in fact one of the biggest reasons for consignment delays, costing the economy between Rs 9 and Rs 23 billion ($225,000–575,000) a year in lost truck operating hours.[6] *The Economist* quoted Vineet Agarwal of the Transport Corporation of India as saying that the 2150 km

---

[6] 'Road Transport Efficiency Study 2005', World Bank, India.

journey from Calcutta to Mumbai took almost eight days, at an average speed of 11 kilometres per hour, with 32 hours spent waiting at checkpoints on the way. Naturally, establishments catering to truckers, like dhabas, garages and brothels, sprout up in places where trucks are expected to stop. Until recently, Panjipara stood perfectly placed between Siliguri and the border checkpoint near Harda. Truck clearance on the Bengal border is rather slow, as the state government has a special tax for multi-axle trucks, which increases processing time. Now, with the broad four-lane expressway coming to the village, Panjipara has become a bit of a dead zone.

If business continues the way it has, Pinkie believes that the sex workers of Panjipara might have to leave the relative security of their brothels, and take to the streets to service clients en route from one halt point to another. Sex work takes many forms along transport routes. Truckers say that while sex work in Bengal is largely confined to brothels, it is far more street-based in other states. Sex workers and their clients have two basic concerns—where to find each other, and where to go together. Brothel based sex addresses both concerns, as clients know where to find sex workers, and the establishment offers rooms for sexual intercourse.

For truckers in particular, the network often operates out of roadside dhabas, where the dhaba owner functions as an intermediary between the drivers and sex workers. Some dhaba owners even have small rooms built adjacent to the dining area where truck drivers can enjoy a degree of privacy. Over a period of time, certain dhabas along the route are identified as establishments where sex is easily available. Along our route for example, Sanjay pointed out a few 'hotels' in Islampur, a halt point just out of Siliguri, where the dhaba owners and sex workers have reached an agreement which allows sex workers to solicit and service clients on the premises in exchange for a percentage (usually between 20 and 30%) of their earnings.

At large trucking yards—often called transport colonies, such as the one on the Delhi–Ghaziabad border, local pimps divide up the areas amongst themselves and bring in sex workers to work their territories. Pimps usually take 30% of all earnings, some of which is paid to the local police station as protection money. Encounters often take place in trucks, under trucks, and in the narrow alleyways between trucks.

Out on the highway, sex workers are often picked up along the roadside. 'It usually happens around dusk and through the night,' said one driver. 'You see a pimp flashing a torch on the side of the road.' The sex worker then either gets into the truck and travels along for a few kilometres, or asks the driver to leave his truck and accompany her to a secluded spot away from the highway. However, this is a much riskier form of business for both. Sex workers say they find it harder to negotiate fair rates and condom use in such situations; at times, the consequences for drivers are equally drastic.

In February 2008, a twenty seven year old truck driver was driving through Gujarat when he saw a torch flashing on the side of the road. He pulled over, thinking it was a sex worker. Instead he was beaten to death by a gang of men who then proceeded to break into his truck and attack his helper. The transport industry has grown to accept attacks on their convoys as a part of doing business in Uttar Pradesh and Bihar; however, drivers point out that attacks on truck drivers are increasing in frequency and brutality. 'Earlier, gangs would simply rough us up and leave us by the roadside,' says Sanjay. 'But now you hear of a lot more cases where drivers and helpers have been killed for no apparent reason.' Figures are hard to obtain regarding these incidents, as most of the crimes go unreported.

'You must realise that the trucking business is built solely on reputations,' says MR Walia of the Rajkamal Transport Company. 'Which is why most transporters prefer not to publicise the theft or loss of their consignments.' Walia himself became a victim of highway robbery when his Uttar

Pradesh bound truck, carrying Rs 8 lakhs ($20,000) worth of pharmaceuticals, disappeared in January 2005; neither the driver nor helper were ever seen again. No one I spoke with could provide a convincing reason for the increase in attacks, but some pointed to the general breakdown in law and order in the UP–Bihar belt; an issue that formed a central plank in Mayawati's successful run for chief minister of Uttar Pradesh. This dispersed fear of violence is the reason why Sanjay, Kamlesh and I have spent the last few hours arranged nose to toes in the truck cabin, instead of sleeping outdoors under the stars.

The knocking and shouting outside the truck has grown too loud for even Sanjay to sleep through. It seems the convoy has assembled. Sanjay jumps into the driver's seat and starts up the engine. Lights turned low, engines tuned down to an ill-tempered grumble, chasses emblazoned with cryptic incantations to ward off the evil eye, five tarpaulin-cloaked trucks creep noiselessly along the unlit highway towards the border checkpost, our truck in the lead. Suddenly, Sanjay flicks on the high beam, floors the accelerator and charges straight at the barricades in our path. Time slows for a terrifying instant as policemen skip out of the way, Sanjay's feet glance off the pedals as the truck skids through the barricades, and powers down the highway. The rest of the convoy follows suit, the last truck tipping over the barricades as it bursts through. Now cruising safely along in Bihar, Sanjay turns to me with a wry smile. 'You see, Amanji, trucker's life is full of risk.'

'But what did you jump that checkpost for?'

'Motherfucker wanted a bribe.'

'How do you know?'

'I just know,' he maintains obstinately.

While riding with Sanjay, every border crossing, checkpost and barricade seems to transform from an innocuous display of bureaucratic red tape into a nest of predatory policemen. If drivers and transporters are to be believed, every district in the country levies its own informal transit fee. According to sources in the industry, the entry rate for Uttar Pradesh currently stands at Rs 10,500 ($260) per truck per month, while checkposts in Bihar charge between Rs 1500 and 2000 ($38–50, approximately $45) per entry for each district. In fact, a report[7] on surface transport efficiency in India values 'facilitation payments' made at checkpoints at between Rs 9 and Rs 72 billion per year ($225,000–$1,800,000). The payments are usually made to circumvent the hundreds of regulations set down by the Indian Motor Vehicles Act of 1988 and the Central Motor Vehicles Rules of 1989, as well as their amendments and notifications. The primary reason, though, for these payouts is that most trucks exceed their load limits. According to the rules, two axle trucks are allowed to carry a maximum of 9 tonnes (including the weight of the truck) while three axle trucks are allowed to carry 25 tonnes. However, most three tonne trucks carry up to 40 tonnes of cargo—making them prime targets for the police force. Overloading is so rampant a problem that some states like Uttar Pradesh attempted to tap into the vast amounts of bribes paid to highway policemen by introducing an amnesty scheme called the 'Gold Card', which allowed cardholders to load above the allowed weight limit on payment of a penalty amount to the state government. In effect, the Gold Card reflected an acceptance that transporters were going to overload their trucks anyway, so the state government might as well earn revenues by allowing transporters to legally break the law. The Gold Card was finally shot down by the Supreme Court in 2005, on the grounds that it was patently illegal.

All drivers are given a lump sum of between Rs 8–10,000 ($200–250) for bribes and expenses to cover the cost of food, repairs, and alcohol. But since drivers' salaries are so minimal—Sanjay makes only Rs 3500 ($88) per month—most prefer to jump checkpoints and pocket the money rather than hand it over to the police. Transporters know that drivers

---

[7] Ibid.

jump checkpoints, and so refuse to raise their salaries on the grounds that drivers skim enough off the expenses. With salaries frozen at subsistence levels, drivers have no option but to jump checkpoints; the police have no option but to fleece whoever they can stop.

This morning, Sanjay is loath to talk about sex or HIV. Early morning, a time for introspection and prayer, is an inappropriate moment to speak of such matters. This morning, Sanjay feels I should consider the other problems that inform a truck driver's life. Chief among them: the risk of accidents—trucks are involved in half of all roadside accidents in India.[8] With an accident comes the risk of being beaten to death by an irate crowd gathered at the accident site. But hovering over the more tangible dangers of a truckers' life is a bigger issue: a constant and continuous exposure to harassment that leads to the overall lack of izzat, or respect, in a truck driver's life. I sense that the absence of respectability in the driving profession is something that he too has difficulty in addressing. Why are truck drivers stigmatised? And is this something that has changed over the past few decades, since the days of the ustaad?

'Well most of these young drivers are to blame, high on something or the other, playing their loud disco music; of course they are going to have accidents.' Sanjay does not play music in his cabin; he doesn't even have a radio—a lifestyle choice he is rather proud of. Like so many other professions, driving too seems to be going through a phase where the old guard blames the young guns for bringing disrepute to the profession. 'Back in the day, no one had the nerve to say anything to us. My ustaad once slapped the entire staff of a dhaba when they refused to light a stick of incense when he sat down to eat. These days? No one has the nerve to say anything to anyone.'

'Why do you think that is?'

---

[8] 'Overloaded Trucks are Death On Wheels', Cooshalle Samuel, *Hindustan Times*, November 26 2007.

'Everything seems to have dissipated. Some do drugs, some blow up their money on whores, some—like me—are a few steps from becoming full blown alcoholics.' He thinks for a moment, and then says something that reflects a confusion that arises when attempting to understand, in one shot, an issue that can only be comprehended piecemeal. 'I suppose it is modern life,' he says. 'Earlier people lived to be a hundred, today no one crosses seventy.' As a statement, it is easily disproved by those who know statistics on life expectancy; people today live longer than they ever did. But as an experience, it is hard to contradict.

Is it just 'modern life'? When finding answers to such complex questions in a country infested with faux holy men, one must turn to the sole oracle of truth—Bollywood.

In the superhit film *Gadar: Ek Prem Katha* (Gadar: A Love Story), Tara Singh the truck driver, played by trucker demi-god Sunny Deol, is asked a poignant question by Partition refugee Sakina, played by Amisha Patel. 'Tara Singhji,' she asks as she expertly ties his turban, 'why don't you get married?' To this, Tara Singh shakes his turbaned head, and gives her an answer that made practically every truck driver in India nod his head approvingly and say 'Wah!'

'Madamji,' says Tara Singh, 'I live in Khana Buddur; today my truck is parked here, but tomorrow I might be in Delhi. After all why would anyone want to marry a truck driver?'

Though the movie is set in 1947, Tara Singh's question touches upon an issue that is relevant even today. Truck drivers aren't particularly discriminated against when it come to marriage partners[9]; but some of the younger drivers I spoke

---

[9] A study among transport workers on the Siliguri–Guwahati Highway found that 61% of transport workers in their sample group were married. 'HIV Infection Among Transport, Workers Operating Through Siliguri–Guwahati National Highway, India.' Bal et al. J Int Assoc Physicians AIDS Care (Chic Ill).2007; 6: 56–60.

Data from the National Family Health Survey-3 (produced in 2006 by the Ministry of Health and Family Welfare) suggests that 62.4% of all respondents to the survey were currently married.

with said that finding matches was becoming harder and harder.

I watched *Gadar* on the recommendation of Sanjay and some of his friends. Played out against the backdrop of the Partition riots in 1947 in the border states of India and Pakistan, *Gadar* tells the tale of how a heroic Jat-Sikh truck driver rescues a wealthy Muslim girl from a rampaging mob; wins her trust, marries her, rescues her once more—this time from her rampaging father—and finally settles down, in a happy ending. While several films have had their heroes careen up and down highways in trucks, the heroes are rarely truck drivers; the truck just happens to be the closest vehicle at hand to make good their escape, rescue their lovers, or run over their enemies. *Gadar* is perhaps the only mainstream hit in which the protagonist is a truck driver who proves to be a good husband, father, patriot, and all round nice guy.

Unfortunately, *Gadar* too starts with Tara Singh accepting that fate has dealt him a poor hand by making him a truck driver. He obligingly sings and dances and plays the part of the happy trucker, but he understands the distance between him and the object of his desire. As he says, 'Even if I wanted to, I can't touch the moon, can I?' The rest of the plot is a story of redemption—of proving that truck drivers are honourable, powerful, and patriotic.

Why does truck driving lack izzat? Why are truckers victims of negative stereotypes? Is it class? Is it their association with a high-risk behaviour group? Does, in fact, being categorised as a high-risk group stigmatise them even further? From *Gadar* to their portrayal in the Indian press, truckers are regarded as rough and ready and reckless, dirty and dissolute. Prone to drink, driving accidents—and now disease.

Izzat can mean different things to different people. Perhaps the truck drivers' values were extravagance, arrogance, and excess. A code of honour steeped in a machismo of drinking, driving, whoring and smoking was probably as good an indicator of their lives as an izzat of chastity and virtue is of middle class lives. The very qualities for which a driver today is stigmatised, were in fact the ideals he would have aspired to in the past. But this code is no longer relevant, indeed it is an anathema today. The end of the ustaad era signalled more than a structural change in the trucking industry; maybe it signalled a shift in the way that truck drivers viewed themselves.

Sanjay could be a confused man primarily because the death of ustaad izzat has left a vacuum in the lives of truckers. As appealing as their uninhibited excesses may be, the era of the ustaads offers few lessons on engaging with 'modern life', and all its accoutrements of price inflation, sexually transmitted diseases and road accidents. It is entirely possible that in time, another honour code shall evolve in response to the challenges truck drivers face today, but for now it is up to Sanjay and his contemporaries to muddle their way through what promises to be a turbulent future.

We pull into Harda for breakfast at 6 in the morning. Barauni—the point at which Sanjay and I part ways—is only another 200 kilometres away, but is expected to take all day. The convoy of four trucks pulls in behind us. Everyone except Kamlesh piles out; he is still sleeping on his tiny shelf. Dispensing with his morning tea and other pleasantries, Sanjay pours himself another round of Shot 70 with Sprite, and promptly falls asleep on a hay mattress laid out on the floor. 'We shall resume at 8:30 and drive nonstop,' he proclaims as he closes his eyes. I walk around the highway—stretching my limbs, gently massaging my back. Towards the east, dawn is breaking. After the constant noise of the engine, the surroundings are almost unsettlingly quiet. En route we stopped at a collection booth for a toll bridge.

Sanjay straightened his collar and flattened his salt-and-pepper hair. 'Ex-serviceman,' he declared, glaring at the tiny man in the toll booth. 'I served the country for more than 15 years.'

'What service?'

'Army.'

'ID card?'

'ID card? You think I spent my time in Kashmir only to be questioned by a maderchod motherfucker like you? Would you like to see my bio data?'

'In that case it will be Rs 200 [$5]!'

'You see, you see? I hope you are noting all this corruption,' said Sanjay, noticing I had stopped scribbling on my notepad. 'The fuckers don't even spare the army!'

'But you're not from the army,' I protested.

'That isn't the point. The point is that I could well have been.'

LOVE IN THE TIME OF POSITIVES
Nalini Jones

'…he was overwhelmed by the belated suspicion that it is life, more than death, that has no limits.'

Gabriel García Márquez, *Love in the Time of Cholera*

On the day I arrived in Bangalore, I was ushered into a small, uncluttered office. The women seated around the table looked up expectantly. They were poor but made enough to live in small houses—a room or two, perhaps—and to put something aside to educate their children. Some had been to school themselves, through the 9th or 10th standard. Some had been trained for a trade; others, at home, for marriage and motherhood. Most were young, in their twenties or thirties, although one, with a few strands of silver in her coarse dark hair, was nearing forty. She greeted me in English; the others smiled and nodded.

I sit beside such women on the hard wooden benches of commuter trains. We sway into each other's shoulders in the 'ladies only' car, brushing away the children selling packets of hair elastics, batteries, sweets. I pass women like these outside temples or near school gates at dismissal time, waiting for their children to appear. If you are in India, you have seen them too, in streets and parks, waiting in bus shelters, haggling with cobblers over new soles for their slippers, strolling along promenades in the corn-silk evenings, perhaps with a few other women, perhaps with a young man.

On this day, only one man joined them. He was tall with a thin chest; his button-down shirt hung from the points of his shoulders. He sat with his hands folded in the manner of a student about to be examined, though I guessed he was in his late thirties. His wife had accompanied him, a woman with a small chin and firm round cheeks who did not appear likely to speak.

I had come to Bangalore to learn about the stigma faced by wives and husbands, daughters and sons, who discover they are HIV positive. I met with housewives primarily, women whom epidemiologists consider outside the high-risk behaviour groups, women to whom AIDS seemed so distant, so impossible, that many found it difficult to believe their own diagnoses. In every case, the virus had been passed to them by their husbands; in almost every case, they learned their status during pregnancy. I also spoke to Basavaraj, the man who had brought his wife for support, who was diagnosed when he was a bachelor.

Most Indians with HIV face far more than the threat of disease. In villages and cities, kitchens and bedrooms, they live in the grip of a stigma so powerful that families frequently reject their own. Children are sometimes barred from attending school. Healthy people are subjected to a kind of cultural quarantine, as if AIDS might be transmitted by touch. Far too often, people who are HIV positive are treated as little more than walking infection.

This is the way the people I met once viewed themselves: as time bombs, ticking down to a death. Basavaraj didn't think he was going to last very long when he was first diagnosed; he quit his job in a provisions store and waited for the disease to overtake him. A widow described her husband's response when his blood test came back positive—'he had imagination that HIV is death,' she said. This misconception was strengthened considerably when his doctor gave him three months to live, even though he had no symptoms. He too quit his job in a fit of despair; a suicide attempt was unsuccessful but alerted his family to his status, and they began to avoid the couple and their children. 'We thought a doctor's words are very much correct, like a god's words, but my husband survived three years, not three months.' I wonder how long he might have lasted without the blow of a death sentence.

I was soon awash in their tales. An hour later, the room seemed crowded with frightened young wives, tight-lipped in-laws, curt doctors, despairing husbands, resolute widows. I looked up and saw that Basavaraj was watching me. His moustache drooped just enough to make him seem tired, and his expression, grave and patient, never wavered. His wife Jayanthi, several years younger, turned to him occasionally, and he acknowledged her gently, moving his head from side to side in reassurance, sometimes speaking to her in a hushed voice. She smiled when I met her eyes but had not said a word all afternoon.

I was eager to hear something different, something happy. 'How did you meet?' I asked the couple, and in an instant all the women around the table were transformed, laughing like sisters, ready to chat. Jayanthi put a hand to her cheek, sweetly bewildered by this new course, and at last Basavaraj smiled.

The man I met, Basavaraj, began his life in a hospital corridor. Three or four years after his HIV diagnosis, he sought treatment in a government hospital in Belgaum for ongoing skin infections. At the time, he had not revealed his HIV status to anyone in his life: his parents, his sisters, his friends. He was sent for blood tests, and when he went to retrieve the results, he recognised the person who was collecting receipts from all the patients—a relative who would surely expose his secret. He hesitated, shocked. His first instinct was to run away, but instead he kept his head down, avoided eye contact, hid his identity. He took the first name that came to mind, the name of his best friend from childhood. 'Since then I am Basavaraj,' he said.

We'd left the office, but a small group had decided to keep talking. Basavaraj and Jayanthi live several hours away in a village near Belgaum in the north of Karnataka; for them, a trip to Bangalore is a holiday. When I asked where they'd like to go, Jayanthi stood on tiptoe to whisper in her husband's ear. He conferred with her briefly; then suddenly, in English, 'Zoo!' But the zoo was closed, so we settled for a park at sunset. We strolled beneath towering stands of bamboo that fell into each other's arms, creating a high dark canopy overhead.

When people hear about HIV, Basavaraj explained, they think immediately of sex. He also used to assume that men who had AIDS must necessarily be of 'loose morals'. Now he feels differently.

Basavaraj's father is a heavy smoker whose habit led to debilitating illness. The whole family tried to persuade him to give up smoking, but his father refused. 'He has a difficult personality,' Basavaraj said quietly. His father continued to fall ill at great cost to the family, and finally Basavaraj tried to take a stand. He and his father fought, and Basavaraj decided he could no longer remain in the household. He went to stay in a lodge, an inexpensive hotel that also houses long-term guests. This was in 1995, when Basavaraj was twenty three years old.

He watched me, gauging my reaction. The lodge was frequented by sex workers, a ready-made supply for the guests. Basavaraj had been profoundly shaken by the rift with his family, and when the manager offered him a girl, he accepted.

'I was a boy,' he said. 'I didn't know many things.'

Clearly he considers this decision a departure. Usually Basavaraj is reticent, not prone to confrontation, so the fight with his father left him in a daze. It is easy to imagine this mild young man devastated by an argument, bewildered by the sudden estrangement from his family, uncertain what to do next. In a culture that relies upon family ties, a man who turns his back on his parents might feel dangerously unmoored from all the roles that contribute to his sense of self. Basavaraj felt he was falling, as if gravity itself had failed. He landed in a lodge; there, he did what people in lodges do.

The next day, as soon as he woke up, he began to think of his family. He is the only son, he has younger sisters, and he feels a strong sense of duty toward them all. He knew he had to reconcile with his father and returned home at once. The rift he felt so deeply lasted only one night.

To me this has the terrible lilt of a fairy tale—or the sibilant whisper of my teacher's silk blouse as she closed the text in a class called 'Family Life' and leaned forward to issue a veiled warning to hushed, bewildered Catholic girls: one night, just one night, is enough to ruin you. Perhaps Basavaraj was thinking along similar lines. He told us that sometimes he wonders: if he had not been so upset, would he have succumbed? He shrugged, a small, prevaricating gesture. This is how he knows when he contracted the virus. It was the only time he let himself go.

Even in one of Bangalore's celebrated green spaces, a gritty haze hung over the park. While we talked, light drained from the sky like dirty water. Jayanthi had answered a few questions about her life with Basavaraj, but her story emerged only after nightfall, as if she were waiting for darkness to screen her. When she had finished, she tried to laugh while dabbing away tears with the back of her hand. 'For so long I say nothing and then everything comes at once!'

Her family was poor. When she was seventeen, a more affluent family approached them, looking for a wife for their son. They agreed to provide the young couple with a large sum of money, but in exchange they insisted that the marriage take place at once. In arranged marriages among the upper class, the parties are usually given a chance to meet and agree before a match is settled, but Jayanthi did not have time to consider her groom before her parents had given their word. They were no doubt relieved that their daughter would be well provided for. Jayanthi consented because she felt their honour was at stake.

The groom's family arrived at her house at 6 in the evening, and by 1 in the morning Jayanthi was married. The rushed wedding was not so uncommon that it gave rise to alarm. He was older than she, and eager to find a wife, his parents said. Now she realises they must have known he was infected, but at the time no one in her family suspected any sort of subterfuge. AIDS would never have occurred to them.

Her husband was a tractor driver. Soon after she was married, Jayanthi heard stories about him, that he had 'bad habits'. The taboo against discussing sex is so powerful that Jayanthi seemed unlikely to elaborate, but with a sudden spark of energy she announced that he visited women. He was often sick and she cared for him, but she did not realise he had AIDS for a long time. She looked after him even when his family began to shun her. After he died, they sent her back to her own family; they would not keep her in their house.

I wondered if Jayanthi's return to her family had offered some relief, if she felt glad to be back with her own parents. She said she had been unhappy in her marriage. But the shame of being sent home overwhelmed her. In the village life that Jayanthi knows, to the women she meets at the temple or market, such rejection could only mean she had failed as a wife and daughter.

Jayanthi was composed when she described her disastrous marriage, matter-of-fact when she revealed the results of her blood test, steely when she explained that she had to resort to a formal claim with the local magistrate to compel her in-laws to pay the money they had promised her. But the humiliation of being an unwanted widow haunts her still—she stopped on the path and began to cry. Basavaraj put an arm around her shoulders; her friend Ashwini touched her arm; and even I moved closer to her, as if to staunch a wound.

But after a minute or two, she consoled herself. Leaning against her second husband, without even needing to look at him, she smiled. 'See, he knows everything that has happened. We know everything that has happened to the other.'

Later, when I asked if she is ever afraid, I expected to hear that she dreads the onset of symptoms or the death of her new husband. After all, Basavaraj admitted to fear; he does not want to leave his aging parents destitute or his wife alone. But Jayanthi threw back her head and said she has no more reason to be afraid than I do. A bus might hit me tomorrow; am I afraid today? It is her past, not her future, that distresses Jayanthi. And if her most troubling burden is the stigma she faces, then she has found her greatest comfort in witness: in the husband who knows her history and has given her his own.

Basavaraj has escaped death three times, in a series of rescues perfectly suited to an Indian hero: once by chance, once by a film, and once by love. As a young man, living with his parents and sisters in a village near the city of Belgaum, he kept a provisions store and was earning well. Two years after his night in the lodge he realised he had herpes and sought treatment, but it was not until several months afterwards, when he was admitted to the hospital in Belgaum with severe chest pains, that his blood was tested. He found out he was HIV positive in 1997.

Indians do not associate AIDS with blood transfers or drug use, Basavaraj pointed out; to most people, it simply means sex. And not just any sex—sex with girls for hire, sex that is not mentionable, sex that gives even a good son a bad reputation, sex that is deadly. The disease functions as a scarlet letter. And so, overcome by shame and convinced he soon would die, Basavaraj kept his diagnosis secret. He abandoned the grocery and fell into a depression so severe that he was unable to find other work. He slept and ate in his parents' house but spent his days roaming in the parks, avoiding their questions. His despair lasted for years.

During this period, he thought frequently of suicide. One night he took a bottle of sleeping pills, washed it down with alcohol, and lay across the train tracks near his village. The next day he woke up a little distance from the rails with no memory of what happened. Someone must have dragged him to safety.

For a few years, Basavaraj surprised himself by remaining in good health. Then, slowly, skin infections began to set in. He visited local medical centres sporadically but ignored advice to seek regular treatment until 2006, when the lesions were so bad that he finally contacted an AIDS network in Belgaum. He began attending support group meetings where, for the first time, he openly shared his status—nine years after he learned he was HIV positive.

By then he was in poor health. His doctor insisted that he start antiretroviral (ARV) treatment right away, but this required a journey to the Karnataka Health Institute and several days' accommodation. Basavaraj had been out of work for years and his savings had drained away. His only remaining possession was a gas cylinder for cooking, which he sold for Rs 1000 ($25) to finance his trip. Once he reached the Institute, he learned he might be denied admittance because he needed a witness from home to vouch for him before he would be eligible for free treatment. He quickly enlisted another man in the waiting room to pose as his relative. After three days of tests, he began ARV treatment. But he was dispirited to learn that his CD4 counts were low, an indication of a weakened immune system. He began once again to think of suicide.

The second time, he left nothing to chance. He stockpiled sleeping pills, hypertension pills, whatever he could find. Then he bought several bottles of alcohol and kept his stash ready. On the day he planned to die, he decided to spend his last afternoon at the movies.

Basavaraj described the film he saw at great length—a family drama starring Amitabh Bachchan called *Baghban*. It is the story of loving parents who give everything they have to their sons and look forward to a happy old age. But their children have grown selfish, caught up in their own concerns, and the parents are left destitute until an unlikely saviour, a street boy the couple had adopted and educated, comes to their rescue.

Sitting alone in the theatre, Basavaraj began to worry about his own parents. He realised he was their only son, their best hope for 'a good old age'. He wanted to be like the adopted boy in the film, the only one who doesn't forget what he owes his family.

Basavaraj went home, threw out the pills, poured away the alcohol, and cast himself as the unlikely saviour—the son who is secretly HIV positive. He resumed ARV treatment. He returned to the support network in Belgaum, and through their contacts, eventually found a job in a field which must once have been unthinkable to him—as a counsellor for the HIV positive community in his home district. For two years he has been employed by a large NGO, and he noted with quiet satisfaction that he was quickly promoted to team leader.

In this role, Basavaraj oversees other counsellors and helps organise outreach programmes for those who are positive and those who are grieving. He leads educational workshops about transmission of the disease, responsible sexual behaviour, and protection. Perhaps most importantly, he shares his own experience with others who have learned they're positive, in the hope that they won't feel the same despair from which he has emerged at last. It is in this way, day by day, that Basavaraj has engineered his own best rescue—for love of his sisters, who now know his status, and of his parents, whom he has never told because he cannot bear to make them suffer. The love of his wife is not what saved him—finding Jayanthi was a surprise, the sort of surprise that comes to those who are not afraid to live, who wonder what might happen next.

Basavaraj has the gentle melancholy of a Faiyum portrait and Jayanthi is resolute; while I was with them, I was struck by the sense that both had emerged from a long darkness. Two days later, on a bright sunny morning in Mysore, Ashwini told me her story.

Ashwini is a fresh-faced woman in her mid twenties who has been a widow for four years. Her husband's health began to deteriorate a few months before the birth of their son, and he died when the baby was fifteen months old. Her husband used to drink heavily and had a history of liver problems, she told me. He gave her no reason to wonder about any other cause for his illness, even when his family began to travel with him to health facilities all over the country.

Ashwini is easygoing, quick to laugh, energetic. Her eyes are lit with humour and intelligence. But I realised I was bracing myself as she described her husband's death. The discovery she never suspected cast its long shadow back so inexorably that it threatened to colour her whole history. Later, when she showed me her wedding photos, I could not look at her husband without bitterness. I lingered on a shot of the couple together: an ox-headed groom, large and brutish, oily-eyed, stood beside a tender-skinned bride, her gaze cast down, a yoke of gold filigree around her delicate neck. I marvelled at Ashwini's equanimity as we studied the picture. Perhaps she recalled a different flavour to that day, a time when her husband represented the promise of a new life, adulthood, children. Perhaps, a finger tracing the fold of her wedding sari, she was simply pleased by her own loveliness. Then she turned to a bridal portrait, smiled fondly at the girl in the picture, and shook her head. Ashwini's face is unlined, her hair thick and black, but she is no longer that girl.

It is the custom for young wives to return to their parents' homes for the last stages of pregnancy and childbirth. When Ashwini went home for her son's delivery, her father learned about the trips his son-in-law was taking all over India and persuaded the sick man to stay home and accept his own assistance. He began accompanying his son-in-law to a nearby foundation, and in this way came to know what Ashwini had not been told: that her husband had AIDS. He was aware that the virus is sexually transmitted and realised his daughter had been at risk for more than a year, at the very least. There was no doubt in his mind that she was already infected.

At this time, the baby was only a few days old. Ashwini's father worried that the shock of such news would endanger his daughter and grandchild. He kept her husband's secret for a few weeks, and then a few more. Ashwini and the child returned to her husband's home, and still her father said nothing. He knew she was unhappy with her in-laws; perhaps he hoped to spare her further pain when she would have no one to comfort her. Perhaps he was giving her husband a chance to tell her, or perhaps he saw no point to exposing her husband when Ashwini had to spend every day taking care of him. Perhaps he feared she might do something drastic and this was the only way he could contrive to protect her. For more than a year he said nothing. When her husband finally died, Ashwini assumed his liver had failed.

She performed the customary funeral rites in the home she and her husband shared with his parents and married sister. At the end of those 15 days, her father came to take Ashwini and the baby home for a visit. She packed a few clothes for herself and her son but left most of her belongings behind.

Her father tried to break the news gently, she said. First he mentioned that her husband had gone to a foundation that treats alcoholics. Ashwini accepted this quite easily. Then he explained that the foundation also helps people with other problems. After a few days he brought up the counselling programme for HIV positive patients. Finally he told her.

I met Ashwini's father, a genial man, full of affection for his children and grandchildren, and clearly proud of the daughter whose disposition so closely echoes his own. I watched as he gathered Ashwini's five year old son Nithin into his lap, unwrapping a chocolate for the boy, who was still half asleep from his nap, and laughing warmly when the child came back to life with a sudden darting grab for the candy. He and Ashwini play chess together, and he shrugged comically when he admitted that she often wins.

There is no fear of contagion in his household, no tension among the pretty sisters, no separation between Nithin and his infant cousin. Ashwini, who is keenly observant but often quiet outside her home, emerges as a force inside these three rooms. Her mother is welcoming and sweet but essentially a home body, illiterate, retiring, shy. Her father has made a point of educating his daughters as well as his son, and Ashwini is outgoing and confident, teasing the little boys, urging the girls to speak. Her portrait hangs in the place of honour on the wall, a recent shot of her giving an address to HIV counsellors.

The contrast between this loving household and the life Ashwini described with her in-laws must have shocked her as a young bride. Her husband's family kept very much to themselves, a mindset imposed upon Ashwini. She was discouraged from speaking with neighbours or maintaining any friendships, and confined as much as possible to the home—restrictions that reflected the sort of lifestyle her mother-in-law considered suitable, and which were maintained long before any health concerns. During her engagement (at sixteen), her husband promised she could continue her education, but once married, he changed his mind and Ashwini was forbidden to attend any classes. If she wanted to visit anyone, she had to beg permission from every member of the household. Her father witnessed this petty humiliation and felt it keenly.

When her husband became ill, Ashwini's in-laws must have been privy to his diagnosis; they travelled with him in search of alternate treatments and consulted with doctors on his behalf. But their care for him did not extend to Ashwini or the baby she carried. They colluded with their son in keeping his status a secret from his wife. Once they decided she was a health risk, they quietly found ways to isolate her. Her food and clothes were kept separately. When Ashwini or Nithin used a glass for water, they put it aside; no one else would touch it. Her mother-in-law made excuses to prevent her from cooking. Her sister-in-law was a midwife, a health worker who must have received training in how the virus is transmitted, but even she persisted. Ashwini's days were spent tending to her husband, and after he died, they blamed her family for the treatment her father had advocated.

They did not exactly throw her out, but eventually she realised they would never call for her to come back. When she had recovered from the blow of this dismissal, Ashwini was forced to enlist the assistance of a women's help line to help restore her property—her clothing, her gold. Her husband's parents have only come once to see their grandson and she does not anticipate another visit. 'They are fine to let him go,' Ashwini said quietly. Nithin is HIV positive.

A few weeks after her husband's death, Ashwini's father took his daughter and grandson to the foundation for blood tests, but Ashwini decided to go alone to receive the results. It was a shock, she said, but she never felt the sort of despair Basavaraj experienced. 'A lot of bad things were happening,' she explained. 'But at the same time a lot of good things were happening.' She listed them: more independence, love and encouragement from her family, support from counsellors, and eventually a job with the network. Ashwini is now a counsellor herself, a role that gives her enormous fulfilment. She has adopted a strategy with new clients of listening first to all their fears and worries before revealing her own status. They can hardly believe it, she told me, because no one suspects that a woman who is strong, fit, successful in her job, and happy with her family could also be HIV positive.

To her clients, Ashwini must represent a new and startling possibility. But to me, Ashwini seems restored to the life that always ought to have been hers, the life she was deprived of pursuing during her marriage. She is a lively, intelligent, curious woman who must have felt cut off not just from her community but from her true self in her in-laws' dour home. She does not dwell on that time, but described it briefly as 'torture'. And such restrictions and ill-treatment, she believes, would only have intensified after her husband's death.

'I might not be living now,' she said, 'if I had stayed with them.'

Every morning, Ashwini eats breakfast with her son and then makes a game of her goodbye, peeking back around the door to surprise him before she leaves him with her mother. She carries a satchel provided by the network, which contains a meticulously kept log book of her meetings and laminated diagrams to use as teaching tools. She works at a centre in a nearby village, about 90 minutes away by bus, and occasionally makes house calls. Her clients might be anyone who is HIV positive, but most are women like herself: housewives in modest households, young widows, mothers. Many widows come with their children, she said, and there are 250 positive orphans in Mysore. Once a week she visits a hub office in the city, with large hand-drawn maps on all the walls. These serve as charts of the villages, which are constantly updated and employ a coding system of adhesive bindis within small brown boxes that represent houses. A green bindi might signify a pregnant woman, a black teardrop a widow, a round red dot a man who is positive.

I visited a similar centre in Bangalore. We walked up a dim flight of stairs and stepped past a mound of shoes tumbled together outside the door. A large room had been divided into small offices and a meeting hall where four or five dozen people sat on the floor for a support meeting. At first the group was comprised mostly of women, but a thin line of men soon formed along the room's perimeter, leaning against walls, listening avidly. One consulted a bulletin board which displayed pertinent notices in several languages. A recent clipping described a proposal to grant HIV positive people discounted rail fare.

For the first hour, they were addressed by various speakers in Kannada. One gave a detailed update on 60 pending applications which the network had submitted on members' behalf; HIV positive families are eligible for free housing.

Another struck an inspirational note, explaining how she came to know she was positive, and encouraging others to reveal their status—not frivolously but whenever necessary to receive services. In a discussion of the upcoming elections, it became clear that this group—made up predominantly of housewives and widows—was determined to wield its political power fiercely.

Before they split into small group activities, parents were given a quick tutorial about how to begin special savings accounts for their positive children and how to buy insurance, in both cases with assistance from various corporations and charities. A camp was announced for the upcoming weekend, during which children could receive free blood tests; all were encouraged to attend. The meeting was full of children, I noticed; they sat, kicking idly in their mothers' laps or ran among the folding chairs in the back. Some were older: a school girl with long braids, a bookish-looking boy with glasses, and I wondered how much they understood.

Nithin is too young to know his status, although Ashwini realises she will have to tell him some day. At the moment his CD4 count is fine, and he takes half a tablet of Septran each morning to help ward off opportunistic infections. She laughed when she admitted that of greater concern are his teeth, which have already suffered from his love of chocolate. His milk teeth have all fallen out early, though a dentist has advised her not to worry; new ones will come soon.

Her only real fear, she said, is that some harm will come to her son. But she took care to express this in a way that does not suggest anything beyond a mother's typical worry. If, as for Basavaraj and Jayanthi, the virus came with requisite loads of shame and dread, Ashwini refuses to bear such burdens any longer. She has left them behind, perhaps in the same rooms where she lived with her husband. Now she carries herself with remarkable lightness—she will handle whatever comes.

But she is determined to keep herself and Nithin strong until a better treatment—'a cure'—is found. Her faith in this outcome is so strong that she speaks of it quite naturally, in the same tone she uses to describe her son's adult teeth—they have not yet grown in, but she only has to wait.

Just before we went to meet her family, I asked Ashwini if there was anything else I ought to know, anything I had neglected to ask her. She considered for a moment, then gestured toward my notebook. 'You can write that I had a daughter,' she said.

The baby came during Ashwini's first year of marriage, premature by several weeks. She died within a month. Ashwini recovered slowly; she felt weak for a long time and had difficulty conceiving again. Eventually she and her husband consulted doctors to determine if they could have another child, and as part of a standard screening, blood was drawn from both of them. Ashwini asked why, and her husband told her it was a test for AIDS.

Her husband was twenty six when they married, nine years older than Ashwini. He was a driver by profession, frequently away from their home in Bellary. She knew that he indulged in alcohol and tobacco. But it was only after his death that people came to her with reports of his infidelity. She learned that he visited women in other cities, and she was aware, of course, that he had access to sex workers while travelling. She believes this is how he contracted the virus.

When they received their results, Ashwini was confused to see two dots on her husband's record, and only one on hers. She asked why and he convinced her that a different code was used for men. At the time, with no idea they were at risk, she believed him. Now she realises that he was positive and did nothing to protect her, did not even consider the children they intended to have. Ashwini looked at me steadily when she said that she thinks of this sometimes. She regrets not having taken precautions during her pregnancy. She did not mention Nithin's name when she said that maybe if she had known, things would be very different.

328

Her family's home is bright blue, with a kitchen, a common room large enough for half a dozen people to sit cross-legged on mats, and a small shaded bedroom where a sleeping mat has been unrolled beneath the window for Nithin's nap. Nithin's cousin, Ashwini's baby nephew, swings from the low ceiling in a fabric cradle until he is brought out to meet us, blinking in surprise, a fist to his eye. Nithin keeps a few small toys lined up near the TV, and once he is convinced that we have no more chocolate, he pushes a little wooden truck across the cement mosaic floor. Ashwini shows us her Singer sewing machine, where she spends her evenings stitching salwar kameezes and sari blouses for local women; she supplements her income with tailoring work. The television is in one corner; Ashwini explains that Nithin is upset with his grandfather because the neighbours have a DVD player and his family does not. He wants to watch films, to sing and dance along with his favourite stars. Every time Ashwini leaves for work, he reminds her to bring one home. 'Naughty boy,' she said with relish.

When we arrived, her mother had prepared tea for us. Her father was home from his shift at a nearby factory. He used to run a restaurant in Bellary, which has recently closed, but the family still earns enough to indulge their taste for meat once or twice a week. Her young brother, barely a teenager, was still at school, but two of her three younger sisters had come home to meet us—one studies computer programming, and the other, a new mother, is training for electrical work. Her infant son stared at our troupe of newcomers with the fierce expression of a tiny hawk, and Ashwini held out her arms to him, laughing and teasing until his face creased in a sudden smile.

She doesn't think she wants more children. When I asked what she does want, she paused. To make sure her little brother is educated, she said, and to help her youngest sisters marry. And for herself? At first she demurred, but when I pressed she said there is someone in the city where she used to work, a man who is also HIV positive, also a counsellor. She hopes he will speak to her father soon. She would like to marry again.

For Basavaraj, marriage came as a surprise; he had supposed he would remain a bachelor forever. He and Jayanthi met through their support network. Basavaraj had an opening on his team, and Jayanthi, a positive widow in need of work, insisted on an interview. He hired her after one conversation. He said he realised at once that she had the confidence to support others.

Their courtship was conducted as a kind of dialectic. As they grew to know other, Jayanthi began to pepper him with questions. Why had he never married? Did he ever want to get married? As someone who is positive, he must know life can be difficult—didn't he think it might help to be married? Finally he countered with an unexpected answer. 'You've asked me this so many times, maybe you should marry me.'

Jayanthi hesitated, murmuring about the problems that might arise. In fact, she had gone to her family about Basavaraj, and they disapproved, citing caste differences, Basavaraj's lack of property, and, unexpectedly, his HIV status. Her parents had used the entire settlement she won from her husband's family, Rs 1.5 lakhs ($ 3750) that they badly needed, to send her for ayurvedic treatment. They believe she is cured—that all the money they had, a small fortune by their standards, must surely have been enough to save her. In their eyes, she is no longer infected. 'Don't marry this positive man,' they told her. 'We will find you a negative husband.'

Jayanthi did not have the heart to dissuade them, but she knew she could never marry according to their wishes. 'Then I would spoil another life,' she said.

When she told Basavaraj no, she mentioned caste—she is Brahmin and he is Lingayat, a branch of Hinduism that does not recognise caste. He said, 'If that is how you feel, then you do your work and I'll be doing my work, and in that way only we will go on. But don't ask me about marrying.'

That state of affairs lasted two months. By then Jayanthi was convinced that no one would ever understand her as well as Basavaraj does. 'I live and die with him,' she decided. They married without her family's consent, in a temple, with the full support of their counselling programme. I met them just before their first anniversary.

Since then her father has come to visit twice and her mother once. But the split with her family has not broken Jayanthi, as a similar rift might once have broken Basavaraj. Her parents' disapproval stems from a misconception about HIV, heartbreaking in light of their sacrifice, and from traditional concerns about caste and property. But in some sense, Jayanthi and Basavaraj are living outside tradition, in a new world where their alliance is paramount. They understand what others cannot; they have made journeys that their families, no matter how well-meaning, cannot comprehend.

And perhaps they have changed the world around them, in small and unexpected ways. Jayanthi recounted with pleasure a slow turning in her community's thinking. Before, they were not interested in learning about HIV or transmission— all they saw when Jayanthi came into view was a deadly disease. Now they see a married woman with a good job, leading a normal life. Even her first husband's family have begun to treat her with respect. Lately they have tried to contact her, she said. She is not interested in visiting them, but she is glad to know she has made them wonder.

Two of my favourite aunts live in Bangalore, and that night I went to a family party. I was reaching in my bag for a dose of cold medication and came upon the water bottle I'd shared with Basavaraj and Jayanthi in the park. I realised my blunder at once and was so annoyed at myself that I muttered aloud, 'I might have passed on my cold to people who need to be careful about infection.' A few minutes later one of my cousins gently approached me. I had shared a bottle with people who are HIV positive? Didn't that put me at risk?

I looked up in surprise but reassured her. A few minutes later I felt a current of whispers and turned to my aunt who is famously bold, certain she would ask whatever was on her mind.

'But darling, doesn't it come through fluids? Through saliva?'

And then, 'Can you be certain?'

Their shock mirrored my own. I had come, I thought, prepared to encounter tales of this stigma. But I had not been prepared for how widespread it is, how comfortably it has taken up residence in the homes of educated professionals, in hospitals and private clinics, around dinner tables. Basavaraj was kept outside the doors of a clinic when he required an injection, but for men, he believes, the most debilitating shame is self-imposed. Men are the bread winners, the protectors, and so they are especially vulnerable to the assumption that a man who has AIDS deserves his fate. For years Basavaraj regarded his condition not just as a disease but as a disgrace—one that could pollute those around him if his status was known. He saw no choice but isolation, a half-life whose main purpose was silence.

Even now, married, counselling, well accustomed to telling his story, he has shielded his parents from the truth. It seems surprisingly easy for him to keep his secret, perhaps because his parents' relief in his change in circumstances is so great that they don't ask many probing questions. Basavaraj has described his job only in the broadest terms, and they have accepted quite happily the explanation that he works for the community. They are thrilled that he has married at last, they have welcomed Jayanthi as a long-awaited daughter, but they have no idea the couple is HIV positive. Basavaraj does not plan to tell them. Both his mother and father are in fragile health, and he worries they might not recover from the shock. And Basavaraj knows they are waiting for good news—for a grandson to carry on the family line. He and Jayanthi have decided not to have children, but he does not want to deprive his parents of such hopes. He hates the thought of disappointing them.

Jayanthi understands his decision. She has seen the pain that her status caused her parents, and she knows how powerful the fear of AIDS can be. During her first marriage, she experienced a chilling ostracism: shunned by other women in her village and kept out of the temple, no longer a part of festivals or religious functions. Even before her husband died, her in-laws refused to have meals with her. They forced her to use a different bathroom and did not let her care for the children of the household. Jayanthi was treated as a pariah by the neighbourhood children, who were not permitted to come near her. She bought them sweets, she told me, but they were still told to keep away.

Now she and Basavaraj are advocates for the HIV positive children in their area. The couple has interceded on the children's behalf with the local school and visit periodically to make sure that the children whose status is known are being treated fairly. They are happy with their friends, Jayanthi reports. Everyone plays together.

I was thinking of all this when my aunt asked her questions, surprised but glad that she was wondering too.

On our last day together, I sat with Basavaraj and Jayanthi at a picnic table. Planes taking off from a nearby airport rumbled overhead, and Jayanthi craned her head to see them go by. Once, her face filled with wonder, she waved.

I asked if she would ever like to fly on a plane and she smiled, uncertain, but amused by the notion. Her hopes are closer to home. She wants her own house with a large enough garden for flowers and vegetables. The couple both speak of adopting HIV positive orphans. Basavaraj dreams of running an orphanage for children affected by AIDS, a project which will take years to be realised. For the moment, they revel in the little ones they see on their rounds through the villages. They flock to Jayanthi, Basavaraj reported, and she flung her arms open wide when she said, 'They are all my children!'

I walked out with them through the gardens, teasing Basavaraj that he must take his wife shopping for their first anniversary. She looked hopeful, then turned to me with the shy exultation of a newly-wed. 'I like shopping,' she said, 'and he likes dancing.'

At home, in the evenings, they listen to the radio. When Basavaraj hears one of his favourite songs, he can't help himself—he stops whatever he's doing because he must dance. Jayanthi laughed, well pleased with her husband's grinning admission. 'He knows many songs.'

When they left me she was still smiling. They walked close together, their arms at their sides. Once she turned and lifted her hand, the same small fluttering gesture with which she waved to the plane, as though not quite sure I was still watching. I was. It was difficult to resist the pair of them, strolling to the edge of the park, pointing out a dog or a flower, pausing to face each other. She perched on the curb while he steadied her with one hand, their eyes at the same height. I kept watching until I could no longer see their faces, until they might have been any young couple in love in a park— and then they passed through the gates, into the crowded street and out of sight.

Acknowledgements

Many people have come together to make this anthology possible.

First and foremost, heartfelt thanks are due to the individuals from the various communities in India who opened their lives and allowed their stories to be told. Their voices were captured by the 16 authors who generously volunteered their time and talent. These stories are as important to understanding the epidemic as are the numbers and statistics by which we define HIV/AIDS.

Many thanks to the NGOs who served as a link between the community members and authors, and are responsible for much of the excellent HIV prevention and care work in India. A thanks to: Care India, Centre for Advocacy and Research, Constella-Futures, Corridors Project, Durbar Mahila Samanwaya Committee, Family Health International, Heroes Project, Hindustan Latex Family Planning Promotion Trust, Indian Network for People Living with HIV/AIDS, International HIV/AIDS Alliance, Karnataka Health Promotion Trust, Lawyers Collective, Naz, Pathfinder International, Population Council, Population Services International, Project Orchid, Project Parivartan, Tamil Nadu AIDS Initiative, and Transport Corporation of India Foundation.

Chiki Sarkar, editor-in-chief of Random House India, infused the anthology with energy from the early days of the project and acted as a co-editor and partner in every aspect of the book's creation—without Chiki, this anthology would not have happened. Ashok Alexander, director of Avahan, saw the potential in this project, carved the space under which the book could evolve, and has been its steadfast supporter. Parmeshwar Godrej helped open many doors and propelled the book from a mere concept to reality. As part of a longstanding commitment to India, Richard Gere and Carey Lowell brought together a small group to discuss the Indian HIV epidemic, which was the first time the anthology idea was floated. And Gita and Sonny Mehta were an invaluable sounding board, helping to get the anthology off the ground.

Prashant Panjiar's easy way of working with community members produced a vivid collection of photographs that were used in this book and beyond. Jonty Rajagopalan who worked on all aspects of the project—from devising field visit itineraries, to tirelessly travelling with authors—all with a smile and an offer to make aloo paranthas for any and all. The Avahan team in India, in particular Renu Verma and Penny Richards were particularly generous with support, as was the Communications and Global Health Public Affairs team of the Gates Foundation in Seattle. The Wylie Agency took on the anthology as a charitable project, and among its many contributions helped to broaden the book's accessibility and reach. A special thanks to Rajni George who lent her keen eye for detail, and the unique partnership between Random House India, Anchor US and Vintage UK who worked across continents to produce this book in record speed.

May the hard work of all these individuals and the stories they helped tell infuse our commitment to understanding and containing the AIDS epidemic.

Negar Akhavi